When the Answer Is NO

When the Answer Is No

Dandi Daley Knorr

BROADMAN PRESS
Nashville, Tennessee

Dewey Decimal Classification: 248.3
Subject Heading: PRAYER
Library of Congress Catalog Card Number: 84-21427
Printed in the United States of America

Library of Congress Cataloging in Publication Data

Knorr, Dandi Daley.
   When the answer is no.

   1. Prayer.   I. Title
BV220.K66   1985   248.3′2   84-21427
ISBN 0-8054-5801-8

To Jenny and Katy, the answer to all our prayers. "Behold, children are a gift of the Lord" (Ps. 127:3).

Contents

1

"Success" or "Failure" in Prayer

The first specific answered prayer I can remember concerned a pencil, or rather my lack of a pencil I felt I needed right then. I said my prayer, looked down, and found a pencil lying on the ground.

A few days later, I prayed I would get a seat, a window seat, on my airplane flight home. I was flying stand-by fare, returning home from a Christian conference on Labor Day weekend. The airline attendant instructed me to wait. A few minutes later, he walked over and told me he thought there would be room after all. And would I like a seat by the window?

Since that year, when I began my personal relationship with Jesus Christ, I have seen God answer yes to countless prayers. I could spend several chapters recounting prayer "success" stories: working with Campus Crusade for Christ following my graduation from the University of Missouri; falling in love with my terrific husband Dave; our adventures in having a ministry with college students; seeing God provide all our needs; becoming missionaries overseas; receiving God's special gifts in the forms of our lovable daughters, Jenny and Katy. "The Lord has done great things for us; we are glad" (Ps. 126:3).

But this book deals with the prayer "failure" stories, those times when God says no to our prayers. How should we handle so-called unanswered prayers? What should we do or think when we pray for something and it does not happen? Or how can we take it when we pray something will *not* occur, but it does?

Early listings in my collection of rejected prayers are the times I prayed my phone would ring and the right person would be holding the other end of the line (most likely dates that never materialized).

Then there was the time my roommate Mary and I prayed that Campus Crusade for Christ headquarters would reassign both of us to Houston. We were rookie staff members working on the University of Houston campus. We thought we made a good team and wanted another year together. We even put out a plea in our prayer letters to our financial supporters: "Please pray that Mary and Dandi would be reassigned to Houston next year!"

I was assigned to Dallas that year. Next prayer letter, I announced my new assignment, avoiding any mention of God's negative answer to our prayers.

Dave and I, because of our changing ministries, have lived in twelve different homes in our eleven years of marriage. Recently a friend, as she opened her address book to cross out Chicago and write in Evanston under Dave and Dandi Knorr, suggested that for Christmas we give all our friends ten "K" pages for their address books. Our moves and apartment hunts usually spur us to sincere prayer. On one such hunt, after moving from Toledo to Michigan, we thought we had found the perfect little chalet cottage in the country. Well, I prayed we would get that apartment. Several other couples were applying at the same time. The cottage went to one of the other couples.

Each prayer story we have survived has drawn Dave and me closer to our Master. Perhaps the best learning lab in the school of prayer comes when we receive a no answer from God. God has our full attention. We need to take advantage of the opportunities in this learning laboratory. If we will seek the Lord in reverence and in the right spirit, we can discover more about God, more about ourselves, and more about our circumstances.

Prayers are not unanswered. We fail to hear and understand the answers divinely given us. We need to gain a sensitivity in prayer. Listen to God's promises to answer our prayers, and see if they sound as if God wants to turn down all our prayer requests.

"Ask, and it shall be given to you; seek, and you shall find; knock, and it shall be opened to you. For every one who asks receives, and he who seeks finds, and to him who knocks it shall be opened" (Matt. 7:7-8).

"And everything you ask in prayer, believing, you shall receive" (Matt. 21:22).

"Truly I say to you, whoever says to this mountain, 'Be taken up and cast into the sea,' and does not doubt in his heart, but believes that what he says is going to happen, it shall be granted him" (Mark 11:23).

"Therefore I say to you, all things for which you pray and ask, believe that you have received them, and they shall be granted you" (Mark 11:24).

"And whatever you ask in My name, that will I do, that the Father may be glorified in the Son" (John 14:13).

"If you ask Me anything in My name, I will do it" (John 14:14).

"If you abide in Me, and My words abide in you, ask whatever you wish, and it shall be done for you" (John 15:7).

"Until now you have asked for nothing in My name; ask, and you will receive, that your joy may be made full" (John 16:24).

"And this is the confidence which we have before Him, that, if we ask anything according to His will, He hears us. And if we know that He hears us in whatever we ask, we know that we have the requests which we have asked from Him" (1 John 5:14-15).

Do these sound like promises God would make if He wanted

to say no to all our requests? Yet God loves us too much to say yes to some of our prayers. Every Christian seems bound to pray for something he will never receive. How we take God's no for an answer can affect our Christian walk and the way we view God. We may get angry with other people or at our circumstances. We might even get mad at God.

It's dangerously easy to develop a warped view of God. What kind of a God would fail to answer my request? By the time I met Kathy, she had formed her own picture of God. "Why should I let you talk to me about God? I prayed that my mother wouldn't die and she died anyway. So even if there is a God, I don't want anything to do with Him."

If we are good Christians and won't let ourselves get angry with God, we may choose to ignore His denial and try to forget we ever asked. But there's a better reaction to God's refusal. We can accept God's no answer with open eyes. We can choose to respond in faith when God turns down our request because we trust in God and His characteristics. We can place our confidence in what we know to be true about the God of the Scriptures. This is the response illustrated by the lives of Jesus, Paul, Job (eventually), and David.

Jesus

The night of Christ's arrest in the Garden of Gethsemane, He prayed, "My Father, if it is possible, let this cup pass from Me; yet not as I will, but as Thou wilt" (Matt 26:39). As we know, the cup did not pass from Jesus. He endured suffering and separation on the cross to pay the penalty for our sins. Jesus could have become angry. He might have chosen to go back to heaven, ignore the Father's will. He could have abandoned His earthly mission.

Yet in His second prayer in the Garden, Jesus responded in faith and confidence in His Father. "My Father, if this cannot pass away unless I drink it, Thy will be done" (Matt. 26:42).

Luke recorded that Jesus prayed in such earnestness that His sweat fell like drops of blood to the ground.

Jesus responded in total faith and submission to the Father because He knew God's character. He knew the Father, whose perfect will for Him included "drinking the cup." Earlier Jesus had taught, "All things have been handed over to Me by My Father; and no one knows the Son, except the Father; nor does anyone know the Father, except the Son, and anyone to whom the Son wills to reveal Him" (Matt. 11:27). Jesus' intimate knowledge of God the Father invoked a trusting response. He responded in faith because of His confidence in the Father's nature.

Paul

A second illustration of how to take God's no for an answer comes from the life of the apostle Paul. In his letter to the Corinthians, Paul explained that he was given a thorn in the flesh, an infirmity. One widely held view suggests that Paul suffered from "chronic ophthalmia," a disease of the eyes. Although the ailment would not have caused Paul extreme pain, at times the symptoms would have made him repulsive in appearance.

Whatever the exact infirmity, Paul had not asked for it! In fact, he had entreated three times for the Lord to take it away. God's answer was no, and His reason: "My grace is sufficient for you, for power is perfected in weakness" (2 Cor. 12:9).

How did Paul respond? Who could blame him if he had gotten angry! After all, Paul had spent his life serving his Master. He had been beaten, stoned three times, whipped, and thrown into prisons. He lived in constant danger from the sea and from his enemies. Frequently, Paul went hungry, thirsty, without sleep—all for the sake of the gospel. Didn't he have a right for God to answer him in the affirmative and take away this thorn in the flesh? Paul had healed others. Even handkerchiefs and aprons touched by Paul had effected miraculous healings. Couldn't he now heal himself?

Paul chose to respond in faith to God's answer. When God refused to answer his prayer affirmatively, Paul accepted God's promise that grace was sufficient, that God's power would be made perfect in his weakness. And so Paul wrote: "Most gladly, therefore, I will rather boast about my weaknesses, that the power of Christ may dwell in me" (2 Cor. 12:9).

Paul knew the nature of the God he petitioned. He constantly reminded his friends of the kind of God they were dealing with. Paul began his second letter to the Corinthians, "Blessed be the God and Father of our Lord Jesus Christ, the Father of mercies and God of all comfort" (2 Cor. 1:3). Earlier he had written them, "God is faithful, through whom you were called into fellowship with His Son, Jesus Christ our Lord" (1 Cor. 1:9).

It was in Corinth that the Lord spoke to Paul in a vision and told him not to fear. Why? "For I am with you" (Acts 18:10). Paul knew his omnipresent, compassionate, faithful Lord. Later, when that same Lord rejected his request to take away his thorn in the flesh, Paul could respond in faith. He had confidence in his Father's nature. He knew God's power, love, and protection; he trusted God's wisdom and mercy.

Job

Job learned a valuable lesson when God said no to him. Poor Job lost family, possessions, and finally his own health. How did he handle it? From Job's response in Job 19:6, "Know then that God has wronged me," he was brought to a point of submission and understanding. In the final chapter Job professed, "I know that Thou canst do all things,/And that no purpose of Thine can be thwarted./. . . /I have heard of Thee by the hearing of the ear;/But now my eye sees Thee;/Therefore I retract,/And I repent in dust and ashes" (Job 42:2,5-6).

What brought Job to this attitude of faith? God revealed His own character to Job with a lecture on the power and authority of the Almighty. And Job finally saw God clearly. A good, solid view of God elicited a good, solid response of faith from Job.

David

Perhaps the most vivid example of a no answer from God concerns King David. David had committed adultery with Bathsheba, Uriah's wife. Later, Nathan the prophet came to David and pointed out his sin. After Nathan left, God struck the child that Bathsheba had borne to David; and the child became very ill.

David pleaded with God for his child. He fasted and spent the nights lying on the ground. He refused to eat or to get up from the ground. But on the seventh day, God gave David His answer: The child died.

David's servants were afraid to give him the news of his child's death for fear he might do something desperate. But David's response surprised his servants. When he learned the child was dead, "David arose from the ground, washed, anointed himself, and changed his clothes; and he came into the house of the Lord and worshiped. Then he came to his own house, and when he requested, they set food before him and he ate" (2 Sam. 12:20).

David's worshipful response perplexed his servants. "What is this thing that you have done? While the child was alive, you fasted and wept; but when the child died, you arose and ate food" (2 Sam. 12:21).

David's answer gives us a glimpse of the depth of his knowledge of God: "And he said, 'While the child was still alive, I fasted and wept; for I said, "Who knows, the Lord may be gracious to me, that the child may live." But now he has died; why should I fast? Can I bring him back again? I shall go to him, but he will not return to me'" (2 Sam. 12:22-23).

David prayed ardently for his desire. But when God's answer came back a definite no, he submitted to God's will. He knew God's justness, compassion, and love. David responded in faith because he trusted in God's character and sovereignty.

In all these situations, the Lord Jesus, Paul, Job, or David could have responded in anger to God's negative answer to their requests. They might have ignored the situation or rejected the idea that this was God's will for them. Yet each one chose to respond in faith because he had confidence in the nature of God. Jesus prayed for the will of the Father to be accomplished in Him. Paul chose to rejoice in his weakness. Job acknowledged the unsearchable wisdom and power of the Almighty. David submitted to the Lord's sovereignty.

When we receive a no answer from God, we have these same choices. We can take it in faith, confident of our Lord. Or we can capitulate to our unbelief.

Before we can begin to learn from God's no answers to our prayers, we must first take a look at God's nature, His characteristics, and see how they relate to prayer. We don't pray in a vacuum or to ourselves. We pray to God. How we understand prayer and God's answers to our prayers reflects our view of God. What do God's sovereignty, goodness, omnipotence, and holiness mean to me when I pray? How can a firm grasp of God's characteristics help me when He turns down my prayer request? Let's step into God's special school of prayer, those so-called "unanswered prayers."

Study Questions

Study Passages: Matthew 7:7-8; Matthew 21:22; Mark 11:23; Mark 11:24; John 14:13-14; John 15:7; John 16:24
1. Choose one of the above verses and memorize it.

2. List as many prayer promises as you can find in the Bible.

3. List ten specific yes answers to your prayers.

4. List three answered prayers from last week.

5. Has God ever said no to your prayers? When and for what?

6. Can you think of any reasons why God did not answer yes to your prayers in Question 5?

7. What do you usually do when you pray for something and it doesn't happen?

2

Reasoning from God to Our Circumstances

When I was a senior at the University of Missouri, having already served as a bridesmaid seven times, my desire was finally to have the lead role in my own church drama. So I prayed to my Father in heaven for a husband. None came. I prayed I would get engaged right after graduation. Instead, I was once again a bridesmaid.

My disappointment tempted me to look at my situation and reason from the circumstances that God wasn't very caring. Given my extended maidenhood, I could easily begin to draw certain conclusions about this God to whom I had made my plea. Maybe God couldn't work in the real world, the physical realm. Or perhaps He could do something, but He just didn't want to help. Maybe God had no concern for my needs or desires. He didn't understand loneliness. All God had in mind for me was missionary work—and don't let anything interfere with my service! Considering the circumstances, I might have drawn all sorts of conclusions about God's character.

Or, in the incident of the lost cottage, when our dream chalet was given to other tenants, we might have focused on our disappointment, and from there let our imaginations design what God must be like. Evidently, God must have lacked the resources to secure us that house. Or He just didn't care about a life detail so insignificant to His grand design for mankind. He had bigger and better projects to occupy His time.

Reasoning from circumstances to God is not only dangerous, but extremely inaccurate. Circumstances change and situations differ; God remains the same. My feelings about life, about myself, about God change; God remains the same. If I want a solid faith, I will have to place my faith in God, the unchangeable Truth, and not·trust in my own unreliable feelings.

We need to direct our faith toward facts, rather than feelings or circumstances. A fact is something which is absolutely true and never changes. Feelings, on the other hand, change from day to day. And although sometimes our feelings reflect truth, often they can be deceiving and unreliable. Have you ever *felt* as if you hated your parents, spouse, kids, or a friend; but you knew better? You were just angry or hurt. I remember feeling things would never work out, but they did. Some mornings I wake up, drag myself out of bed, and feel the whole world is against me. (But probably it's not; chances are, someone is still for me.)

If my faith rests on feelings, my life will be a roller coaster of highs and lows. Instead, I need to place my faith and trust in facts, in what I know is true about God, and not just what I may feel about God at any given moment from considering the circumstances.

Trusting in God's character over visible circumstances is always essential for Christian growth. But it's even more crucial when we face disappointments. To determine the truth about who God is and what he is like, we need to form our opinions from what God has said about Himself in the Bible. Then our faith can be steady, consistent, unchanging, and true. The Bible teaches us the facts about God's character. And these facts are unchanging ("Heaven and earth will pass away, but My words will not pass away"—Mark 13:31) and true ("Thy word is truth"—John 17:17).

What things can I take as absolute truth about God, even when He turns down my request? Let's look at four of God's characteristics (and four more in the next chapter), which we might be tempted to call into question when we feel God has let us down.

Goodness

"Give thanks to the Lord, for He is good;/For His loving-kindness is everlasting" (Ps. 136:1).

"The Lord is good to all,/And His mercies are over all His works" (Ps. 145:9).

"The Lord is good,/A stronghold in the day of trouble,/And He knows those who take refuge in Him" (Nah. 1:7).

Goodness is one of God's characteristics, undeniably part of His character at all times. God is never bad or evil. Consequently, God *does* good.

"If you then, being evil, know how to give good gifts to your children, how much more shall your Father who is in heaven give what is good to those who ask Him!" (Matt. 7:11).

God is our Father who waits to show us His goodness. Yet God's goodness is one of the characteristics easiest to question when our prayers get a no answer. In the summer of 1975 Dave and I were attending a Campus Crusade for Christ staff training in Fort Collins, Colorado, when the Colorado flood struck. The morning after the Big Thompson River overflowed up in the mountains, nearly two thousand of us gathered safely down in Fort Collins to begin our training. Then came the announcement: Fifty staff women had been up in the canyon for a leadership retreat. All were now missing.

In that room sat the husbands of some of those women. They looked disheveled, exhausted from searching hospitals and morgues all night. Then, under the leadership of Bill Bright, whose wife Vonette was one of the missing, we lifted our voices to the Lord and began to sing:

> God is so good.
> God is so good.
> God is so good,
> He's so good to me.

We knew God, and we knew for a fact: God is good, no matter how circumstances might work out. When it was all over, we praised God for His goodness in returning forty-three of the women; and we praised Him for His goodness in taking seven women home to heaven.

Years earlier, another group of believers gathered to celebrate God's goodness with almost the same song: "For He is good, for His lovingkindness is upon Israel forever" (Ezra 3:11).

The remnant of Israel had returned from captivity to Jerusalem. Under Ezra's direction, the builders laid a foundation for the new Temple. Priests with their trumpets and Levites with cymbals took their places to praise the Lord. Emotions were mixed: Some shouted with joy at the completion of the foundation. Many older men who had seen the former Temple in its glory wept aloud at the comparison. But in praise and thanksgiving, all sang, "He is good."

In Psalm 27 David described his fearless trust in God. "I would have despaired unless I had believed that I would see the goodness of the Lord/In the land of the living" (Ps. 27:13). Believe and trust God to show you His goodness—not only in eternity, when we'll experience the culmination of His goodness, but right now too!

If the fact of God's goodness doesn't overwhelm you, maybe you haven't involved yourself with Him enough to see how good He really is. I never suspected the depth of goodness in a certain woman from our church. I barely knew her until I asked her for help one day. I needed someone to baby-sit so I could meet a writing deadline. She not only baby-sat that afternoon, but volunteered again and again. She offered me meals she had prepared for my family to relieve my time pressures. She showed her goodness again and again. I had no idea what a sincerely good person she was until I gave her a chance to show me. God is infinitely good. We need to be involved with God enough for Him to show us His goodness.

How should a grasp of God's goodness affect our prayers?

Since God is good, His act of saying no to our prayers is an act of goodness. We shouldn't feel like martyrs or resent God's refusal. We can praise Him because we know He acted out of complete goodness.

Omnipotence

"Once God has spoken;/Twice I have heard this:/That power belongs to God" (Ps. 62:11).

"Behold, I am the Lord, the God of all flesh; is anything too difficult for Me?" (Jer. 32:27).

"With men it is impossible, but not with God; for all things are possible with God" (Mark 10:27).

God is able. He is omnipotent, all-powerful. When God fails to answer yes to our prayer, the problem is never that He can't do what we ask. God can always do what we ask, and far more than we could ever imagine. What an insult to the Almighty God for us to question His ability or power!

When Moses questioned God's promise to feed the Israelites meat in the wilderness, meat for a whole month, this is how God answered him: "Is the Lord's power limited? Now you shall see whether My word will come true for you or not" (Num. 11:23). We can't believe God is God and suggest limits to His power.

God merely spoke, exerting no effort, and the worlds were made. We need to pray as Jeremiah prayed: "Ah Lord God! Behold, Thou hast made the heavens and the earth by Thy great power and by Thine outstretched arm! Nothing is too difficult for Thee" (Jer. 32:17).

Jesus chided the Pharisees for their mistakes and attributed their error to a lack of knowledge about the Scriptures and the power of God. Paul prayed for the Ephesians that the eyes of their hearts might be enlightened so that they could know God's incomparably great power, the same power God exerted when He raised Christ from the dead.

In John's vision in Revelation 19, he saw a throne and heard the voice of a great multitude shouting: "Hallelujah! Salvation and glory and power belong to our God" and "Hallelujah! For the Lord our God, the Almighty, reigns" (Rev. 19:1,6). In heaven, God's power is fully recognized and praised.

Omniscience

A long time ago I saw a cartoon depicting a small prayer meeting. A little boy, peeking at a stately man in the middle of a long prayer, was whispering into his mother's ear, "Mommy, who's that guy explaining things to God?"

Sometimes our prayers reflect our low view of God. We may feel God doesn't understand; He just doesn't know what we're going through, and we can't explain it.

But God's omniscience, the fact that He knows everything, should assure us that He does understand. Hebrews 4:15 explains how Christ can know and understand all about us. "For we do not have a high priest who cannot sympathize with our weaknesses, but one who has been tempted in all things as we are, yet without sin."

Knowing that God does understand our weaknesses and temptations should give us more confidence to pray to Him. Even if no one on earth knows what I'm going through, Jesus knows.

In Psalm 139:1-5 David painted a picture of God's omniscience. "O Lord, Thou hast searched me and known me./ . . . /Thou dost understand my thought from afar./ . . . And art intimately acquainted with all my ways./Even before there is a word on my tongue,/Behold, O Lord, Thou dost know it all."

If I can't put my prayer into words when I come before my Father, I know He's omniscient. He knows my thoughts and searches my heart. Because he is omniscient, God knows me better than I know myself.

Sometimes when I sin and take back the controls of my life, if I lose all patience, or doubt God, I feel ashamed for letting

God down. I feel He must be so disappointed in me that He wouldn't want my fellowship. But God's omniscience teaches me that God is not surprised. He knows me; He knows what is in my heart. And still, Christ chose to die for me, and God drew me to himself. No matter how badly I mess up my life, God is not surprised. He is not pleased! And neither am I. I want to please God; but knowing that God isn't shocked by what I've done keeps me from giving up.

God's omniscience underlies His wisdom. When God says no to your request, remember His omniscience. He knows something you don't know. God knows our future as well as our past or present. His refusal comes from total knowledge of what would happen if He granted your petition.

Omnipresence

Did you ever pray when your prayers seemed to bounce off the wallpaper? Have you ever started to pray, but felt you were talking to yourself? Be careful! Just because we may feel God is far off, that we're alone, or that He doesn't hear us when we pray, we can't give in to a false notion of the Almighty and omnipresent God. The Bible teaches us that God is everywhere present. We are surrounded by God, whether we acknowledge His presence or not.

"Where can I go from Thy Spirit?/Or where can I flee from Thy presence?/If I ascend to heaven, Thou art there;/If I make my bed in Sheol, behold, Thou art there./If I take the wings of the dawn,/If I dwell in the remotest part of the sea,/Even there Thy hand will lead me,/And Thy right hand will lay hold of me" (Ps. 139:7-10).

" 'Am I a God who is near,' declares the Lord,/'And not a God far off?/Can a man hide himself in hiding places,/So I do not see him?' declares the Lord./'Do I not fill the heavens and the earth?' declares the Lord" (Jer. 23:23-24).

Our God is always present. Elijah counted on God's omnipresence when he confronted the prophets of Baal on Mount

Carmel. What a contest! The false prophets prepared a bull for sacrifice and tied it on the altar. They called on the name of their god to accept their sacrifice with fire. As they futilely beseeched Baal from morning until noon, Elijah mocked them. " 'Shout louder!' he said. 'Surely he is a god! Perhaps he is deep in thought, or busy, or traveling. Maybe he is sleeping and must be awakened' " (1 Kings 18:27, NIV).

When Elijah's turn came, he prayed, and immediately God consumed his sacrifice with fire. Elijah knew his God was always close. He trusted in an omnipresent God.

How should an understanding of God's omnipresence influence our prayers? God is always near to us. Take advantage of His presence. We tend to keep God "in his place," confining Him to church on Sundays. We may keep Him around for other special appointments: a daily quiet time or devotional, special times of Bible study or prayer. What a waste of God's omnipresence! We could enjoy constant communion with the Father all during our day, washing dishes, driving to work, running errands, everywhere.

In college I once attended a fraternity party where, if God would ever choose to be absent, that might be the place. As the evening wore on, and more people became drunk and rowdy, I called on the Lord to shelter me. God was omnipresent. I could sense His protection, even in such unholy circumstances. (But I didn't go there again.)

"For what great nation is there that has a god so near to it as is the Lord our God whenever we call on Him?" (Deut. 4:7).

"Thou art near, O Lord,/And all Thy commandments are truth" (Ps. 119:151).

"The Lord is near to all who call upon Him,/To all who call upon Him in truth" (Ps. 145:18).

When we pray, we can count on God's goodness, His omnipotence, His omniscience, and His omnipresence. If He denies our request, we can trust Him, no matter how circumstances look to us.

The next chapter continues our exploration into the character of our Heavenly Father and how His characteristics affect our prayers.

Study Questions

Study Passage: Psalm 46

1. What are some wrong conclusions we could draw when God turns down our requests?

2. How does God's goodness affect your attitude when you pray?

3. What does God's omnipotence have to do with our prayers?

4. What does God's omniscience have to do with our prayers?

5. What does God's omnipresence have to do with our prayers?

3

Getting to Know You, God

In chapter 2 we looked at several characteristics of God and how they affect our perception of no answers to prayer. In this chapter we will examine four more characteristics: God's justice, kindness, love, and holiness.

Justice

"Far be it from Thee! Shall not the Judge of all the earth deal justly?" (Gen. 18:25).

"The Rock! His work is perfect,/For all His ways are just;/A God of faithfulness and without injustice,/Righteous and upright is He" (Deut. 32:4).

Have you ever told God, or maybe confided to a friend, "It's just not fair!"? You prayed for a job promotion; you sincerely believed yourself the best qualified for the position; but someone else got the spot. Or you prayed your friend would recover from his illness, but he did not. God said no, and it just did not seem fair.

God's fairness or justice is another quality we tend to question when circumstances don't satisfy us. It happened to the prophets. Jeremiah knew God was planning to punish the Israelites. He also knew that men were plotting to take his life because he warned of the impending destruction. So Jeremiah cried out to the Lord: "Indeed I would discuss matters of justice with Thee:/Why has the way of the wicked prospered?/Why are all those who deal in treachery at ease?" (Jer. 12:1). Jeremiah didn't believe people were getting what they deserved; he questioned God's justice.

Yet the Bible teaches us: God is just. Not only is He just, but whatever God does is justice. There doesn't exist some moral or just law to which God must conform. There is no moral principle outside of God's own nature. God's nature *is* justice.

In *The Knowledge of the Holy* (A. Wilson Tozer, 1961; Back to the Bible Broadcast, p. 93), Tozer writes:

> It is sometimes said, "Justice requires God to do this," referring to some act we know He will perform. This is an error of thinking as well as of speaking, for it postulates a principle of justice outside of God which compels Him to act in a certain way. Of course there is no such principle. If there were it would be superior to God, for only a superior power can compel obedience."

Everything God does is just; everything He does is fair. If we believe God acts unjustly, then we should worry about our reason, not His justice. Through Ezekiel, God rebuked the people:

"But the house of Israel says, 'The way of the Lord is not right.' Are My ways not right, O house of Israel? Is it not your ways that are not right?" (Ezek. 18:29).

"Yet your fellow-citizens say, 'The way of the Lord is not right', when it is their own way that is not right" (Ezek. 33:17).

Jesus recounted the parable of the laborers in the vineyard. A landowner hired several groups of workers at different hours throughout the day. The first group worked the entire day, hours longer than the last group. At the end of the day, all the workers filed by and received the same day's wages.

Well, Group Number 1 was furious. "These guys only worked one hour, and you've made them equal to us. We worked all day in the scorching heat. It just isn't fair! It's not just!"

The owner of the vineyard answered their complaints. "Friend," he said, "I am doing you no wrong; you got the fair wage we agreed upon. But I want to give this last man the same as you. Isn't it all right for me to do what I wish with what is my own? Or is your eye envious because I am generous?" God can do whatever He pleases with His infinite resources. And whatever He does is just.

Our attitude of subtle pride makes us feel we deserve something better than what we've been handed. We've tried our best, but look what it's gotten us. Paul, writing to the Romans (Rom. 11:35-36), quelled that argument with the following praise: "Or who has first given to Him that it might be paid back to Him again? For from Him and through Him and to Him are all things. To Him be the glory forever. Amen."

Deuteronomy 32:4, contained in the Song of Moses, proclaims: "The Rock! His work is perfect,/For all His ways are just;/A God of faithfulness and without injustice,/Righteous and upright is He."

How does God's justice affect our response to His no answer? If we understand God's justice, we should humbly accept His refusals. We won't storm before God's throne and demand our request. Whatever God does is just.

Kindness

The kindness of God is usually the first characteristic I doubt when I take my eyes off the facts of God's nature and place them on my circumstances. Can God really be kind and make me move to a big city when I hate cities and pray for a spot in the wide-open spaces? Can the same God who allows the death of our friends' baby daughter be called kind?

Yet kindness is integral to God's nature. In Psalm 136 the psalmist assured us twenty-six times that "His lovingkindness is everlasting." Our English language is inadequate at this point in attempting to interpret the Hebrew word *hesed* as lovingkindness. *Hesed* occurs well over two hundred times in the Old Testament and is translated by English versions of the Bible in different ways: loving-kindness, kindness, wonderful kindness, mercy, favor, loyalty, love, goodness, sure mercies, faithful mercies, steadfast love, unfailing love, great love.

Hesed is a rich word. It reveals a special facet of God's attitude toward us. There is a definite covenantal aspect of God's loving-kindness, His steadfast love. *Hesed* emphasizes the loyal nature of God's love for His children, a love that endures despite occasional rebellions from us. God's kindness is not conditioned on our good behavior.

Psalm 89 exalts the covenant God made with David to establish his seed forever. God promised David that even if his sons abandoned the Commandments and forced God to punish their transgressions, David could rest in the confidence that God would not break off His loving-kindness or violate His covenant.

In the Psalms, *hesed* expands to mean not only God's loyal and faithful nature, but also His mercy. Paralleled with words such as truth, salvation, mercy, and righteousness, *hesed* embodies the Old Testament concept of God's grace, His mercy and forgiveness.

How can God's *hesed* help me when I run up against a no answer to prayer? God's *hesed* points me to the depth of His love and mercy. When God says no to my request, He is doing the kindest thing for me. I may feel, from the circumstances I can see, that God does not care about me. But the fact remains: His loving-kindness never fails. God's acts of kindness are not merely passing whims of well-doing. They reflect His deliberate faithfulness and loyalty.

What else should a clear understanding of God's kindness do for me? Should it give me the excuse to go on sinning, to do what I want, to pray unthinkingly for anything I want because I know God will forgive me? No. "Or do you think lightly of the riches of His kindness and forbearance and patience, not knowing that the kindness of God leads you to repentance?"

God's kindness should lead us to repent, to feel sorry for things we've done wrong. And God hears the prayers of a repentant child, as a shepherd sacrificially sees to the best interest of his sheep. His *hesed* endures forever. His loving-kindness is better than life.

Love

How can I take no for an answer from God? I admit that my first response is not to declare God's love. But it should be! Few truths are spelled out more precisely than God's love.

"For God so loved the world, that He gave His only begotten Son, that whoever believes in Him should not perish, but have eternal life" (John 3:16).

"See how great a love the Father has bestowed upon us, that we should be called children of God; and such we are" (1 John 3:1).

"By this the love of God was manifested in us, that God has sent His only begotten Son into the world so that we might live through Him. In this is love, not that we loved God, but that He loved us and sent His Son to be the propitiation for our sins" (1 John 4:9-10).

"But God demonstrates His own love toward us, in that while we were yet sinners, Christ died for us" (Rom. 5:8).

God loves us. He tells us over and over again. He proved His love absolutely by giving up His Son. Jesus loved us enough to suffer an agonizing death on the cross, to be separated from His Father. Paul argued in Romans 5 that Christ's death proved God's love for us. Someone, he argued, might be found to die for a good and righteous man. But Christ died for us while we were sinners, hostile to Him, with nothing pleasing about us.

To a child, a mother's insistence to put away toys, a father's command not to touch the hot stove, or the denial of late-night privileges may not seem like love. We are God's children. No matter what the circumstances indicate to us, God is love, His actions those of a loving parent.

What does God's love mean to us as we pray? God says yes to some of our prayers because He loves us. And He says no to other prayers because He loves us. A no answer doesn't mean God has stopped loving us. He is exercising His role as loving parent, protecting us from ourselves. If it hadn't been for God's loving no answers to some of my petitions, I would have married the wrong man, lived in the wrong city, chosen the wrong career, had the wrong children at the wrong time!

Holiness

"For I the Lord, who sanctifies you, am holy" (Lev. 21:8).

"There is no one holy like the Lord,/Indeed, there is no one besides Thee,/Nor is there any rock like our God" (1 Sam. 2:2).

God is holy. He is set apart from humans, set apart from the world He created. He is not like us. He will not change His mind, won't break His promises. He is without sin. We may find God's holiness harder to understand than any other characteristic because we reflect so little of it. God is set apart from anything evil.

The prophet Isaiah's vision revealed seraphim proclaiming God's holiness. Jesus was called "The Holy One" by angels before His birth and by followers and enemies during His earthly life. Even the demons and unclean spirits recognized His holiness.

How should God's holiness affect our prayers? Frail humans should not *demand* things from a holy God. When we question God, or condemn Him for not giving us what we want, we have lost sight of God's holiness. We should yearn for the intimate friendship with God that Abraham, Moses, and David experienced. But familiarity with God should foster sincere reverence and awe, not flippant companionship with "the Man Upstairs."

During His earthly ministry, Jesus gave some of His highest

praise to a Gentile, a Roman centurion who understood Christ's holiness. One of the centurion's slaves was dying. The officer had heard of Jesus and decided to send several Jewish elders to ask Jesus to come and heal his servant.

As the elders pleaded with Jesus, they lauded the centurion: "This man deserves to have you do this," they urged, "because he loves our nation and has built our synagogue" (Luke 7:4, NIV).

The centurion had a different perspective. As Jesus approached the home of the centurion, He was met by friends who relayed this message: "Lord, don't trouble yourself, for I do not deserve to have you come under my roof. That is why I did not even consider myself worthy to come to you. But say the word, and my servant will be healed" (Luke 7:6-7, NIV).

The elders considered this centurion worthy of Jesus' help. The centurion felt unworthy even to see Jesus or to have Him as a guest in his home. The officer recognized power and authority in Jesus. He knew Jesus was different, set apart, holy.

How did Jesus respond to the centurion's respect and faith? Luke said that Jesus was *amazed* at him. Turning to the crowd, He said, "I tell you, I have not found such great faith even in Israel" (Luke 7:9, NIV).

Appreciation for God's holiness should build our faith in what our holy God can do. Think of God's holiness when you pray, and believe that His answers are always in keeping with His holiness. Sometimes God's no answers are what we need to conform us to His image, His holiness. "He disciplines us for our good, that we may share His holiness" (Heb. 12:10).

Besides those characteristics we have discussed, we know that God is always righteous, eternal, transcendent, perfect, immutable, merciful, infinite. The characteristics I have singled out are the ones we tend to call into question when God doesn't say yes to our prayers.

God possesses all characteristics at all times. He never changes. You won't catch God on a bad day when He is just, but not loving. His love never contradicts His justice; His kindness does not oppose His righteousness. David understood this when he exclaimed to God, "Righteousness and justice are the foundation of Thy throne;/Lovingkindness and truth go before Thee" (Ps. 89:14). Every characteristic of God holds absolutely true at all times and in all circumstances.

An accurate knowledge of God is a prerequisite to any serious consideration of prayer. We must come to know intimately the God who hears our petitions. For the fear of the Lord (knowledge of His holiness to the extent of deep reverence) is the beginning of knowledge. Unless we believe God and trust in His faithfulness, love, wisdom, and sovereignty, we can't learn from our prayers.

The great men of the Bible knew God. They appealed to the facts of God's character when they humbled themselves in true prayer. David, after his sin of adultery with Bathsheba, addressed God in what we call the "Sinner's Prayer." "Be gracious to me, O God, according to Thy lovingkindness;/According to the greatness of Thy compassion blot out my transgressions" (Ps. 51:1). David didn't need to look to his circumstances to draw conclusions about God's character. He *knew* God and appealed to God's unfailing love, His mercy and compassion.

When Daniel went before the Lord to petition his forgiveness for the children of Israel, he began: "Alas, O Lord, the great and awesome God, who keeps His covenant and lovingkindness for those who love Him and keep His commandments . . . " (Dan. 9:4).

At that time in history, the Israelites were captives in Babylon, exiled from their Promised Land. Daniel had not simply deduced from his circumstances that God keeps His covenants and is great. He knew these facts more deeply from His knowledge of God. Without such an intimate friendship with God, a conviction based on facts, not on circumstances, Daniel could not have appealed in believing prayer to the great and awesome God.

If Daniel had not known his God, he might have focused on his own circumstances, the as-yet-unfulfilled promises of God, his own exile, and he might have developed a warped view of God. But Daniel lived in close fellowship with God and could appeal to Him in prayer.

Nehemiah was another of the exiles in Babylon after Israel fell to that empire. As he was serving in the king's court, a messenger brought word to Nehemiah that Jerusalem lay in destruction, his people in great distress. Immediately, Nehemiah prayed before the God of heaven: "I beseech Thee, O Lord God of heaven, the great and awesome God, who preserves the covenant and lovingkindness for those who love Him and keep His commandments, let Thine ear now be attentive and Thine eyes open to hear the prayer of Thy servant which I am praying before Thee now, day and night" (Neh. 1:5-6).

Nehemiah knew God and could invoke his loving-kindness (*hesed*), even when circumstances looked tragic.

How well do you keep in mind the facts of who God is, His nature and characteristics? Where do you get your picture of God, your ideas about Him? Did you ever stop to think that you might be worshiping an idol? An idol can be any image of God created by persons. When we draw our conclusions about God from our circumstances and formulate our own ideas of what God is like, we create a false image of God.

Instead, we need to begin with God and what He tells us about Himself. Then we can reason *from* God *to* our circumstances and not *from* our circumstances *to* God. But in order to do this, we have to know God as revealed in the Scriptures. Then we can fix our eyes on Jesus and focus on our God. "Ascribe [give, reckon as true fact] to the Lord the glory due to His name" (Ps. 29:2).

One characteristic of God stands out in any analysis of

prayer: God's sovereignty. I don't think we can ever understand prayer until we grasp the unqualified sovereignty of God. This one characteristic is the subject of our next chapter.

Study Questions

Study Passage: Psalm 31

1. How should the concept of God's justice affect our prayers?

2. Explain the biblical idea of *hesed*. How should God's *hesed* affect our view of His no answers to our prayers?

3. Name as many proofs of God's love as you can.

4. What should it mean to us that God is holy?

5. Give a definition of idolatry. Have you ever been guilty of formulating a false picture of God?

6. How can you begin to develop an accurate picture of God?

4

Prayer and the Sovereignty of God

I doubt if we can understand prayer until we grasp the unqualified sovereignty of God. A no answer to prayer is a no answer from God. If we accept God's refusal, we are submitting to God. If we reject God's no answer, we are rebelling against God.

Most believers affirm the idea of a sovereign God who holds complete power over nature and humanity. But we start to squirm when we talk about God's sovereignty affecting our daily lives. Did I miss that bus because God wanted me on the next one? Does God's sovereign will restrict me to one person in the world I should marry?

Some people subscribe to the "watchmaker's concept" of God's sovereignty. According to this view, God created the world, wound it up, and now watches it run down, never intervening in the mechanics of the world.

The Bible speaks of God's sovereignty and includes the idea of God as Sustainer and Ordainer of all things. We affirm God as Creator. But the Bible teaches that God's sovereignty extends to the minutest details of life. God intervened in human affairs throughout biblical history.

God's sovereignty lies at the root of many of our tough questions about prayers we may call *unanswered*. Is a no answer to our prayers really a no from God, or merely the working out of natural processes and circumstances? Does God say no, or do things hoped for simply fail to materialize? If God is in complete control, why do we bother to pray? Is prayer just a mental exercise for our benefit, or a meditation to enhance communication with God? Can prayer really *do* anything, accomplish or effect change? In other words, what are we doing when we pray; and what is God doing?

First let's examine the sovereignty of God, straight from the Scriptures. If we want to develop an accurate idea of God, we go to the Bible. Theologians sometimes define God's sovereignty as "universal"—a complete reign and ownership over all created things; and "personal"—having complete control in daily affairs of men and nations. These divisions might prove helpful for us in our study.

Universal Sovereignty of God

In the Old Testament, God is praised as a King who rules over His kingdom.

"The Lord is King forever and ever;/Nations have perished from His land" (Ps. 10:16).

"The Lord reigns, He is clothed with majesty;/The Lord has clothed and girded Himself with strength;/Indeed, the world is firmly established, it will not be moved./Thy throne is established from of old;/Thou art from everlasting" (Ps. 93:1-2).

"He rules by His might forever;/His eyes keep watch on the nations;/Let not the rebellious exalt themselves" (Ps. 66:7).

"Thy kingdom is an everlasting kingdom,/And Thy dominion endures throughout all generations" (Ps. 145:13).

Another recurrent picture of God in the Old Testament is the image of Yahweh as owner of the earth. Moses told Pharaoh the purpose of the plagues: "that you may know that the earth is the Lord's" (Ex. 9:29). On Mount Sinai God told Moses, "For all the earth is Mine" (Ex. 19:5). Later Moses warned the children of Israel, "Behold, to the Lord your God belong heaven and the highest heavens, the earth and all that is in it" (Deut. 10:14).

Psalm 95:3-5 sums up the Old Testament portrait of God the sovereign king, owner of all the earth: "For the Lord is a great God,/And a great King above all gods,/In whose hand are the depths of the earth;/The peaks of the mountains are His also./ The sea is His, for it was He who made it;/And His hands formed the dry land."

The New Testament confirms our view of God as king and owner of the universe. The Lord God declares himself to be the Alpha and the Omega, the first and the last, the beginning and the end. That about covers it! Study these New Testament excerpts.

"For the earth is the Lord's, and all it contains" (1 Cor. 10:26).

"Now to the King eternal, immortal, invisible, the only God, be honor and glory forever and ever. Amen" (1 Tim. 1:17).

"He who is the blessed and only Sovereign, the King of kings and Lord of lords; who alone possesses immortality and dwells in unapproachable light; whom no man has seen or can see. To Him be honor and eternal dominion! Amen" (1 Tim. 6:15-16).

God owns and directs the universe. But when we pray, we need to know that His sovereignty is personal as well as universal, that He intervenes in our circumstances.

Personal Sovereignty

"See now that I, I am He,/And there is no god besides Me;/It is I who put to death and give life./I have wounded, and it is I who heal;/And there is no one who can deliver from My hand" (Deut. 32:39).

"O Lord, Thou hast searched me and known me./ . . . /Thou dost understand my thought from afar./Thou dost scrutinize my path and my lying down,/And art intimately acquainted with all my ways./Even before there is a word on my tongue,/ Behold, O Lord, Thou dost know it all./Thou hast enclosed me behind and before,/And laid Thy hand upon me./ . . . /How precious also are Thy thoughts to me, O God!/How vast is the sum of them!/If I should count them, they would outnumber the sand./When I awake, I am still with Thee" (Ps. 139:1-5,17-18).

In 2 Kings 19 King Hezekiah needed God's personal intervention. The Assyrian king Sennacherib had conquered every nation in his path. Jerusalem was his next prey. Assyrian messengers delivered threats and abuse within the hearing of all the inhabitants of Jerusalem. As Hezekiah turned to the Lord for help, he began his prayer with recognition of God's sovereignty and of God's sovereign activity in the world:

"O Lord, the God of Israel, who art enthroned above the cherubim, Thou art the God, Thou alone, of all the kingdoms of the earth. . . . Incline Thine ear, O Lord, and hear; open Thine eyes, O Lord, and see; and listen to the words of Sennacherib, which he has sent to reproach the living God" (2 Kings 19:15-16).

Hezekiah knew he was talking with God. He expected God to be tuned in to his predicament: "God, listen to what that man is saying to insult you!"

Like Hezekiah, many of the great men of the Old Testament show us through their prayers their firm belief in God's power to intervene into their personal circumstances. When Jehoshaphat was king in Judah, an army of Moabites and Ammonites made war on Jerusalem and all Judah. The people of Judah came together from every town to seek the Lord. King Jehoshaphat prayed for deliverance and began his prayer by praising God's sovereignty:

"O Lord, the God of our fathers, art Thou not God in the heavens? And art Thou not ruler over all the kingdoms of the nations? Power and might are in Thy hand so that no one can stand against Thee. . . . O our God, wilt Thou not judge them? For we are powerless before this great multitude who are coming against us; nor do we know what to do, but our eyes are on Thee" (2 Chron. 20:6,12).

The Bible shows God active in the daily affairs of persons,

responsible for circumstances, able to change events of history. It was God who chose Abram, who led Israel out of Egypt, who parted the Red Sea, who spoke on Mount Sinai. God led His people into the Promised Land; He led them into captivity and back again. God's supreme intervention, coming to earth in the form of a bond servant and dying for our sins, proved His absolute personal sovereignty.

Reconciling Sovereignty and Prayer

The Bible reveals God as a personal God who can answer specific requests. He is not simply everywhere and in everything. A belief in a personal God should lead to the conviction that God answers our prayers.

But we may get confused when we consider the relationship between God's sovereignty and our own role in our prayers. Here are some of the most obvious comments:

1. If God is sovereign and will do His will anyway, why should I pray?

2. If everything that happens is God's will for me, what good is prayer?

3. Doesn't God know my needs before I ask Him?

4. Maybe I should just let God do what's best for me and not bother making any requests.

5. Am I just talking to myself in prayer?

6. What is prayer anyway? Am I:
   —informing an all-knowing God?
   —persuading God?
   —changing His mind?
   —urging Him on, hurrying Him up?
   —letting Him know my desire?
   —using God to get my will?

The more we focus on God, the clearer our spiritual vision and the easier it will be for God to teach us to pray. Our finite minds will never grasp all that goes on when we pray, but God has given us all we need to pray effectively. We have a responsibility to pray. Let's look more closely at that responsibility.

Communication

An easily reconcilable role of prayer lies in our communication with the Father. The great prophets in Israel's history learned to know God through prayer. They listened to God and pleaded on behalf of Israel. Read their prayers to see how intimately they knew their Creator. Communication with God wasn't an exercise for them—it was a way of life.

Jeremiah delivered a message from the Lord against false prophets. God condemned them for prophesying falsely and creating visions in their own minds. They had not communed with God and did not know Him. Jeremiah prophesied accurately because he knew God.

" 'But who has stood in the council of the Lord,/That he should see and hear His word?/Who has given heed to His word and listened?/ . . . /But if they had stood in My council,/Then they would have announced My words to My people,/And would have turned them back from their evil way/And from the evil of their deeds./ . . . /Can a man hide himself in hiding places,/So I do not see him?' declares the Lord./'Do I not fill the heavens and the earth?' declares the Lord" (Jer. 23:18,22,24).

Jeremiah had stood in God's council of prayer. Prayer is our avenue of communication with our Father. If we limit our prayers to asking for things, then we miss God's companionship, His comforting. We will never come to an accurate knowledge of God without communing with Him in prayer.

Asking

Part of our role in prayer is to ask. We may never fully understand why our omniscient God wants us to ask Him for things in prayer, but He does. God commands us to ask. Many of God's greatest prayer promises include the requirement: Ask!

"You do not have because you do not *ask*" (Jas. 4:2).

"*Ask,* and it shall be given to you; seek, and you shall find; knock, and it shall be opened to you. For every one who *asks* receives, and he who seeks finds, and to him who knocks it shall be opened" (Matt. 7:7-8).

"How much more shall your Father who is in heaven give what is good to those who *ask* Him!" (Matt. 7:11).

"And everything you *ask* in prayer, believing, you shall receive" (Matt. 21:22).

"And whatever you *ask* in My name, that will I do, that the Father may be glorified in the Son" (John 14:13).

"If you *ask* Me anything in My name, I will do it" (John 14:14).

"If you abide in Me, and My words abide in you, ask whatever you wish, and it shall be done for you" (John 15:7). (Not, "If you abide in Me, whatever you wish will be done for you," but, "If you abide, *ask,* and it shall be done for you.")

In 1 Kings 3:5 the Lord appeared to Solomon and told him, "Ask what you wish me to give you." God granted his request for wisdom, but Solomon had to ask for it.

Ask! We need to pray and ask. Prayer works. It's not an exercise for our minds. "The effective prayer of a righteous man can accomplish much" (Jas. 5:16). Whether or not we understand the dynamics, our prayers count! They change circumstances. Jesus directed His disciples to pray and ask, even for their daily bread.

Preparation

A third role of prayer: *Prayer prepares us to receive God's will.* It is in prayer and through faithful study of God's word that we discern God's will. God can change our motives while we're praying. He remains constant, sovereign; we change. Persistent prayer for something that lies within God's will for us cements our conviction that He will answer and prepares us for His answer.

Paul explained in Romans how Abraham grew in confidence as he waited and prayed. Abraham awaited the fulfillment of God's promise for an heir. He didn't waver in unbelief, but was strengthened in his faith, giving glory to God. He knew God would keep His promise. When we pray for something outside of God's will, God can use our times of prayer to change us. He can turn our hearts and make us desire His will for us. He can prepare us for His answers.

Prayer involves submission to God's will. God's sovereignty clarifies some aspects of prayer for us. God is our king. We are not His electorate. He's not a president, responsible to us for His actions. We are His subjects. We don't advise the king; we obey Him. We should never enter into prayer with the attitude or notion that we are in any way advising or counseling God.

Our attitude in prayer should reflect our submission and obedience to the king, no matter what His will. "Thy kingdom come, Thy will be done" is the right attitude for a servant, an underlying submission of "not my will, but Thine be done." True prayer roots and grows in obedience.

God Gives Responsibilities

God had promised the land of Canaan to the Israelites, descendants of Abraham, Isaac, and Jacob. He had given them His absolute, sovereign promise that the land would be theirs. Yet Israel was called upon to participate and to obey. Israel had a responsibility to *possess* the land, even though God had promised to *give* the land to them.

Read Moses' account in Deuteronomy as he related what the Lord God said to Israel at Horeb: "See, I have placed the land before you; go in and possess the land which the Lord swore to give to your fathers, to Abraham, to Isaac, and to Jacob, to them and their descendants after them" (Deut. 1:8).

Israel's plight resembles our prayer dichotomy: God's sovereignty plus man's responsibility. God's gift of the land to Israel was sovereign and absolute. But Israel had a responsibility to participate in the conquest of the land. God could have zapped the Canaanites and subdued any obstacle that might have kept Israel from possessing the land. In the days of Noah, God had destroyed an entire world; He could certainly handle a few heathen without any help. Yet God established a partnership with Israel, blending their responsibility with His sovereignty.

In Joshua's farewell to Israel, he delivered a warning. This warning gives us insight into—not God's will or His sovereignty—but into Israel's participation in God's will.

"See, I have apportioned to you these nations which remain as an inheritance for your tribes, with all the nations which I have cut off, from the Jordan even to the Great Sea toward the setting of the sun. . . . For if you ever go back and cling to the rest of these nations, these which remain among you, and intermarry with them, so that you associate with them and they with you, know with certainty that the Lord your God will not continue to drive these nations out from before you; but they shall be a snare and a trap to you, and a whip on your sides and thorns in your eyes, until you perish from off this good land which the Lord your God has given you" (Josh. 23:4,12-13).

Do you see the co-existence of both truths? God is sovereign. He accomplishes His eternal will. The land would belong to Israel. Yet Israel had a responsibility, a role in bringing about God's will. Those Israelites needed to work hard to drive out the nations from the Promised Land. God used them to help accomplish His will. He demanded their obedience. Likewise, our involvement in God's will depends on our obedience to that will.

This same dichotomy between God's sovereignty and our responsibility is reflected in our attitude toward evangelism. We know that God's grace alone saves persons. No one can come to God unless God draws him. It was God who chose us before the foundations of the world. And yet He has chosen to have Christians play a part in the evangelism process. Clearly we have a responsibility to tell others about Christ.

Paul wrote the Romans (1:14), "I am under obligation both to Greeks and to barbarians, both to the wise and to the foolish." Paul explained to the Corinthians that he was under compulsion to preach the gospel as a stewardship entrusted to him. We have a responsibility to tell Christ's message. God will hold us accountable for doing our job, even though His will is sovereign.

God's will is sovereign in every detail of our prayers. Yet He has given us the responsibility to pray. Prayer is not just a nice thing to do. Prayer is part of the outworking of God's will.

God in His wisdom, from His infinite resources, has conditioned many of His free blessings upon our asking. Some things we will never possess because we will never ask in prayer. Those blessings in which we choose to participate through our obedience in prayer will mean more to us because we will have seen God work in us and through our circumstances.

Chapter 5 shows us a man who learned a valuable lesson about the nature of God. He learned it the hard way: poor Job.

Study Questions

Study Passages: Psalm 24; 1 Timothy 6:13-16; 2 Chronicles 20

1. Write your own definition for *sovereignty*.

2. What did you learn from the study passages about God's sovereignty and our responsibility to pray?

3. What questions have you had about God's sovereignty?

4. What is the "Watchmaker's Theory"? How can we be sure this theory is false?

5. Why do we need to believe in and understand God's sovereignty before we can effectively pray?

6. If God is sovereign, why bother to pray?

7. Name several benefits from prayer.

5

Poor Job

Can we talk about adverse circumstances and God's no answers without coming to Job? Poor Job. Imagine yourself in his sandals: Suddenly you lose everything. You pray things will get better. They get worse. Maybe, like Job, you accept your trials initially, as you know you should. But the situation prolongs, problems persist, and it looks as if there's no way out.

You begin to doubt God's goodness, His power, His justice. How could a loving God treat you this way? How unfair! You don't deserve this! What's the sense in praying? Either God doesn't hear, or He doesn't care. Poor Job.

In the opening chapter of the book of Job, God gives Satan permission to test Job. Satan wants to see if Job will curse God to His face. What's about to happen to poor Job is not a result of his sins. These trials are instigated because of Job's righteous conduct! Satan picked on Job because he was God's blameless servant.

If we ever needed proof that suffering is *not* always God's punishment on us for our sin, this is the text. Job is described as blameless and upright, fearing God and shunning evil, the greatest man among all the people of the East. God commends Job, calling him "my servant Job," and explaining to Satan that there is no one on earth like Job.

The first tragedy hits—and what a catastrophe! Job's sons and daughters had been feasting at the oldest brother's house.

A messenger runs to Job with the tragic report: The Sabeans have attacked Job's servants in the field and carried off all his oxen and donkeys, killing all his servants there, except this one messenger.

While the first messenger is still speaking, a second man runs in to inform Job that fire fell from the sky and burned up his sheep and servants.

While the second messenger is still speaking, a third man rushes in with news of the Chaldeans carrying off Job's camels and killing the servants. In other words, Job's entire fortune and his earthly security have been wiped out. And, as if that were not enough, still another messenger comes in to tell poor Job that a mighty wind swept in from the desert and struck the house, causing it to collapse and kill his sons and daughters.

Satan didn't waste any time! God had forbidden Satan to harm Job, but Satan did everything else he could. Later God lifted that prohibition and allowed Satan to attack Job's body; but in God's first instructions to Satan, God banned bodily injury to Job. First Corinthians 10:13 explains that God will not let us be tempted beyond what we can bear. It's a relief to have God's promise that He won't allow anything unbearable to happen to us.

Jesus honored this same restraint with His disciples right before His arrest and crucifixion. "I have many more things to say to you, but you cannot bear them now" (John 16:12). Later, when God's Spirit came to indwell the believers, the disciples would be guided into *all* truth.

Job's first response to his tragedies adds credence to his reputation as blameless and upright. After showing signs of grief, Job fell to the ground in worship: "Naked I came from my mother's womb,/And naked I shall return there./The Lord gave and the Lord has taken away./Blessed be the name of the Lord" (Job. 1:21).

Job could have claimed his "rights." He might have complained of injustice. Everything he had worked for and lived for had been destroyed in a night. Yet the last verse in chapter 1 gives us a glimpse of Job's reactions: "Through all this Job did not sin nor did he blame God" (v. 22).

What would it mean to *blame* God? In the beginning of the chapter we learned that Job regularly made sacrifices of burnt offerings to God for his children, in case they had sinned or cursed God in their hearts. Job had prayed for his children. He might have blamed God for letting his children perish despite his faithful prayers and sacrifices.

When something bad happens, or when we don't get what we've wanted and prayed for, we may accuse God, or at least our circumstances, of being unfair. (For some reason, bad circumstances always appear unfair, while good circumstances seem well deserved!) Not Job. At least, not yet. After this first grueling attack, Job still would not blame God.

Now we come to the second test. Few of us have ever had so many consecutive tragedies. Still, at times our problems pile up on us, almost like a one-two punch, or boxing's *"double whammy."*

When Dave and I were living in Toledo, he talked me into accompanying him to the Golden Gloves Boxing championships. "All in fun," he promised. "Little kids with giant gloves throwing wild punches. Nobody ever gets hurt."

Well, I made it through the first few bouts watching the little tykes. Every now and then one of the kids would land a pretty good blow, but never two punches in a row. The kids always had time to recover, and no one got hurt.

But the contestants kept getting older and bigger. By the time the fifteen-year-olds stepped into the ring, I knew I'd better scurry out for some fresh air. Those juvenile boxers had learned the art of the ol' one-two punch. They relied on a combination of hits to fell their opponents. And two, or three, or four punches, landed one after the other, was often enough to knock down a hulking opponent.

If we haven't recovered from an initial setback, we may be

more vulnerable to a second attack. If we're still reeling from one problem, it won't take much to finish the job. Instead, submit immediately to God and focus on the truth about God's nature. We can't afford the luxury of waiting until we feel better. We can't wallow in self-pity. We have to submit to God and brace ourselves for other attacks.

The opposition the apostle Paul faced in spreading the gospel often arrived in a one-two combination. Paul delivered a sermon in the synagogue of Pisidian Antioch (Acts 13). The next Sabbath the whole city turned out to hear him preach. But certain jealous Jews attacked Paul verbally. They blasphemed and contradicted everything he said. Paul and Barnabas overcame that opposition, answering them boldly.

Then came the second opposition. The Jews aroused prominent women and leading men of Pisidian Antioch and instigated a persecution against Paul and Barnabas, driving them out of the city. The opposition's first blow had been a verbal attack; their second blow was physical. In Iconium (Acts 14), unbelieving Jews stirred up the Gentiles and poisoned their minds against the disciples. Paul and Barnabas continued to speak boldly with reliance upon the Lord. Later Iconium's second blow came from Gentile and Jewish leaders. They plotted to stone Paul and Barnabas. The disciples learned of the plot and helped Paul and Barnabas escape. Here, if they had still been reeling from their first opposition, they might never have survived this second blow. Instead, they just kept preaching the gospel in those surrounding cities.

I'm afraid I've buckled under some lightweight one-two punches. Several years ago, as Dave and I were returning home from a Christian conference in the dead of winter, a not-so-funny thing happened. As we limped into our driveway, I decided everything would come out OK. After all, we had a second car, a beat-up Volkswagen, but it always ran. There it sat, impacted in ice. Torrential rains and dropping temperatures had turned our tires into ice cubes, gluing "Old Faithful" to the ground. In the ensuing battle to free our car from the ice with shovel and spade, Dave broke through the ice, but ran the spade through the back tire.

I might have gotten by if the trial had ended there. It did not. When I retired to our house and turned on the faucet to brush my teeth, no water. Our pump was frozen. Well, that did it. God had no right to go that far! After all, we had given up our time to teach the Bible (*His* Bible)! Why should we have to go through this? I was knocked out by consecutive blows.

Now Job must face his second blow. It is another day; we're not told how much later. Satan afflicts Job with painful sores from the soles of his feet to the top of his head. Scholars have speculated on Job's affliction, diagnosing everything from boils to leprosy. Job had to scrape himself with broken pottery as he sat in ashes. Add to this scenario the loving encouragement of his devoted wife: "Curse God and die, Job!" and we could expect Job to do just that.

Instead, Job's second response is profoundly insightful. He answers his wife, "You speak as one of the foolish women speaks. Shall we indeed accept good from God and not accept adversity?" (Job 2:10).

Few of us agonize over the good things that happen to us. We seldom accuse God of being unfair because he has given us more blessings than we deserve. We adjust quite easily to happy benefits and accept them without question, without being troubled over the injustice of it all. Why don't we do the same when trouble comes?

This section of Job 2 concludes by assuring the reader that in all this Job did not sin in what he said. Whether or not he sinned in his thoughts at this point, or held any wrong attitudes in his heart, we're not told; but the text does not indicate any sin.

Up to now, Job has responded so well, blamelessly, that we are surprised to read the opening of chapter 3.

"Let the day perish on which I was to be born,/And the

night which said, 'A boy is conceived.'/May that day be darkness;/Let not God above care for it,/Nor light shine on it./
. . . /Why did I not die at birth,/Come forth from the womb
and expire?/ . . . Why is light given to a man whose way is
hidden,/And whom God has hedged in?/For my groaning
comes at the sight of my food,/And my cries pour out like
water" (Job 3:3-4,11,23-24).

What happened to Job to turn his calm acceptance of suffering and loss into the bitter cursing we read in chapter 3? At
least seven days had transpired, maybe more. Job's three
friends, when they heard the news of his tragedies, came
together to "sympathize with him and comfort him." When
they saw Job, they wept aloud and tore their robes. Then they
sat with him for seven days and nights, without saying a word.

After this interlude, we find Job cursing and complaining.
The Bible doesn't tell us why Job changed. He may have sensed
the judgmental attitude of his three friends, even through their
silence. When they do speak, they reveal their thoughts: Job
brought this on himself and must be terribly sinful.

I think it's safe to assume that this seven-day waiting period
affected Job. Job waited; he may have prayed; but his suffering
did not relent.

Have you ever faced a tragedy with initial strength and
confidence? Or have you ever begun praying fervently and full
of hope, but as time wore on and you saw no changes in the
situation, your hope diminished into despair, and despair to
cynicism?

Job descends into the depths of cynicism, provoked by the
poor or inapplicable advice offered by his friends. His speeches
and rebuttals waver back and forth between extreme despondency and anger. He attacks his friends and denounces life and
God's injustice. Yet for a few scattered moments, Job seems to
look up, above his circumstances and come away with some
profound truths.

When I read the middle portion of the book of Job, I can see myself vacillating between truth and error. I may know the right answers, the truth about God, but still allow my focus to shift to my circumstances, and let my feelings fall. If I sink far enough, I might complain to my poor husband: Why would God let this happen? Why would God continue to say no to my request? Dave will be a good husband and tell me he understands. But sooner or later he'll say, "Now, Peep, you know the right answers."

And I do! I know that God is always just and kind; but that knowledge rests on one end of a teeter totter, offset by my feelings of injustice, that I've been wronged. Apparently, Job also knew the right answers. Interspersed amid his hottest complaints, traces of deep wisdom and spiritual understanding try to spring up.

Job astutely describes mankind's position. He admits we all sin; if we got what we deserved, we would be in serious trouble. "Who can make the clean out of the unclean?/No one!" (Job 14:4).

Job knows the right answers about God's power and wisdom. "Wise in heart and mighty in strength, . . . /Who alone stretches out the heavens,/And tramples down the waves of the sea;/Who makes the Bear, Orion, and the Pleiades,/And the chambers of the south;/Who does great things, unfathomable,/And wondrous works without number" (Job 9:4,8-10).

"If it is a matter of power, behold, He is the strong one!/And if it is a matter of justice, who can summon Him?" (Job 9:19).

As Job focuses on his hideous circumstances, his physical losses, he blurs his picture of God. The more he complains, the more distorted his ideas of God become, until he ends in paranoia. Job complains that God is always there: "Wilt Thou never turn Thy gaze away from me?" (Job 7:19). Then he whines that God is too far away: "Oh that I knew where I might find Him,/That I might come to His seat! . . . Behold, I go forward but He is not there,/And backward, but I cannot perceive

Him;/When He acts on the left, I cannot behold Him;/He turns on the right, I cannot see Him" (Job 23:3,8-9).

Job accuses God of mocking the despair of the innocent, covering the faces of judges to give land to the wicked. The harder Job tries to figure out why he's suffering, the deeper he sinks into despair and sin, formulating wilder and grosser distortions in his mind of what God must be like. He pictures God watching him, waiting to club him if he makes one false move. Complaining to God, Job laments:

"Yet these things Thou hast concealed in Thy heart;/I know that this is within Thee:/If I sin, then Thou wouldst take note of me,/And wouldst not acquit me of my guilt./ . . . /And should my head be lifted up, Thou wouldst hunt me like a lion;/And again Thou wouldst show Thy power against me" (Job 10:13-14,16).

Near the end of his arguments, Job expands on the idea of God's injustice. Defending his own integrity, Job questions the integrity of God. He tells his friends: "Know then that God has wronged me,/And has closed His net around me./Behold, I cry, 'Violence!' but I get no answer;/I shout for help, but there is no justice" (Job 19:6-7). Job clings to his own righteousness at the expense of denying God's righteousness. He refers to God as the God "Who has denied me justice."

The tables begin to turn back to their upright position when a fourth friend, Elihu, takes the floor. He has been sitting quietly, hoping the three older friends would answer Job's questions. Now it's his turn. He will begin to open Job's eyes to the erroneous conclusions Job has drawn about God.

"For Job has said, 'I am righteous,/But God has taken away my right;/ . . . /Therefore, listen to me, you men of understanding./Far be it from God to do wickedness,/And from the Almighty to do wrong./ . . . /Surely, God will not act wickedly;/And the Almighty will not pervert justice" (Job 34:5,10,12).

Elihu vindicates God's justice and reproves Job. Then God

steps in and takes over. He reveals Himself to Job in a lecture Job would never forget.

First, God exposes Job's small perspective of his Creator. Just where was Job when God was laying the earth's foundation or setting the limits of the seas, ruling over the darkness and the light, snow and ice, stars and skies? Then God gives Job an oral exam:

"Where is the way to the dwelling of light?/And darkness, where is its place,/That you may take it to its territory,/And that you may discern the paths to its home?/You know, for you were born then,/And the number of your days is great!/ Have you entered the storehouses of the snow,/Or have you seen the storehouses of the hail . . . ?" (Job 38:19-22).

Next, God rebukes Job for discrediting God's justice. Job was guilty of condemning God to justify himself. In the middle of this oration, God pauses to ask the accused to answer him. Job's reply echoes great men of the Bible who were never the same once they saw God clearly. Job answers sheepishly, "Behold, I am insignificant; what can I reply to Thee?/I lay my hand on my mouth./Once I have spoken, and I will not answer;/Even twice, and I will add no more" (Job 40:4-5).

By the end of the book, Job has gained a clearer understanding of God. Before his sufferings, Job had heard of God; but now his eyes have seen the Almighty. Job's restoration from God, a doubling of his former prosperity, is more than a physical restoration. God restored Job spiritually.

It's never too late for us to pick up our so-called unanswered prayers and lay them humbly at the feet of our Lord. God can use our failures and disappointments to draw us into a closer friendship with Him.

Study Questions

Study Passages: Job 40; Job 42:1-9

1. Has anything ever happened to you that you considered unfair?

2. Explain the "one-two punch" syndrome. Have you ever run up against a double whammy?

3. What's the best way to stand up against multiple disappointments, no answers to our prayers, or tragedies? Be specific.

4. Memorize 1 Corinthians 10:13. Write down five practical applications of this verse.

5. In what way did Job's three friends fail him as counselors? If you were Job, how would you like your friends to act?

6. Pick out one piece of good advice from each of Job's three friends, advice that would be great, if applicable.

Eliphaz the Temanite:

Bildad the Shuhite:

Zophar the Naamathite:

7. What line of reasoning did God take when He answered Job?

8. What can you do when you start to believe that God is unfair or unjust?

6

With Thanksgiving?

We all know we *should* be thankful. Parents try to teach kids to be grateful. Most of us learned to "say grace" at the dinner table, even if we didn't like the food.

In *Great Expectations* (Centennial Edition: Heron Books, pp. 27-28), Charles Dickens catches the spirit of shallow thankfulness through the eyes of a young boy. Pip, raised by his cantankerous sister, is about to get a lesson in gratitude:

> It began the moment we sat down to dinner. Mr. Wopsle said grace with theatrical declamation—as it now appears to me, something like a religious cross of the Ghost in Hamlet with Richard the Third—and ended with the very proper aspiration that we might be truly grateful. Upon which my sister fixed me with her eye, and said, in a low reproachful voice, "Do you hear that? Be grateful."
>
> "Especially," said Mr. Pumblechook, "be grateful, boy, to them which brought you up by hand."
>
> Mrs. Hubble shook her head, and contemplating me with a mournful presentiment that I should come to no good, asked, "Why is it that the young are never grateful?" This moral mystery seemed too much for the company until Mr. Hubble tersely solved it by saying "Naterally wicious [vicious]." Everybody then murmured "True!" and looked at me in a particularly unpleasant and personal manner.

"No" answers to prayers do not lead naturally to thanksgiving. Before Dave and I were able to adopt our terrific daughters, Jenny and Katy, we prayed persistently for God to give us children. For four years, I prayed every day (and usually more than once a day) that I would be pregnant. Then, when I would learn my prayers had failed again, my automatic response was not "Thank You."

Is it unrealistic of God to expect gratitude from us when He doesn't answer our prayers? How can we be thankful when disappointed? What makes thanksgiving a partner to effective prayer? Whatever we decide to do when God says no, we're commanded to do it with thanksgiving, "always giving thanks for all things in the name of our Lord Jesus Christ to God, even the Father" (Eph. 5:20). God commands our thankfulness.

"In everything give thanks; for this is God's will for you in Christ Jesus" (1 Thess. 5:18).

"And let the peace of Christ rule in your hearts, to which indeed you were called in one body; and be thankful" (Col. 3:15).

"But we should always give thanks to God for you, brethren beloved by the Lord, because God has chosen you from the beginning for salvation through sanctification by the Spirit and faith in the truth" (2 Thess. 2:13).

We could end this chapter here. God never owes us an explanation. He has commanded us to give thanks in all circumstances (even when He says no). *Anything* God gives us is infinitely better than what we deserve. Jeremiah wrote: "Why should any living mortal, or any man,/Offer complaint in view of his sins?" (Lam. 3:39).

Yet, when God turns down our requests, we usually feel more disappointed than thankful. Then our act of giving thanks can serve as a sacrifice to God. Our obedience will please God more than bubbly enthusiasm.

"Through Him then, let us continually offer up a sacrifice of praise to God, that is, the fruit of lips that give thanks to His name" (Heb. 13:15).

"He who offers a sacrifice of thanksgiving honors Me" (Ps. 50:23).

An Attitude of Thanksgiving

"Devote yourselves to prayer, keeping alert in it with an attitude of thanksgiving" (Col. 4:2).

Thanksgiving should pervade all our prayers. Not only in our prayers, but in everything we do, God calls for an attitude of thanksgiving.

"And whatever you do in word or deed, do all in the name of the Lord Jesus, giving thanks through Him to God the Father" (Col. 3:17).

Let's consider thanksgiving *before, during,* and *after* a prayer request.

Before

We should begin all our prayers in an attitude of thanksgiving. If we get off to a good start, we may respond better when we see God answer no to some of our prayers.

The Psalms urge us to begin prayer in an attitude of thanksgiving:

"Let us come before His presence with thanksgiving" (Ps. 95:2).

"*Enter* His gates with thanksgiving,/And His courts with praise./Give thanks to Him; bless His name" (Ps. 100:4).

When you first place your request at God's feet, thank Him. Thank Him for listening to you, for allowing you to enter His Throne Room because Christ has covered your sin. Thank Him for His characteristics: His power, His wisdom, His grace. Thank Him that he is able to do whatever you ask and caring enough to do what's best for you.

During

You've gotten off to a good start, presenting your requests with an attitude of thanksgiving. Now what? During your waiting period, the minutes or years you'll wait to see how God will answer your request, maintain your attitude of thanksgiving. Paul wrote the Ephesians that he *never ceased giving thanks for them,* while he mentioned them in his prayers regularly. He told the Colossians to devote themselves to prayer, keeping alert in it with an attitude of thanksgiving.

We can lose our thankfulness when we feel God is delaying our answer. If we don't continue in an attitude of thanksgiving, we make it harder to give thanks if God does say no. If we have given thanks since the inception of our prayer, and have continued in an attitude of thanksgiving, then we stand in a better position to graciously take God's no for an answer.

After

Thanksgiving is the same for all prayers in their beginnings and during the waiting period because we don't know if God will say yes or no until later. Giving thanks for answered prayers shouldn't puzzle us. That's an easy assignment, unless we forget our own request and ignore God's answer.

But how can we give thanks when, after asking with thanksgiving, and waiting with thanksgiving, we still don't get what we want? We know God commands us to give thanks in *all* things. It's easier to fulfill that command when God says yes than when He says no. How can we do it?

Sometimes, if we will take time to evaluate our circumstances from God's perspective, we can see the outline of solid reasons for God's denial. We can see why God said no to our petition.

God says no to some of our requests to teach us lessons. He may deny a frivolous prayer to give us a deeper insight into eternity. In Deuteronomy Moses explained why God let the

Israelites go hungry for a time, why He did not serve them steaks and leeks in the desert.

"And He humbled you and let you be hungry, and fed you with manna which you did not know, nor did your fathers know, that He might make you understand that man does not live by bread alone, but man lives by everything that proceeds out of the mouth of the Lord" (Deut. 8:3).

Depriving the Israelites of roast beef and gravy taught them that man could not live on bread alone. Sometimes I think God may be continually denying my plea for a fireplace to teach me that woman cannot live on fire alone. I have learned that one (so may I *please* have a fireplace now?).

One aid in boosting our thankfulness after God turns us down is retrospect. When I first realize God has answered no, that no looms gloomily in front of my nose and prevents a farsighted gaze. After a time, looking back on my prayer and God's answer might reveal God's wisdom in saying no.

My friend Mandy thought she had found Mr. Wonderful. She thanked God for bringing him into her life. Then Mr. Wonderful found a different Mrs. Wonderful.

Before her initial shock subsided, Mandy thanked God. She didn't look or feel very thankful; but she knew enough about God's faithfulness to permit her to thank Him sincerely. Within two years, Mandy had found Mr. Right and now literally lives happily ever after.

I have seen these same circumstances repeated so often that I have to restrain a show of excitement when a girlfriend informs me she has broken up with her boyfriend. I know God has someone terrific in store for her.

In retrospect, I am thankful God ignored my request to stay in Houston the year Dave and I were engaged. I poured myself into my campus ministry in Dallas, while Dave continued his ministry in Houston. The distance didn't prevent us from seeing each other most weekends (back in the good ol' days of 70 MPH speed limits and thirty-cents-a-gallon gas). God prepared each of us individually for marriage and spared us the struggles of ministry versus time together.

Think back. If God had granted all your requests, what would your life look like now? What might you have missed? Can you see more clearly why God said no? A friend of mine habitually tackles more than she can sanely manage. If God had answered all her prayers yes, she would be holding down two full-time jobs and one part-time, running in local elections, working out for the Olympics, taking correspondence classes, and raising twelve children.

We shouldn't need to depend on retrospect for our thanksgiving, but it helps. Joseph came to understand God's intricate design for his life. Thrown into a well, then sold into slavery by his own brothers, young Joseph may not have seen much reason for thanksgiving. But he grew to become a mighty ruler in Egypt, second in power to Pharaoh. When Joseph and his brothers were reunited years later, Joseph had a new perspective on his circumstances:

"Then Joseph said to his brothers, 'Please come closer to me.' And they came closer. And he said, 'I am your brother Joseph, whom you sold into Egypt. And now do not be grieved or angry with yourselves, because you sold me here; for God sent me before you to preserve life. . . . And God sent me before you to preserve for you a remnant in the earth, and to keep you alive by a great deliverance. Now, therefore, it was not you who sent me here, but God; and He has made me a father to Pharaoh and lord of all his household and ruler over all the land of Egypt' " (Gen. 45:4-5,7-8).

Joseph learned the secret of looking beyond circumstances to God, beyond the intentions of man, to the sovereign intentions of God.

"And as for you, you meant evil against me, but God meant it for good in order to bring about this present result, to preserve many people alive" (Gen. 50:20).

The better you know God, the easier it will be for you to give Him thanks in all circumstances.

I doubt if Joseph felt thankful when he stood trapped in an abandoned well, or even when his brothers got a good price for him on the open market. But by the time he met his brothers in Egypt, Joseph had acquired God's perspective on his life. He could see then that God had taken circumstances they had intended for evil and had turned them to amazing good. His bitterness and resentment had melted into thanksgiving.

Dave and I are completely thankful for what used to seem like our most distressing circumstance, and God's biggest no. We prayed and prayed to have children. God has now answered those prayers, though not in the way we originally petitioned. Children enter families in one of two ways: natural birth or adoption. We always assumed God would give us our children "naturally." But God had a better plan. If God had answered our prayers for natural kids, we wouldn't be the proud parents of the children God picked out for us before the beginning of time. God knew what he was doing! He knew what he needed to do to bring our kids to us. (If you could meet Jenny and Katy, you'd understand what makes us so wholeheartedly thankful!)

In retrospect, frequently we can see our circumstances through God's eyes and understand why we should be thankful. Sometimes God lets us understand why He turned us down. *Other times, He does not.*

For the life of me, I don't know why God hasn't given me a fireplace, let me win a Publishers' Clearing House Sweepstakes, or have a poem published. I don't know why my friend's grandfather died before accepting Jesus. I can't understand why some missionaries are expelled from hostile countries where people desperately need the gospel. But I know that God knows why.

We would be presumptuous to expect to understand all of God's answers. God's thoughts are not our thoughts; His ways are not our ways. As the heavens are higher than the earth, so God's ways and thoughts are higher than ours. God doesn't expect us to understand—only to obey and give thanks. Our lack of understanding when God turns down our prayer request reflects *our* weaknesses, not *His.*

When It's Hard to Give Thanks

How can we give thanks when, even in retrospect, we don't *see* anything that looks worthy of thanksgiving? How could Joseph have given thanks while he stood in the well, or sweated as a slave, before he rose to favor in Egypt? Could he have given thanks if he had remained a slave or rotted to death in prison?

What's the secret for accepting God's no with thanksgiving? If you have paid attention to the early chapters of this book, you know the answer. Trust in all you know to be true about God (His nature and character). *When you can thank God for who He is, you can thank Him for what He does.*

We need to give thanks by faith, but not just a blind, cross-your-fingers variety of faith. We can place our faith solidly on facts about God. For example, if God is loving, compassionate, good, then God's answer is loving, compassionate, good. Even if I can't comprehend His actions, I know God well enough to know that His acts are consistent with His nature.

Submitting to God and admitting His divine nature, thanking Him in spite of apparent circumstances, can let you reap blessing instead of disappointment. One long winter in the middle of an unrelenting campus ministry in Toledo, Ohio, Dave and I decided we deserved a weekend off. We headed north to Michigan, laden with cross-country skis and visions of snowflakes dancing in our heads.

Of course, I prayed for good ski conditions and a winter wonderland of fresh snow. It rained continuously Friday, Saturday, and most of Sunday. As we inched our car through the Friday evening downpour, we faced the hard truth that if we wanted to ski, we'd better trade our snow skis for water skis.

Finally we pulled into a roadside motel. We weren't even sure where we'd stopped. But we prayed and thanked God for the rain and for what he, as the all-knowing, all-powerful Creator, had in store for our weekend. We knew His plans would be better than ours. And they were! We look back to that weekend as one of our best and most refreshing weekends.

God had arranged for a special date with us. For two days we had no time pressures—not even self-imposed uses for our time like skiing or TV. I remember reading until tired; then we would simply take a nap. We'd study until Dave got hungry, then get a bite to eat, no matter what the hour. If we didn't feel like eating at 7 AM, 12 PM, and 6 PM, we kept doing whatever we were doing. We uncovered a unique joy from having God as our sole entertainment that weekend.

God calls us to give thanks in all circumstances. Learn to *know* God, to *know* Christ, to let Christ be at home in your heart. Paul said he considered knowing Christ of more value than any physical acquisition. He pressed on to know the Lord. Knowing God as omnipotent, omniscient, holy, righteous, loving, kind, and good makes thanking Him for everything the next logical step.

How can we take God's no for an answer and give Him thanks? Know him. Paul urged Timothy: "Continue in the things you have learned and become convinced of" (2 Tim. 3:14). Timothy's mother and grandmother, and Paul himself, had taught Timothy the Scriptures. Paul knew that was not enough. Timothy would have to continue in that knowledge and become *convinced.*

Are you convinced of God's goodness and kindness? Are you convinced He's powerful, just, and loving? If you are, then you will be able to give thanks to God, even when His answer is no.

Study Questions

Study Passages: Genesis 45:1-8; Colossians 3:16-17

1. What did you learn from the study passages about giving thanks to God?

2. Why should we give thanks when God says no to our requests?

3. List some no answers from God for which you did not feel thankful.

4. In any of the above situations, is it now clearer why God said no?

5. In retrospect, how would your life be different if God had answered yes to *all* your requests?

6. How can we give thanks at the beginning of our prayers?

—during our prayers?

—after our prayers are answered?

7. What characteristics of God especially reassure us that God's no answers are something to be thankful about?

7

Maybe Yes, Maybe No: WAIT

Be careful. God doesn't always answer yes. He doesn't always say no. He may hand you a third answer: "Wait!" And for a twentieth-century American on the go, a "wait" answer may be harder to handle than a no answer. What can you do with a prayer in a holding pattern?

My language studies program in college arranged for me to spend my junior year at a French university. All that year in southern France, I depended on the French people who were unfortunate enough to live near me. Generous strangers took the time to guide me through their country and customs.

So, when on my flight home I found myself seated next to a Frenchwoman, I wanted to try to repay international courtesies. We were not flying Air France; we were on an American transport. As soon as we crossed the waters, I felt compelled to point out *my* ocean, *my* country. "There you see the Statue of Liberty," I announced proudly; although I couldn't see to be sure. I had only spent twenty-seven hours in New York. "And there's one of our tallest buildings. Now we see the New York harbor."

As we flew off over water again, I continued my tour: "Ah, this looks like the ocean. And there's the Statue of Liberty, and one of our tallest buildings."

Twenty minutes later, I was still pointing out these now-familiar landmarks.

When the stewardess explained over the speaker system that our plane had been assigned a holding pattern, I passed along the information to my friend. "Nothing to worry about," I assured her. "The airport is busy and we have to wait our turn."

Half an hour later, my French friend began to squirm in her chair. "You are sure *your* pilot knows what he is doing?"

I feigned laughter and tried to look absorbed in the latest edition of *In Flight.*

An hour later I had given up defending this ignorant pilot who had lost us all in space. I had passed through extreme boredom to acute fear and finally arrived at pure anger. How dare America welcome me back with a long wait in a holding pattern! I deserved better!

Just as I lost faith in that pilot, we can strain our faith in God when He puts our prayers in a holding pattern and makes us wait. How can we handle a prayer that's not answered yes or no? Frequently we say prayers are *unanswered* when God says no. Actually He *has* answered, though not with the answer we wanted. The closest thing to unanswered prayer comes when we don't know if God will answer yes or no. God hasn't given us a final answer; we have to wait.

God holds a special class session for us in His school of prayer when He makes us wait. Every Christian has to wait for some things. We wait for Christ's return, His second coming. We wait for Christ's kingdom, a New Heaven and a New Earth, our resurrection bodies. Christ hasn't revoked or altered His promise to return to earth in glory.

"For the Son of Man is going to come in the glory of His Father with His angels" (Matt. 16:27).

"For just as the lightning comes from the east, and flashes even to the west, so shall the coming of the Son of Man be" (Matt. 24:27).

God will keep those promises, but right now we *wait* for their fulfillment, not knowing the dates the Father has set by His own authority.

In our time-oriented society, we crave to know *when,* and to make *when now.* We have a coin-operated mentality. Put in your quarter and get your answer instantly. But God cares more about our spiritual growth through the process of waiting than He cares for instant answers.

Why do some Christians pray and sell their houses quickly, or find an apartment overnight, while others apartment hunt for six months before settling on a little shanty, or end up with a house on the market for three years? When Dave and I took a missionary assignment overseas, we needed to find temporary housing in Vienna, Austria, for several weeks. When we arrived, we learned that our friends had spent thirteen months searching for housing.

The next day, we met another Christian couple. They cheerfully related their overnight success story. The day after their arrival in Vienna, God answered their prayers for a five-room flat (with a view).

Why did God answer one couple's prayer instantly, but make the other family wait? I don't think God found the second couple more spiritual and deserving than the first. Why do the Smiths have to wait for seven years to have their first child, but the Joneses get three in three years? Why does God answer some money needs immediately, but let us struggle longer with other financial problems? For his reasons, God makes some people wait, and makes all of us wait at different times. He has carefully constructed a curriculum for each of his children. Some lessons are best learned through waiting on God.

The Waiting Room

Adam and Eve

Let's look at some of the Old Testament people God ushered into his waiting room. Ever since Adam had to wait on Eve, God has been teaching His children by making them wait for the answer to their prayers. God created Adam, but didn't follow directly with Eve. Instead, He assigned Adam the task of naming the animals.

I imagine Adam felt ready for a companion that resembled him more closely than the giraffe or the duck. But there he sat, tossing out animal names as they all filed by: "Bear, monkey, elephant."

By the time God got around to making Eve, ol' Adam had fallen asleep (with God's help). When Adam woke up, his waiting period had ended. He saw the woman God had created for him and declared, "Wow! This is more like it—bone of my bone and flesh of my flesh!" He believed she was worth the wait.

Abraham and Sarah

Now, for Couple #2. Abraham and Sarah were two of our most famous people in God's waiting room. They were waiting for a child. God had promised them an heir, descendants as numerous as the stars in the sky. Yet they didn't even have one baby.

We can almost imagine Abraham's struggles as he sat in God's waiting room:
On the one hand:
God has promised to make a great nation from me!
On the other hand:
It's still just Sarah and me.
On the one hand:
God has always come through for us.
On the other hand:

I have no descendants.

On the one hand:

God said he would make my descendants as the dust of the earth, as numerous as the stars in the heavens!

On the other hand:

I am almost one hundred; Sarah's nearly ninety; and we're not getting any younger.

When Abraham reached eighty-six years and still had no children, he and Sarah took matters into their own hands. They felt they had waited long enough. Sarah gave Abraham her servant, Hagar; and Ishmael was born. Their tragic mistake came during their waiting period.

God told Abraham that Ishmael was not the promised child. He would still conceive a son by Sarah. When Sarah overheard the angel promise Abraham that he and Sarah would bear a son by that same time the following year, she laughed.

Sarah must have struggled to believe God while she sat helpless in His waiting room. But the book of Hebrews records her ultimate triumph.

"By faith even Sarah herself received ability to conceive, even beyond the proper time of life, since she considered Him faithful who had promised" (Heb. 11:11).

And how did Abraham fare while waiting for his son? Read Paul's commentary on Abraham in Romans 4.

"In hope against hope he believed, in order that he might become a father of many nations, according to that which had been spoken, "SO SHALL YOUR DESCENDANTS BE." And without becoming weak in faith he contemplated his own body, now as good as dead since he was about a hundred years old, and the deadness of Sarah's womb; yet, with respect to the promise of God, he did not waver in unbelief, but grew strong in faith, giving glory to God, and being fully assured that what He had promised, He was able also to perform" (Rom. 4:18-21).

Let's draw principles from our Couple #2 to see if we can

learn what to do when God says, "Wait." How should we conduct ourselves in God's waiting room?

Lesson #1 from Abraham and Sarah: Keep your eyes on God and His promises—just as when God says no, look at God, not at circumstances. Abraham and Sarah responded in unbelief when they looked at their problem rather than dwelling on God and His promise. Abraham was one hundred; Sarah's womb was "dead." But when they considered God, they responded in belief. Abraham did not waver in unbelief with respect to the promise of God. Sarah considered the God who had promised them a son "faithful."

Lesson #2: Accept God's timing. Abraham and Sarah made a costly mistake when Abraham reached eighty-six years old. They rejected God's timing and tried to force their own time schedule on God's eternal promise.

Submit yourself to God's timetable. Give thanks for His perfect timing, even if you never see the fulfillment of His promise. Hebrews 11 lists unsung heroes, men and women who were mocked, imprisoned, stoned, martyred. "And all these," said the writer of Hebrews, "having gained approval through their faith, did not receive what was promised" (Heb. 11:39). They greeted it from a distance. You may end your earthly life in God's waiting room. Don't sulk. Don't waste time reading magazines until it's your turn. Accept God's timing and delight in His eternal promises. Keep praying.

God's timing is precise, perfect. Jesus came in the fullness of time. Habakkuk promised:

"For the vision is yet for the appointed time;/It hastens toward the goal, and it will not fail./Though it tarries, wait for it;/For it will certainly come, it will not delay" (Hab. 2:3).

Finally, from Abraham and Sarah, *Lesson #3: Waiting can yield an increase in faith.* After twenty-five years of waiting for a son, waiting to begin the great nation God had promised him, Abraham could have given up. He might have lost faith as year after year rolled by and left him childless.

But Romans records that Abraham, while waiting for his son, grew strong in faith, giving glory to God. How could he do that? Abraham knew God. Abraham was God's friend. He was "fully assured that what He had promised, He was able also to perform" (Rom. 4:21).

David

Contestant #3, step into the waiting room, please (and into our examination room). God called David, the man after God's own heart, to spend considerable time in His waiting room. God used that waiting time to refine His servant David.

When did David have to wait? Samuel anointed David as King of Israel in 1 Samuel 16:13. But not until 2 Samuel 5:4 did David begin his reign. David spent twenty chapters in God's waiting room! Instead of celebrations and ticker-tape parades in David's honor after his "election" to the post of King of Israel, David returned to rule over his father's sheep. He knew God had appointed him king; but for now, his job was shepherding sheep.

David's older brothers didn't treat him as a king, even though they had attended his anointing. They were Israelite soldiers. When David's father sent him down to the battle-grounds to check up on his brothers, David's older brother Eliab rebuked him: "Why have you come down? And with whom have you left those few sheep in the wilderness?" (1 Sam. 17:28). That's no way to speak to a king just because he is in the waiting room!

David spent several of his waiting room years, not sitting, not standing, but running. Old King Saul resented David and tried to kill him. David ran and hid in caves. He refused to take Saul's life when he had the opportunity and rejected the chance to hurry up the time of his kingship.

It was during his waiting period that David wrote some of our favorite Psalms. Take a peek at his quiet times and see what God taught him about waiting. Then consider what David can teach us about waiting on the Lord.

"I would have despaired unless I had believed that I would see the goodness of the Lord/In the land of the living./Wait for the Lord;/Be strong, and let your heart take courage;/Yes, wait for the Lord" (Ps. 27:13-14).

"Rest in the Lord and wait patiently for Him;/Fret not yourself because of him who prospers in his way, Because of the man who carries out wicked schemes" (Ps. 37:7).

"I waited patiently for the Lord:/And He inclined to me, and heard my cry" (Ps. 40:1).

What principle can we draw from David's waiting-room experiences? *Lesson #1: Wait patiently.* David could have grown impatient with God. *He* was the rightful king. Why should he have to hide in caves? Yet David waited patiently for God to fix his circumstances. He trusted God to keep His promises.

Lesson #2: Wait persistently. If I had been in David's sandals, I would have gladly returned to those sheep and lived a contented life under the skies writing songs. But God had appointed David king of Israel. David never forgot his calling as he waited for God to fulfill His promise.

Persisting in prayer while in God's waiting room transforms us into the image of Christ. We will all have to wait for God's answers at some point in our lives. During those waiting periods, we can forget all about our prayer requests, give up, or persist as David did. It is hard to persist. We're not naturally single-minded enough to continually focus on the same prayer. The Spirit is willing, but the flesh is weak. Don't lose sight of your promise just because you can't see it yet.

While David waited on God to make him king, God made David into a better king. Because David didn't give up on God's promises, God could mold him and build into David qualities he would need when he took over the kingship of Israel. Dave and I had to wait seven and one-half years for children. During those years, God prepared us to be better parents, and built in us a deeper appreciation of our daughters. God used our waiting time for good, as soon as we trusted Him and His timing.

Lesson #3: Wait expectantly. David wrote, "My soul waits in silence for God only;/From Him is my salvation./ . . . /My soul, wait in silence for God only,/For my hope is from Him" (Ps. 62:1,5). And, "In the morning I will order my prayer to Thee and eagerly watch" (Ps. 5:3).

No matter how long we sit in God's waiting room, we need to eagerly await God's answer. Look how long the Lord's return has been imminent—almost two thousand years. Yet we need to eagerly await His return as if it would be today.

The psalmist in Psalm 130 said that he waited for the Lord more than the watchman for the morning (v. 6). A watchman waiting for the dawn doesn't doubt its arrival. He knows dawn will come; it always comes. While we wait, we need to expect God's answer, as the watchman expects the dawn.

Jude took us a step further and said to wait anxiously: "But you, beloved, building yourselves up on your most holy faith; praying in the Holy Spirit; keep yourselves in the love of God, waiting anxiously for the mercy of our Lord Jesus Christ to eternal life" (Jude 20-21).

Waiting expectantly goes against my grain. I prefer to protect myself from hoping. If I expect the worst, then at least I won't be disappointed. But if I really expect something good, won't I be disappointed when I don't get it?

Years ago I decided I probably would never get married. Then, at least, I wouldn't be disappointed if I ended up an old maid. Yet this is not a response of faith in God and his promises.

Paul addressed the Romans on the subjects of hope and disappointment. "And hope does not disappoint, because the love of God has been poured out within our hearts through the Holy Spirit who was given to us" (Rom. 5:5).

To hope is to wait eagerly. And what about disappointment?

We have the promise that hope will not disappoint. Why? Not because we will always get what we want, but because God pours out His love in us through the Holy Spirit!

Martha and Mary

Couple #3, please step into the waiting room. Martha and Mary, Lazarus's sisters, are about to receive a lesson in waiting. They have a problem.

"Now a certain man was sick, Lazarus of Bethany, the village of Mary and her sister Martha. And it was the Mary who anointed the Lord with ointment, and wiped His feet with her hair, whose brother Lazarus was sick. The sisters therefore sent to Him, saying, 'Lord, behold, he whom you love is sick.' But when Jesus heard it, He said, 'This sickness is not unto death, but for the glory of God, that the Son of God may be glorified by it.' Now Jesus loved Martha, and her sister, and Lazarus" (John 11:1-5).

Imagine you're Martha or Mary. Your brother lies sick and close to death. But you know the answer! Jesus, the miracle worker from God, is your friend. He *loves* your brother!

You've heard how Jesus restored sight to the blind, hearing to the deaf. He has healed hundreds of strangers. Why wouldn't He heal your brother?

You send word to Jesus: "Lord, behold, he whom You love is sick." That ought to do it. Surely He will drop everything and rush to Lazarus's bedside and make everything all right.

So you wait. And you pray. Any moment now you expect a knock on your door. You wait and wait and wait. Martha probably kept herself busy, cleaning and recleaning the house, maybe even preparing a place for the Master in case He would be staying over.

Maybe you remind your friends of what happened with the centurion and his slave in Capernaum. That time Jesus didn't even have to come and see the paralyzed, suffering servant.

The centurion took Jesus at His word, and his servant was healed by long distance.

John recorded what Jesus did when he heard of Lazarus' illness: "When therefore He heard that he was sick, He stayed then two days longer in the place where He was" (John 11:6). Two days! Mary and Martha watched their brother grow sicker and sicker . . . and finally die. They buried him.

It looked as if Jesus had let them down, failed to answer their request. The recorded responses of the two sisters indicate that they may have turned their thoughts toward their circumstances, rather than to Christ.

Martha, when she heard Jesus was coming, ran to meet Him and said, "Lord, if you had been here, my brother would not have died" (John 11:21). A little later, when Mary saw Jesus, she said the same thing.

But Jesus had a plan in mind that would end in more glory for the Father, and more joy to the sisters. He graphically illustrated his claim to Martha that "I am the Resurrection and the Life" by raising Lazarus from the dead. He honored their brother Lazarus by choosing to display in him Christ's resurrection power.

What principles can we learn from Martha and Mary that will help us prepare for the waiting room? *Lesson #1: When God makes you wait, don't think He doesn't care.* Jesus loved Lazarus and his sisters. He did not make them wait because He lacked compassion or affection! Jesus wept at their distress. He knew he would bring Lazarus back to life, that Martha and Mary would be happier than ever; but He still wept at their momentary grief.

Lesson #2: When God delays your answer, don't question His power or ability to answer. Some of the Jews who had come to mourn Lazarus said, "Could not this man, who opened the eyes of him who was blind, have kept this man also from dying?" (John 11:37).

Of course, Jesus could have kept Lazarus from dying! Jesus

can do anything we ask. He *can* give us infinitely more than anything we can think or dream of. But he *will* give us what He knows we need, when He knows we need it.

Lesson #3: When you are tired of waiting, don't doubt God's omniscience. Jesus wasn't surprised to find Lazarus dead and buried when He arrived in Bethany. Before beginning the journey, Jesus had informed the disciples that Lazarus had "fallen asleep." John elaborated that Jesus had spoken of Lazarus' death, although the disciples thought He meant literal sleep. Jesus did not weep because He felt sorry for poking around and letting Lazarus die. When He saw Mary and Martha and the other mourners, then He wept—for *their* distress. He knew His plan. He had a lesson to teach His friends. They would have to wait to learn it.

Do you ever doubt God's omniscience? When you let yourself believe that God could not possibly know how you feel, you question His omniscience. How could God know what it's like to want a baby, to want a house, to go without work? The Bible says that Jesus is our high priest who *knows what it's like* to be tempted in every way as we are. He knows our weaknesses.

Lesson #4: God would not make you wait if it were not worth the wait. God loves you and loves to give good gifts to his children. Dave and I make our kids wait for their birthdays or Christmas to open presents. On a few pre-occasions we have capitulated to their pleas and our own impatience to see their little grinning faces. But anticipation augments the celebration when we wait. The kids will be happier, the day more special, if we make them wait to open their presents. They may complain and whine on December 23 and 24, but on December 25 they are glad they waited.

Waiting on God is neutral. We will all pray for some things that God won't answer immediately. It is what we do during our waiting periods, whether we focus on God or on our circumstances, that will determine whether we despair or grow in faith. Waiting without communion with God equals stress and despair. Waiting in trust and communion with God will yield a crop of spiritual growth and increased faith.

Study Questions

Study Passage: Psalm 130

1. Does God have you in a holding pattern for any particular prayers right now? What are you waiting for?

2. What negative thoughts about God creep into your mind when God makes you wait for something you want?

3. Why do you think Christ is making us wait for His return?

4. What lessons can we learn from the following people whom God made wait?

   A. Adam and Eve

   B. Abraham and Sarah

C. David

D. Martha and Mary

5. What role do you think the Holy Spirit plays in prayer? (This is the subject of our next chapter.)

8

The Spirit and Prayer

How can the Holy Spirit help me in the case of a no answer to prayer? When God says no to my request to win the Irish Sweepstakes, what can the Holy Spirit do about it? 1) The Spirit can comfort me; and 2) The Spirit can change me.

Comfort

"Blessed be the God and Father of our Lord Jesus Christ, the Father of mercies and God of all comfort; who comforts us in all our affliction" (2 Cor. 1:3-4).

If anyone can cheer me up after God says no, it is God himself. A long, hard look at God's kindness, love, mercy, power, wisdom, and grace should console me. God promises that our godly hope will not disappoint us because His love has been poured out within our hearts through the Holy Spirit who was given to us. When you don't see the answer you've been hoping for, ask God's Holy Spirit to pour out His love.

Let the Holy Spirit perform open heart surgery so that He can fill your heart with God's comfort and love. God's Spirit can guide us into all truth, even into the truths about God Himself: God *is* loving and generous; God *does* know what will make us happy; God *is* love and everything He does is loving.

Change

Have you ever prayed for something, but by the time you saw your prayer answered, you had changed your request? The summer before Dave entered his Ph.D. program at Northwestern University, we began praying for an extra summer job. After a few weeks of diligently applying and interviewing, we found ourselves praying that God would make all offers fall through. We wanted to spend the little spare time we had before school started with our family. During the prayer process, Dave and I changed and aligned ourselves with God's best for our family. We didn't know His will when we began praying for a job. God used His Spirit and the Word to bring us into line with His plan for us.

Dave and I at times operate under a principle we dub "the shiny object test." When one (or both) of us sees something we think we want (a new piece of furniture, clothes, sports equipment, and so on), we give it the shiny object test: We wait. After a few days or weeks of praying persistently, four out of five times the desire fades. The shiny object isn't so shiny.

The Spirit and our unanswered prayers can form a powerful alliance to change us and conform us to the image of Christ. If we ask for something that lies outside of God's will for us, the Spirit knows. If we continually submit ourselves to God's Holy Spirit within us, then He can change us and guide us into truth. He can take that unanswered prayer, use it to change our desires, and help us pray according to God's will for us.

The Holy Spirit can help us deal with God's no answers, comforting us and changing us. Now, we want to turn our study of prayer to the positive side. How can the Holy Spirit help me get yes answers from God?

The Holy Spirit and Yes Answers

Understanding the work of God's Spirit within us is the key to unlocking the secrets of effective prayer. The Bible consistently links the Holy Spirit and prayer. Jesus explained to the Samaritan woman that the Father seeks those who will *worship Him in Spirit* and in truth.

Paul told the Ephesian church to *pray in the Spirit* on all occasions. Earlier he had reminded them that it was through the Spirit they had their access to God. In the same way, Jude admonished believers to *pray in the Holy Spirit.*

If we want to understand prayer, we need to understand the Holy Spirit. Three biblical terms can summarize the works of the Spirit we need to evaluate in our study here, if we want to pray and get yes answers: 1) Born of the Spirit; 2) Walk in the Spirit; and 3) Pray in the Spirit

Born of the Spirit

It's impossible to pray in the Spirit if you have never been born of the Spirit. If God never seems to answer your prayers, and you can never discern His will, make sure you have accepted Christ personally and have been born spiritually. Many good and religious people have not been born of the Spirit. They may act the way Christians should act; but if they haven't been spiritually born, they are not Christians.

In John 3 Jesus baffled one of the leading religious leaders of His time. Nicodemus, a ruler of the Jews and a man of the Pharisees, met Jesus and praised Him for all His miracles.

Jesus cut to the heart of Nicodemus' problem with this answer: "Truly, truly, I say to you, unless one is *born again,* he cannot see the kingdom of God" (John 3:3).

Nicodemus didn't understand. "How can a man be born when he is old? He cannot enter a second time into his mother's womb and be born, can he?" (John 3:4).

"Jesus answered, 'Truly, truly, I say to you, unless one is born of water and the Spirit, he cannot enter into the kingdom of God. . . . That which is born of the Spirit is spirit. Do not marvel that I said to you, "You must be born again" ' " (John 3:5-7).

Once is not enough. We're all born physically from our mothers' wombs. But to communicate with God and participate in His kingdom, to become His sons and daughters, we must be born again, this time of the Spirit, not the flesh.

How can we be born of the Spirit? When we accept Christ's death as payment for our sins, believe in His resurrection from the dead, and accept Christ into our hearts, we are born spiritually. At that moment, Christ's Spirit comes to live in us.

Peter explained spiritual birth through Christ's resurrection in 1 Peter 1:3. "Blessed be the God and Father of our Lord Jesus Christ, who according to His great mercy has caused us to be *born again* to a living hope through the resurrection of Jesus Christ from the dead."

If you are not sure whether you have ever been born of the Spirit, make sure. You can't expect to pray effectively if you're not spiritually united with God. Ask Christ to come into your heart. Thank Him for forgiving your sins and filling you with the gift of His Holy Spirit.

Every believer receives the Holy Spirit when he accepts Christ as his Savior. A spiritual birth means that the Holy Spirit indwells the believer. Paul wrote, "However you are not in the flesh but in the Spirit, if indeed the Spirit of God dwells in you. But if anyone does not have the Spirit of Christ, he does not belong to Him" (Rom. 8:9).

When Paul wrote the Roman Christians about the Spirit they had received, he referred to God's Holy Spirit as the "Spirit of Sonship," or the spirit of adoption as sons, by which we cry out, "Abba! Father!"

Abba is a Syriac word for the familiar form of "Father"—like our "Daddy." I'm told that if you walk down a crowded street in any one of several Arab nations, you can hear children calling out to their fathers, "Abba, Abba." Our spiritual birth ushers in our sonship with our heavenly Father. The next step is to learn how to walk in the Spirit.

Walk in the Spirit

"As you therefore have received Christ Jesus the Lord, so walk in Him" (Col. 2:6).

"But I say, walk by the Spirit, and you will not carry out the desires of the flesh" (Gal. 5:16).

"For we walk by faith, not by sight" (2 Cor. 5:7).

Once we have been born of the Spirit, we need to learn how to walk in the Spirit, to live moment-by-moment under the Spirit's control. I wish we could push a few buttons to accomplish a Spirit-filled walk. First, I'd push a button marked "self-destruct" and watch my old self, my old sin nature, go up in smoke. Then I'd punch "Forward" and "Spirit-powered" and breeze through my earthly days until I arrived safely in heaven.

Unfortunately, God is not in the button-pushing business. In fact, the step from birth to walking in the Spirit is a lifelong process. Our old self does not self-destruct. We have to die daily to the flesh and our old sin nature. When we sin, we have to admit it, experience God's forgiveness, and yield back control to the Spirit before any forward progress can be made.

When our oldest girl began to walk, she pursued her course vigorously. In a few days, she was covered with bumps and bruises from toppling over. The day she put two steps together was cause for momentous celebration.

By comparison, spiritual walking makes physical walking look easy! I wish walking in the Spirit were something we could master in a couple of years. We have to put off the old self and put on the new self time and time again.

When we walk in the Spirit, God becomes our resource for everything we do. We draw on God's power in preference to our own. We *abide* in Christ through the Spirit inside us. We live in Him, with our minds controlled by the Spirit, set on what the Spirit desires. This is the abiding life that sees God consistently answer yes to prayers. Christ promised that if we abide in Him and His words abide in us, we could ask whatever we wish and He would do it.

In many ways, our walk in the Spirit equals our life of prayer. Prayer should be an overflow of our relationship with God. We don't pray in a vacuum and utter magic words. True prayer presupposes a relationship with God, an intimate friendship. When we walk with God, we listen to Him and allow His Spirit to direct our hearts.

Four Hebrew words for prayer involve this idea of praying from a relationship with God, invoking His friendship.

Hanan—means "to present oneself acceptably before someone." This is the word used to ask God in prayer for a favor.

Niphal—is a word frequently used in Jeremiah 36—42 for prayer. Literally, it means "to stroke the face of God."

Athar—means "to sacrifice" or "to pray," indicative of the involvement of the whole person.

Shahah—is defined as "respectfully to bow oneself down."

We can't separate prayer from our walk in the Spirit. In fact, our prayers may be our best clue as to whether or not we are walking in the Spirit. When I see all my prayers directed toward me, my short-range problems, personal wants, I'd better concentrate on my walk in the Spirit. The Christian controlled by the Spirit has his mind set on the desires of the Spirit. Effective prayer overflows from oneness with God because we receive His vision of the world.

Pray in the Spirit

To pray in the Spirit means that a believer, born of the Spirit and walking in the Spirit, prays under that Spirit's guidance and influence. Submitting to the will of the Father, the Christian sincerely seeks to pray God's prayers to God. His prayers emanate from his mind set on the Spirit. He requests the desires of the Spirit.

In fact, through the Holy Spirit, God becomes both Author and Answerer of prayers. Prayer is God's work in us. C. S.

Lewis in *Letters to Malcolm: Chiefly on Prayer* (New York: Harcourt, Brace and World, 1964) wrote: "But is it not right in thinking prayer in its most perfect state is a soliloquy? If the Holy Spirit speaks in the man, then in prayer God speaks to God."

Who knows the mind of God but the Spirit of God? God's Spirit within us can reveal God's will and God's mind to us as we pray. I heard a missionary to Africa relate how God's Spirit worked in a little elderly woman, a member of a small church in Pennsylvania that supported his ministry to tribal nations. On his furlough home, he stopped at the Pennsylvania church to speak. After listening to his message, the elderly lady came up and asked him if he had been in any serious danger during the past year. He told her that in February he had been bitten by a snake and nearly died. She opened her prayer book to that exact day in February and showed him what she had written: "God impressed me to pray fervently for physical recovery from danger for Dr. _____, our missionary in Africa." That woman knew God and heard Him pass along to her an urgent prayer need.

Many of us have experienced an overwhelming concern for another person, a burden to pray. I suppose God frequently "puts people on our hearts," or impresses us to pray for a specific request or person. But most of the time we don't hear Him because of a heart overload. Our hearts are already full of our own desires, a new washer and dryer, a raise, our favorite TV show or sports team.

Yet, even though prayer comes from God and returns to God, don't think of prayer as a mystical experience, transcending our earthly experience. God has chosen to reveal Himself and His thoughts through His Spirit and through His Word, the Bible. We don't have to rely on visions and sensations; we have the written Word of God. We can "test the spirits," check out our inclinations to see if they align with God's revealed will in the Scriptures.

The Bible is our manual for prayer. How do we know what to pray? Do you ever feel as though you are composing your grocery list when you sit down to pray? How do you know what you need? The Bible exposes the mind of God. Words are the way we communicate with each other. God communicates to us through the Bible. Then the Spirit of God takes His words and reveals them to us.

Jesus told his disciples that the Spirit would call to remembrance all He had said to them. The promise extends to us, but we need to give the Spirit something to work on. If we never read God's Word, how can the Spirit call it to mind?

What happens when you want to pray in the Spirit, but you cannot discern God's will? Years ago, a young couple came to my husband for premarital counseling. After the interview, Dave felt uneasy about their plans to marry. How should we pray? We could pray for their circumstances to change to allow them to marry, or we could pray that God would break them up.

We didn't know how to pray for the couple. So we simply asked God to do His will in their lives. Romans 8:26-27 says, "And in the same way the Spirit also helps our weakness; for we do not know how to pray as we should, but the Spirit Himself intercedes for us with groanings too deep for words; and He who searches the hearts knows what the mind of the Spirit is, because He intercedes for the saints according to the will of God." When we can't discern God's will, we can trust His Holy Spirit to intercede for us, according to His will.

Praying in the Spirit isn't a fancy option on the Christian life. We have to walk in the Spirit and pray in the Spirit. We play a part in the full-scale spiritual battle being fought all around us. It was in the context of spiritual battle and putting on the fighting armor that Paul exhorted the Ephesians to pray in the Spirit. In our own weaknesses we are no match for the spiritual powers of wickedness. But in the Spirit, our prayers are powerful weapons.

Now, carefully and prayerfully, move into the next chapter where we will cautiously ask the question, "Why did I get that no?"

Study Questions

Study Passage: Ephesians 6:18-19

1. Write down any specific memories of how God comforted you when He said no to your prayer request.

2. Has God ever changed you while you were praying? Did you reverse your request?

3. How can you pray when you don't know God's will?

4. What does it mean (cite Scripture references):

   —to be born of the Spirit?

   —to walk in the Spirit?

—to pray in the Spirit?

5. In what way is prayer an overflow of our walk in Christ?

6. How is prayer "a soliloquy"?

7. Have you ever had an "unexplained" burden to pray for someone or something?

9

Why Did I Get That No?

This isn't a question I ask aloud. This is one of those secret questions my mind rifles repeatedly when I am disappointed I didn't get my way. The words may creep out as unintelligible mutterings in unguarded moments of desperation, but few humans will ever hear me verbalize, "Why did I get that no?"

Naturally, when we make a request of God, we would like Him to say yes. If He says no, first we must focus on God and His character rather than on our disappointment. We need to give Him thanks and allow Him to change us and our desires.

Then, and only after we have safely handled our no answer, we *might* profit from asking the question: "Why did I get that no?" Ask it as a mature Christian, eager to serve God through effective prayer. Don't ask it as a two-year-old just denied a package of candy. God always has reasons for turning down any request. Keep in mind that we may never understand those reasons. We trust His decisions because we trust Him. He owes us no explanations.

Yet, if we have successfully handled our disappointment, and if we are focusing on God and giving Him thanks, He may help us learn from this denial. He may use that no to usher us into His learning laboratory where He can teach us valuable lessons about God, about ourselves, and about prayer.

If you have met the prerequisites for asking why (focus on God, thanksgiving, desire to serve more effectively through prayer), you might begin your lesson in God's learning lab by examining some of His guidelines for prayer. Are you praying according to God's directions? Give yourself a little test with the following checklist. Take the ANSWER test.

<u>A</u>bide
<u>N</u>ame
<u>S</u>ea
<u>W</u>ill ANSWER
<u>E</u>vil Motives
<u>R</u>everence

Abide

Jesus told his disciples, *"If you abide in Me, and My words abide in you,* ask whatever you wish, and it shall be done for you" (John 15:7). What a promise! Not just three wishes, but "whatever you wish!" An effective prayer warrior knows how to abide in Christ.

To abide means to take refuge and protection in, to make a home. We need to make Christ at home in our hearts and take all our nourishment and protection from Him. Have you ever noticed how two people abiding in the same home often take on similar characteristics? My husband and I have gradually acquired the same taste in many areas, from movies to desserts. We still differ in some areas (I love tennis; he loves basketball); but at least I know him so thoroughly, I can predict what he will like and dislike. Abiding with Christ helps us become more like Him.

When God says no to your request, ask yourself: "Am I wrapped up in Christ? Does my prayer originate from Christ living in and through me? Are Christ's words abiding in me? Have I studied the Bible as my manual for living? Am I at home there, and are His words at home in me?"

Name

In Jesus' Farewell Address to His disciples before His betrayal, He made some phenomenal promises. He would answer all
their prayers; but He set up certain conditions to these unlimited promises. Five times Jesus conditioned answered prayer on
praying in His name.

"And whatever you ask in My name, that will I do, that the
Father may be glorified in the Son" (John 14:13).

"If you ask Me anything in My name, I will do it" (John
14:14).

"You did not choose Me, but I chose you, and appointed
you, that you should go and bear fruit, and that your fruit
should remain, that whatever you ask of the Father in My
name, He may give to you" (John 15:16).

"And in that day you will ask Me no question. Truly, truly,
I say to you, if you shall ask the Father for anything, He will
give it to you in My name" (John 16:23).

"Until now you have asked for nothing in My name; ask,
and you will receive, that your joy may be made full" (John
16:24).

With such fantastic promises hanging in the balance, we'd
better try to understand what Jesus meant by "in My name."
Is it enough to tack on the words "in Jesus' name, Amen" to
the end of our prayers? Jesus warned His disciples that one day
many people would clamor for Him, vowing that they had
prophesied in His name, cast out demons in His name, performed miracles in His name; but He would reply that He
never knew them. Praying in Christ's name requires more than
a pat formula with proper phrasing.

I'll bet Jesus' disciples thought they understood how to pray
in His name. They had been with Him for three years. I wonder
how they felt when Jesus entreated them, "Until now you have
asked for nothing in My name; ask, and you will receive, that
your joy may be made full" (John 16:24).

Three years! And yet they had never asked for anything in Christ's name. It's a humbling process to depend on the name of another person. We have to admit we can't get what we want on our own, but have to rely on someone else's name.

I grew up in a small Missouri town where everyone knew me as Doc Daley's youngest. Sometimes Mom would send me uptown to get groceries. Since everyone knew everyone, the grocer automatically put my groceries on my folks' bill, and I'd be on my way.

Until one day. A new checkout girl rang up my groceries. This time as I picked up my bag and began to walk out, she stopped me and expected me to pay the bill. For a few seconds I stammered around, "Uh, uh, I d-d-don't have money—I mean, no money on me."

Then I blurted out, "I'm Dandi." Still undaunted, and quite unimpressed, the checker didn't budge until I added, "Doc Daley's girl." She smiled and let me take the groceries, and I headed home. I had received those groceries in my parents' name. Mine wasn't good enough.

A couple of days ago, I spent one of my most trying mornings begrudging every stroke it took me to scour my husband's scuffmarks from the kitchen linoleum. I set a new decibel record for continuous yelling at children, and I cheated on my diet. By the time I got around to having my morning devotions, it was almost evening. As I began to pray, I felt guilty:

"Lord, there's no reason you should listen to me today. I've been just awful. I don't deserve to enter your throne room or to have you answer any of my prayers. I don't deserve . . ."

Then God interrupted me:

"Dandi, of course you don't deserve to come into my presence and ask me for things. But today's no different than any other day. You will never earn the right to pray to me, even when you have been on your best behavior. Your name is not good enough to open an account here. Christ's name has opened an account for you. You can cash in on His name. He has earned the right of answered prayer. Pray in *His* name."

Check and see in whose name you are praying. Are you making your request, believing you deserve the answer? Or, in childlike trust, are you praying as a child of the King, expecting God's answer because of what Christ has done for you, not because of anything you have done for him?

Sea

"But let him ask in faith without any doubting, for the one who doubts is like the surf of the sea driven and tossed by the wind. For let not that man expect that he will receive anything from the Lord, being a double-minded man, unstable in all his ways" (Jas. 1:6-8).

If you are being tossed about like the surf of the sea, God may turn down your prayer request. Are you sure you want what you're praying for? Or are you double-minded, likely to pray something different under different circumstances? God wants to give good gifts to His children. But how can He, if we won't sit still long enough to receive them?

How can we make requests of faith, without any doubting? Focus on God and His stable promises, not on the sea of fickle circumstances. Peter was doing fine walking on the Sea until He took his eyes off Jesus and focused on the water. Make your petition; then keep your eyes on God—not on circumstances, not even on your request.

Jesus said, "And everything you ask in prayer, believing, you shall receive" (Matt. 21:22). How can we pray, believing? How can we keep from doubting? God doesn't want us to psych ourselves into an emotional fervor. Simply take God at His word. The better you know God, the stronger your focus on His characteristics, the easier it will be for you to trust Him with an unwavering faith.

Will

When God says no to your entreaty, check to see if you've prayed for something out of God's will. How can we know God's will? The simplest way to find God's will is to look for it in the Bible.

Most of our prayer requests should originate from the Scriptures. If God has issued us a command, we know this is His will for us. For example, Ephesians 5:18-21 contains these commands:

—"Do not get drunk with wine
—Be filled with the Spirit
    (speaking to one another in psalms and hymns and spiritual songs, singing and making melody with your heart to the Lord; always giving thanks for all things in the name of our Lord Jesus Christ to God, even the Father)
—Be subject to one another in the fear of Christ."

Right away we know it is God's will for us to be filled with the Spirit, to always give thanks for all things, to be subject to one another. Combine these commands with the promise of 1 John 5:14-15, that God will hear and grant any request that is according to His will. What do we have? If I pray to be filled with the Spirit, God will fill me. Why? Because I have prayed according to His will. If I pray that I will learn how to subject myself to other Christians, I can know God will grant my request.

Know God's will and pray according to that will. Jesus commanded, "Go therefore and make disciples" (Matt. 28:19). It is God's will for us to make disciples. If I entreat the Lord to help me fulfill his command, I can know He will do it.

Try this exercise. In a notebook, write down each command you come across as you read through the Bible. Try using these commands as a source for your prayer time, to help you know how and for what you should pray. Praying from God's revealed will in the Bible helps us pray without doubting. Hold your finger on the verse, not demanding your rights, but standing on God's grace and His promises. You can have faith that God always answers prayers that originate from Him and are directed to Him.

If you are having trouble loving someone, turn to 1 John 4:7: "Beloved, let us love one another, for love is from God"; or 1 John 3:18: "Little children, let us not love with word or with tongue, but in deed and truth." Turn to John 15:12: "This is My commandment, that you love one another, just as I have loved you." Tell God you know He has commanded you to love. Pray for this love and trust Him to answer. By faith, thank Him that He has given you love for that person (regardless of your feelings at that point). Allow Christ to love through you.

If you're worried, turn to Philippians 4:6: "Be anxious for nothing"; or John 14:1: "Let not your heart be troubled"; or John 14:27: "Peace I leave with you; My peace I give to you; not as the world gives, do I give to you." Hold your finger on those verses and pray for God's peace. He has commanded you not to be anxious. He will grant your prayer according to His will.

God not only wants us to ask for things that are according to His will; He may want us to ask for them more than once. The message of the Lord came to Isaiah: "You who remind the Lord, take no rest for yourselves;/And give Him no rest until He establishes/And makes Jerusalem a praise in the earth" (Isa. 62:6-7).

I don't understand all the reasons why our omnipotent, omniscient, omnipresent God wants His feeble and frail children to remind Him—but He does. *God* never has a lapse of memory, but *we* tend to forget His promises. I think, if we could scan our past and see all God's answers to our prayers, we'd be shocked at the number of times we failed to see His answers. Reminding the Lord is one way of "holding our fingers on the verse."

Later in Isaiah, in his prayer for God's mercy, He lamented that there was no one who called on God's name, no one who aroused himself to take hold of God (Isa. 64:7). Be careful. Complacency in our daily lives can lull us into forgetfulness. We need to arouse ourselves to take hold of God and pray for His promises, according to His will.

At least 90 percent of God's will for us has already been revealed in the Bible: We should become Christians; we should marry Christians. We should conduct ourselves as Christian men and women, wives and husbands, raise children according to biblical principles. We should be involved in evangelism and discipleship. We should be good neighbors, workers, friends. God's guarantee accompanies prayers that are in accordance with His will.

But what about those other decisions we face, the ones not spelled out in the Bible? Do I major in chemistry or English lit? Do I take the job downtown or in the suburbs? Do we send the kids to this school or that one? After we've applied every biblical principle, how shall we pray?

Let's examine three terms, or expressions, frequently used when Christians discuss God's will:

1. "God laid it on my heart."
2. "I used my sound mind."
3. "It was the desire of my heart."

God Laid It on My Heart

One evening during Dave's third year as pastor of our church in Chicago, he came home with an idea. "Dandi, I want to have a Bible study in our home on Friday nights."

Instantly, I countered with seven reasons why this was not a good idea. (I could have come up with more, but he caught me by surprise.) Our church was growing already. We already had meetings every Sunday and Wednesday nights. Friday night, as everyone knows, should be date night. What kind of a Bible study could we hope to have with our kids at home? Dave had too many responsibilities already. I couldn't guarantee a spotless house week in, week out. If we were to spawn another meeting, I felt we needed a smaller, more selective discipleship group. I argued well, considering such short notice.

Dave nodded pensively and decided to keep praying about it. After a few days, he was more convinced than ever. God had laid it on his heart. The crying need of our people was to study the Bible; our home was the best place for it. For over a year, that Friday night study proved some of the richest, most spiritually productive hours of the week.

Nehemiah received God's plan via his own receptive heart. When he learned that the city of Jerusalem lay in ruins and the people were in great distress, Nehemiah prayed to God. God gave him a plan to rebuild the city. Nehemiah recorded the origin of his plan. "So I prayed to the God of heaven. And I said to the King . . ." (Neh. 2:4-5).

God laid His plan on Nehemiah's heart. Therefore, Nehemiah could pray specifically for the rebuilding of Jerusalem. When we walk in tune with God, he can place great things on our hearts, supernatural plans, not limited by size or rationale.

I Used My Sound Mind

The second principle for understanding God's will suggests using our sound minds to know how we should pray or what God wants us to do. God created our minds, gave us our reasoning faculties. First Corinthians 2:16 says, "But we have the mind of Christ."

Sometimes we have to fall back on sound reasoning and logic to discern God's will or to know how to pray. My husband and I couldn't give you a chapter and verse reference to prove that our move from Vernon Hills, Illinois, to Chicago was God's will. We can't point to the place in the Bible where it says, "Dave and Dandi, pray for an apartment in Chicago, and I will answer."

Even as we began apartment hunting, we prayed that God would change our minds if He didn't want us to move. Our sound minds told us: We should live closer to our church. We could spend more time in evangelism and discipleship if we lived closer. We would save gas and time.

There's a time and place for the sound mind principle. But, beware! Our minds don't always operate in the right gear, marked "mind of Christ." Our old nature, the mind corroded by sin and the desires of this world, would love to take over. We can rationalize anything if we want it badly enough. When that happens, our reasonings can take us in the wrong direction.

For example, equally logical reasoning in debating our move from Vernon Hills to Chicago might go something like this: Vernon Hills is prettier than Chicago, more grass, more trees, less pollution, more space for the kids to play. Living closer to church will mean more work, more people bothering us and disturbing our privacy. The rent on the new place is higher than our rent at the old place. I personally hate to pack up and move.

A sound mind is valuable only when it is controlled by Christ. How can we trust our sound minds?

"And do not be conformed to this world, but be transformed by the renewing of your mind, that you may prove what the will of God is, that which is good and acceptable and perfect" (Rom. 12:2).

Let Christ renew your mind. Inundate your mind with the Scriptures. Don't let it be conformed to the world. Then you can prove what the will of God is.

It Was the Desire of My Heart

"Delight yourself in the Lord;/And He will give you the desires of your heart" (Ps. 37:4).

How simple! No wonder Psalm 37:4 is such a popular verse! If we delight in the Lord, He will give us everything we want. But if all I need to do in order to have everything my heart desires is to delight myself in the Lord, why am I not living by

the sea, rich and famous and beautiful? I delight in the Lord.
I enjoy His fellowship. I like being close to God. Isn't that
delighting? What is missing?

I think we can gain insight into the mystery of delighting in
the Lord from an unlikely source, Eliphaz the Temanite. He
gave some of the poorest, most misdirected advice to poor Job.
But in the middle of his shallow talk fell some words of wisdom, shedding light on the meaning of *delight.* Read Job 22:21-
30:

"Yield now and be at peace with Him;/Thereby good will
come to you./Please receive instruction from His mouth,/And
establish His words in your heart./If you return to the Almighty, you will be restored;/If you remove unrighteousness
far from your tent,/And place your gold in the dust,/And the
gold of Ophir among the stones of the brooks,/Then the Almighty will be your gold/And choice silver to you./For then
you will delight in the Almighty,/And lift up your face to
God./You will pray to Him, and He will hear you;/And you
will pay your vows./You will also decree a thing, and it will
be established for you;/And light will shine on your ways./
When you are cast down, you will speak with confidence/And
the humble person He will save./He will deliver one who is not
innocent,/And he will be delivered through the cleanness of
your hands."

The passage falls together around verse 26: "For then you
will delight in the Lord." Everything before verse 26 defines
what someone must do if he delights in the Lord. Everything
after verse 26 points out the results of delighting in the Lord.
Here are the conditions he set for delighting.

1. *Yield to and be at peace with God* (v. 21). Delighting includes
submission to God and His will.

2. *Receive instruction from His mouth* (v. 22). How can we be
instructed from God's mouth? Through studying His written
word in the Bible.

3. *Establish His words in your heart* (v. 22). Memorize large por-

tions of Scripture; meditate on each verse and apply God's Word to your life.

4. *If you return to the Almighty* ... (v. 23). When we sin, we need to confess our sin, agree with God we have done wrong, and be restored, accepting the forgiveness Christ bought for us on the cross. We can never delight in the Almighty unless we return to Him for restoration.

5. *If you remove unrighteousness far from your tent* (v. 23). We need to confess our unrighteousness, to be sorry for our sin. Then we must repent, remove it from us, turn away and change our actions and attitudes. If you cheat on your diet and eat a piece of chocolate cake, you don't just need to regret it—you need to give the cake away!

6. *And place your gold in the dust,/And the gold of Ophir among the stones of the brooks* ... (vv. 24-25). These verses talk about our priorities. Any "gold" or possession dearer to us than the Almighty will keep us from delighting in God. Anything that gets in between God and me is an idol. It robs God of my devotion. If I will dethrone this gold from the prominent place of honor it holds in my life, then God can take His rightful place in my heart.

For example, I consider privacy a high priority. But from time to time I place it too high and begin to fight for my privacy. I resent late-night visitors and grumble against long meetings and social obligations. Privacy becomes my gold. I won't delight in the Lord until I give up my privacy to the Lord and choose to have Him be my gold, the one thing I will really seek.

Through the process of yielding, Bible study, memorization and meditation on God's Word, confession, repentance, and making God number 1, we will delight in the Lord. When that happens, we will lift up our faces to God (v. 26), pray and be heard (v. 27), decree a thing and it will happen (v. 28), have light shining on our ways, speak with confidence (v. 29), and help deliver the innocent (v. 30)!

Delight in the Lord, and He will give you the desires of your heart. It's not magic. A heart that sincerely delights in God will share God's desires and see God answer yes.

A final caution before leaving this "W" part of our AN-SWER test. Don't forget that the most reliable source of God's will is the Bible. Whether you're praying for something God has laid on your heart, something you've deduced from your sound mind, or for a desire of your heart, remember that God will never contradict His written Word. Satan is the master deceiver. Take care to whom you listen. Our minds are fallible; desires can be self-generated. Consistently search the Scriptures for God's will.

Evil Motives

Now we come to "E" in ANSWER: Evil motives.

"What is the source of quarrels and conflicts among you? Is not the source your pleasures that wage war in your members? You lust and do not have; so you commit murder. And you are envious and cannot obtain; so you fight and quarrel. You do not have because you do not ask. You ask and do not receive, *because you ask with wrong motives,* so that you may spend it on your pleasures" (Jas. 4:1-3).

If God has said no to your request, check your motives. Why do you want this? What would you do if God granted your request? Are your desires in line with God's, or are you only concerned with your comfort and pleasure?

God must have to shake His head at some of my requests. I'm glad He doesn't automatically grant my every prayer. Occasionally I catch myself in the middle of a prayer request and see how evil my motives are. During summer, Thursday is my library day, a glorious ten hours when my husband keeps the kids at home and I sally forth to the library for study and writing. Last Thursday got off to a bad start when Katy woke up at 1:30 AM, 2:15 AM, and 4:30 AM. Her sister Jenny took over at 5:30 AM.

Dave *finally* got up and finished breakfast so I could make my getaway. As we said our good-byes, he smiled and sighed, "I've been looking forward to today all week. I need a vacation at home."

I was quick to point out that home is rarely a vacation with two children under the age of three. He chuckled something about a piece of cake, and I was out the door.

En route to the library I stopped in the middle of my prayer that was going something like this: "And please, God, take care of Jenny and Katy today. Make them as troublesome and difficult to handle as they can be. Make Jenny whine a lot and Katy cry, just to give Dave a realistic picture of. . . ."

My evil motives in that prayer were easy to detect. But sometimes our motives aren't obvious. Remember when Peter was rebuked by Christ for an evil motive. I'll bet Peter thought he was doing the right thing by telling Christ not to say that suffering and death lay waiting for him. But Jesus fingered Peter's motive: "Get behind Me, Satan; for you are not setting your mind on God's interests, but man's."

How can we guard against evil motives? Be consistent in studying the Bible. The Word of God is "sharper than any two-edged sword, and piercing as far as the division of soul and spirit, of both joints and marrow, and *able to judge the thoughts and intentions of the heart*" (Heb. 4:12). Even if I am not fully conscious of my intentions, the Spirit of God knows. Let God's Spirit speak to you through the Bible and reveal any evil motives.

Reverence

"In the days of His flesh, He offered up both prayers and supplications with loud crying and tears to the One able to save Him from death, and He was heard because of His *piety* [humble devotion, reverent submission, reverence]" (Heb. 5:7).

"Do not be hasty in word or impulsive in thought to bring up a matter in the presence of God. For God is in heaven and you are on the earth; therefore let your words be few" (Eccl. 5:2).

When you pray, never forget that God is God. Christ has bridged the chasm separating us from God. He has put His Spirit inside us so we can have fellowship with him. But he is still the Almighty God, who spoke and the world came into being, who could wipe out the universe in an instant. He is holy and deserves to be treated with respect and reverence.

I don't think God is amused by flippant prayers to the "man upstairs," thoughtless requests, or haphazard pleas. Prayer takes us into God's holy of holies, His throne room. Our attitude should reflect our reverence for God, our respect for His power, His sovereignty, His wisdom.

An antonym for "reverent" might be "presumptuous." Presumptuous is defined as "arrogant, rash, overconfident." If we want to be respectful and show God reverence, we should never be presumptuous. In some advice to the Israelites in Deuteronomy, God warned about "presumptuous prophets." If a prophet says he speaks in the name of the Lord and predicts something, but that something never happens, then that prophet has spoken presumptuously. He has shown arrogance and rash overconfidence. He has spoken for himself, but claimed to be speaking for the Lord.

Be careful in your prayers not to speak presumptuously. Don't say, "God has revealed to me that this will happen" unless you're positive God has spoken it. A mature Christian leader felt impressed of the Lord that his friend would recover from a serious illness. He shared his confidence with the sick man's wife. Two days later his friend died. He had spoken presumptuously.

When Dave and I bought our house, we were happy, but our parents were elated. At last we would settle down just like normal people—for at least three to five years, we assured our families.

Well, after an enjoyable six months as homeowners, we

followed God's leading in another direction—quite a distance. We accepted an overseas missionary assignment.

It was a hard decision. We loved our home and our life in the community; we might never have another chance to own a home. Yet we knew God was calling us overseas to a special ministry. The hardest part would be breaking the news to our poor parents that their kids were back to abnormal.

First step, sell our house. I decided I wanted to grow in my prayer life, to take a step of faith, and pray that we would sell our house in one week, by Thursday. I wanted to make my request specific and see God come through for us. I even shared this request verbally with a couple of friends.

Well, Wednesday night came, but no buyers. "Thursday, Thursday," I prayed. Thursday morning, two couples came to look at the house, but neither was very interested. Finally, at eight o'clock Thursday evening a realtor called and asked if she could show our house. This time I knew God was about to answer, and just in the nick of time. The house hunter thoroughly examined every inch of the building and came out grinning. No question, this was our man!

Later that night, his realtor called and said they were drawing up a sales agreement. I was so happy! It had worked! I prayed for Thursday—and it happened!

Friday morning the realtor called back and apologized. The client was unable to come up with the proper financing. The deal was off. When I hung up the phone, I felt sick inside. I wasn't really afraid that God wouldn't sell our house; but I was disappointed in my failing prayer experiment in faith.

That morning as I picked up my quiet time study where I had left it the day before, God's Word "sharply divided my joints and marrow" and "judged the thoughts and intentions of my heart."

I was reading through Deuteronomy and came upon the verse about the presumptuous prophet. As soon as I read it, God's Spirit convicted me. To sell the house on Thursday was not God's idea. God had not given me Thursday as the day when our house should be sold. I had arbitrarily, or presumptuously, set Thursday and decided to pray for that day. It was very presumptuous! God doesn't play games. He's not bound by my whims.

My mind raced back through memories when I had prayed, or seen others pray, toward a certain date or a given number, and God answered yes. Those prayers had not been presumptuous, but God had given the specifics. My problem this time wasn't that I had prayed specifically, but that I had prayed presumptuously. The next day, we sold our house.

In Psalm 19:13 David said, "Also keep back Thy servant from presumptuous sins;/Let them not rule over me;/Then I shall be blameless,/And I shall be acquitted of great transgression."

In the right spirit you can ask the question, "Why did I get that no?" Run through the ANSWER checklist. Are you abiding with Christ, letting his Word abide in you? Are you praying in His name? Are you being driven with doubt as the surf of the sea? Are you praying according to God's will? Are your motives evil? And are you reverent and respectful to God?

Study Questions

Study Passage: Hebrews 12:12-16
1. List specific instances when you wondered why God said no to your prayers.

2. Did you ever learn why God said no?

3. What is the danger in asking, "Why did God say no?" What can we do to avoid that danger?

4. See if you can recall what each letter stands for in AN-SWER test. Explain what each concept means and how we can learn to pray more effectively.

A

N

S

W

E

R

10

When God Says No, Look Up!

The secret of taking God's no for an answer is: Know God. When God says no, look up. Focus on God, His nature and character, who it is who has decided it's best for you not to have your way this time.

We get ourselves into trouble when we look in directions other than upward. If our eyes wander from our Master, they may land on our circumstances, or on ourselves.

Don't Focus on Circumstances

It's usually easier to focus attention on circumstances than to focus on God. Circumstances crowd around us every day and make us react to them or stumble over them. If God turns down your request for a Friday night date, the fact that you are sitting home alone at 9:30 Friday night stares you in the face.

Circumstances come into focus easily. We have to cultivate a focus that sees God. If we do nothing, circumstances will take over. It doesn't take a conscious choice to fall prey to circumstances; it's what we do naturally.

Guard against a circumstance-centered focus. When God says no, jerk your eyes off your disappointment or your problem, and set your focus on God. The longer we focus on circumstances, the greater the temptation to distort our perception of God. Don't concoct a false image of God by reasoning from your circumstances. For example:

"If God would let my mother suffer like this, He must be cruel."

"Only a God without compassion would allow that fire to burn their house to the ground."

"It's not fair that I should be punished and he should go free. God's not fair."

How can we fight to keep our focus off our circumstances? The best defense is a good offense. First, focus on God. I follow up this chapter with a plan to help you focus on God. If your eyes are riveted to your Lord, they may not be so easily drawn away by a disappointing answer to your prayer.

In addition, every time you find yourself bogged down by your circumstances, confess your misplaced focus as sin. God commands us to trust Him. If we don't, we are guilty of disobedience.

Next, as soon as God says no, give Him thanks. Don't wait until you feel thankful. It may be too late by then.

Don't Focus on Yourself

Focusing inward sets the most dangerous snare for me when I'm having trouble taking God's no for an answer. When I was single, I used to try to figure out what was wrong with me. Most of my friends had successfully prayed for husbands. Where did I go wrong? What was my tragic flaw?

In the years before God gave us our children, Dave and I were tempted to think God didn't deem us fit for parenthood. Should we try to figure out what was wrong with us, why God kept saying no to our prayers for a baby?

There is a place for healthy, tempered introspection in the Christian life, a time when we need to check ourselves and make sure we are standing firm in the faith, walking in the Spirit.

Yet excessive introspection when God answers no to our

prayers can weaken our focus on God by zeroing in on ourselves. Let me give you a few reasons why I think this kind of introspection may be unhealthy:

1. *We already know we're no good* (in ourselves, apart from Christ). If I focus inward and rest my vision on my old sin nature, I shouldn't be surprised when I get discouraged. My sin nature will keep decaying, getting worse and worse until I die and get rid of it.

"For all of us have become like one who is unclean,/And all our righteous deeds are like a filthy garment;/And all of us wither like a leaf,/And our iniquities, like the wind, take us away" (Isa. 64:6).

"For in Thy sight no man living is righteous" (Ps. 143:2). If you are going to look inside, be prepared for what you will see. And don't stay there too long!

2. *God's plan is sovereign.* No matter how hard you try to search yourself for the reasons why God has said no, remember that God is sovereign. God doesn't lend His stamp of approval to your plan if you are very, very good. He doesn't punish you with a no answer because you have been too bad. Rather, God has a plan for you. John 15:16 says: "You did not choose Me, but I chose you, and appointed you, that you should go and bear fruit, and that your fruit should remain, that whatever you ask of the Father in My name, He may give to you."

God chose us. He continually reveals His plans for us as we depend on Him and become more like Christ. As we mature in Christ, our minds and desires should increasingly align themselves with Christ's desires and will for us. Our prayers should become more effective the closer we draw to Christ.

Don't let your excessive introspection rob you of valuable fellowship with God through "unanswered" prayers. Don't pray less, afraid you will only get another no answer. Pray more! But don't be hasty or haphazard. Follow the command of Philippians 4:6: "Be anxious for nothing, but *in everything* by prayer and supplication with thanksgiving *let your requests be made known to God."*

3. *We can't see straight.* Rarely do we emerge with an accurate self-evaluation when we delve deeply into the recesses of our souls. We can be hardened by the deceitfulness of sin, blinded by Satan, and misled by measuring ourselves against others rather than against God's holy standard.

Paul wrote the Corinthians that he had given up trying to examine himself. That was God's job.

"But to me it is a very small thing that I should be examined by you, or by any human court; in fact, I do not even examine myself. I am conscious of nothing against myself, yet I am not by this acquitted; but the one who examines me is the Lord. Therefore do not go on passing judgment before the time, but wait until the Lord comes who will both bring to light the things hidden in the darkness and disclose the motives of men's hearts; and then each man's praise will come to him from God" (1 Cor. 4:3-5).

Focus on God, not on yourself. Let His Word and His Spirit point out your weaknesses. We don't have to scrape down and ferret out our flaws. The Holy Spirit will convict us of sin. Fix your eyes on Jesus, the Author and Perfector of our faith.

Focus on God

Focus on God and his character when God says no to your prayers. Then take it from there. Because God is loving and kind, His refusal is the kindest thing God could do for you. God has the power to grant any request, but He possesses all knowledge. He knows that the best answer to your prayer is a no answer.

Take God up on His invitation to step into his special laboratory in the school of prayer. You will recognize the classroom by the big "NO" on the door, or an adjacent room marked "WAIT." Come on in and listen to God. He will teach you about Himself, about you, and about your circumstances.

A focus on God doesn't come naturally. We don't automatically gain all knowledge of God once we accept Christ as Savior. How can we expect to know God, to see Him as He is? He is not at all like us. His thoughts are not like our thoughts; our ways are not His ways. Don't read your own flaws into God's character. God won't give up on you, stop loving you, or change.

God has revealed Himself to us in the Bible. We have to commit ourselves to daily study and prayer to let God "reprogram" our minds and give us His understanding. We won't just stumble onto the truth. We need to study the truth, to live in God's Word, to fix our minds on Christ Jesus.

We should be students of the Bible. A verse a day won't keep Satan away. You need a plan for studying the Bible. If you are using a system that works for you, stick to it! If you have been closing your eyes and picking a page, or a book of the Bible, you need a system. You may want to try one of the following Bible study methods. They are not original, but represent tips I've picked up over the years.

Read

You might want to begin with a study method that takes you through the Bible in a year. Daily readings average out to only three to four chapters a day, rarely more than ten minutes of straight reading. And every year you will have read the whole Bible.

You could choose from many reading plans. My plan, the last chart at the end of this book, simply combines two or three Old Testament chapters with one New Testament chapter, whenever possible, to keep you in the whole of Scripture. When you read, read with a pen! Underline, scratch questions in the margins, take notes.

Read prayerfully and expect God to meet you through His Word. "Open my eyes, that I may behold/Wonderful things from Thy law" (Ps. 119:18). We can read and study; but the Holy Spirit has to teach us.

O.I.A.: Observe, Interpret, Apply

This method works well if you want to study a passage of Scripture or a chapter or a book of the Bible.

1. *Observe* the text, passage by passage or chapter by chapter. Ask, "Who? What? Where? When? Why?" Write down your answers in a notebook you can save. Look for contrasts, similarities, repetitions, things in a series.

2. *Interpret.* Ask, "What does this text mean?" Try to find the one big idea of the passage. Are there promises to claim? Commands to keep? This interpretation phase may be the most neglected step of Bible study today. Unfortunately, much of modern Christianity prefers to ask, "What does this text mean to me?" without first honestly wrestling with, "What does this text actually mean?" As a result, personal feelings, experiences, and intuition may receive more attention than God's intended Word. Don't skip this step! What does this passage say?

3. *Apply.* Now you can ask, "What does this text mean to me?" "Where do I fall short?" "What do I need to do about this?" "Is there something I need to change? Start doing? Stop doing?" Write down these applications and plan them into your routine.

Horizontal Book Chart

The horizontal book chart helps you view an entire book of the Bible telescopically, to see the big picture. You can summarize, or condense, a book in order to notice at a glance the interrelation of chapters and topics. First, make a chart, divided into the number of sections equal to the number of chapters in the book you plan to study. In my chart on 1 Peter I have divided the page into five sections (for five chapters).

Next, give each chapter a title. (Note the segment on my chart designated "A".)

Divide chapters into paragraphs, and entitle each paragraph (segments "B" in first column of chart).

Subdivide paragraphs as detailed as you want to get in your chart (segments marked "C").

Write applications on the bottom of each section, and pray these into your life (Section "D").

Horizontal Book Chart—1 Peter

	1 HOLINESS IS IN CHRIST	2 SUFFERING IS IN CHRIST	3 LIVING IS IN CHRIST	4 PREPARE FOR SUFFERING	5 EXHORTATIONS TO ELDERS
A					
B	vv. 1-2 Greeting C -to aliens -grace & peace vv. 3-5 Blessed be God -born again -to obtain inheritance -protected v. 6 Distressed by trials -proof of faith -praise & glory -rejoice -salvation vv. 13-21 Exhortations -gird minds -keep sober -fix hope v. 14 don't conform -be holy vv. 22-25 Love one another	vv. 1-3 Long for spir. milk vv. 4-10 Spiritual house -living stones -cornerstone -stumbling block -God's people vv. 11-12 Excellent behavior vv. 13-18 Submit to authority -king's -gov.'s -master v. 19 Suffer patiently vv. 21-25 Christ is example -no sin -didn't revile -bore sins	vv. 1-6 Wives -be submissive -win husbands -chaste & respect -gentle spirit -Sarah ex. v. 17 Husbands -understand -fellow heirs -prayers vv. 8-12 Be humble vv. 13-18 Be zealous -blessed if suffer -sanctify -good conscience -suffer for right vv. 18-22 Victory -Christ -Appeal to conscious	vv. 1-6 Arm yourself -Christ did -God's will -past lusts -in spirit vv. 7-11 With brethren -be of sound judgment -fervent -hospitable -use gift -glory to God vv. 12-19 Preparation -Don't be surprised -Rejoice -You're blessed -Glorify God -Entrust	vv. 1-5 To overseers -Shepherd flock -Be examples -Crown of glory -younger subject to elders vv. 6-9 Commands -Humble self -Cast anxiety -Be on alert -Resist Satan v. 10 God's will perfect confirm strengthen establish vv. 12-14 Greeting
D	v. 2 We're chosen that we might obey Jesus v. 13 Fix hope completely on grace v. 22 How can I fervently love others?	v. 9 Proclaim God's excellence v. 12 Will people glorify God on account of my good deeds?	v. 1 Submissive v. 8 Define the objective Quit nagging!	v. 9 I must be hospitable (even when I prefer solitude) v. 10 Use gifts to serve others	v. 1 Peter was witness of Christ's sufferings Suffer now—glory later Praise now— nothing later

Outline

Example: Ephesians 1:1-4
I. Greetings—verse 1
  A. From Paul
    1. an apostle
      a. of Christ Jesus
      b. by the will of God—Tells how and why Paul is an apostle
  B. To saints
    1. at Ephesus—See also Acts 19; Eph.; Rev. 2
    2. faithful in Christ Jesus
  C. Grace and peace to you—v. 2 - content of greeting
    1. from God our Father—Source of grace and peace
    2. from the Lord Jesus Christ—Source of grace and peace
II. Blessed be the God and Father of our Lord Jesus Christ—verse 3-Praise
  A. Who has blessed us—I need to recognize His blessings
    1. with *every* spiritual blessing—We have *all* spiritual blessings
      a. in the heavenly places
      b. in Christ says *where* blessings are
  B. Just as He *chose* us—verse 4 His will—Links with v. 1, apostle by God's will
    1. in Him
    2. before the foundation of the world—*when* He chose us
    3. *that* we should be holy and blameless
      a. before Him—tells *why* He chose us
      b. In love

Topical (Word) Study

The word study can be one of the most exciting and satisfying Bible study methods. All you do is pick a topic—husband/wife roles, God's will, obedience, love, joy, anything. Next, look up related words in a good concordance. A concordance lists Scripture verses where each word appears. An exhaustive concordance gives all the verses where you can find that word used in Scripture. Compact concordances record major verses. If I were limited to one Bible study tool, I'd choose a concordance.

When I did a study on *wives,* I used a concordance to find every passage in the Bible that might give me needed information. I looked up *wife, woman, family, mother, husband, home, marriage, children.* Then I went to some of the great women of the Bible: *Sarah, Rebekah, Hannah, Abigail, Esther, Priscilla, Elizabeth, Mary.* Your study expands as you gather God's teaching on related topics.

List these passages, either copying the verse or general meanings. Be careful not to pull the verses out of their context. There's an inherent danger in word studies. It's easy to go to the Bible to confirm our own opinion, pull verses out of context, and impose our view on the passage. Look at the passages surrounding your verse, and draw meaning from the whole portion of Scripture. Finally, draw general principles from these verses and think of applications.

A rewarding long-term project would be to make your own limited concordance. Begin with a loose-leaf notebook binder. Decide on a number of topics you want to research. Keep a separate section for each subject and label it: "God's Will," "Love," "Holy Spirit," "Sin," "Forgiveness." Then, pen in hand, as you read through the Bible, jot down verses in the appropriate pages with brief observations and applications. Eventually you'll have your own personal concordance, a ready-made resource of biblical information on several topics.

Biographical Study

Focus on someone from the Bible. Study all passages connected with him or her by using cross-references (found in the margins or between page columns in many Bibles) and a concordance. Draw applications for your own life. Don't forget that the Bible doesn't condone all the actions it records. Biblical characters were real people with real problems. But their lives, even their sins, have been recorded so that we might learn from their mistakes as well as from their successes.

"For whatever was written in earlier times was written for our instruction, that through perseverance and the encouragement of the Scriptures we might have hope" (Rom. 15:4).

Memorization and Meditation

Meditation on God's Word can sharpen your focus on God. I used to think meditation was something you did sitting cross-legged on the floor in a dark room overflowing with incense. But God has always called His people to meditate.

"This book of the law shall not depart from your mouth, but you shall meditate on it day and night, so that you may be careful to do according to all that is written in it; for then you will make your way prosperous, and then you will have success" (Josh. 1:8).

"My eyes anticipate the night watches,/That I may meditate on Thy Word" (Ps. 119:148).

When we meditate on God's Word, we concentrate on what God says to us. Memorization makes the first step of meditation. Once you've committed a portion of Scripture to memory, write out each phrase and list as many applications as you can deduce. For example:

First Corinthians 13:4

Love is patient,
　　—even at red lights!
　　—in grocery stores and bank lines
　　—when I'm ready to go and have to wait on someone
　　—when Jenny pokes on a walk
　　—when Katy knocks over her breakfast

Love is kind,
  —smile and love her, even when she's unkind
  —write letters to someone who's lonely
  —initiate friendships with neighbors
  —give Dave time alone, without making him feel guilty
  —to Jenny, when she won't take a nap
  —to other drivers and shoppers
  —make unnecessary phone calls
  —take time out to hold Katy, even when she's not crying

Love is not jealous,
  —of the success of others (their books)
  —for "my" private time
  —for my time with Dave
  —of comfy homes with fireplaces
  —when the girls prefer Dave

Love does not brag,
  —even when I'm right
  —of articles accepted for publication
  —about Jenny and Katy
  —subtly making known past accomplishments
  —even inwardly
  —or exaggerate

Love is not arrogant,
  —demanding my rights
  —must be teachable, a learner
  —behind the steering wheel
  —to inefficient salespeople.

Pray these applications into your life, and let God's Spirit call His words to mind.

As you begin your Bible studies, don't make the same mistake I made. Someone had encouraged me to write down my biblical work and notes. So I wrote down my studies—on the backs of church bulletins and letters, on napkins and paper of odd sizes. Most of my early scribbles are now lost. I've always regretted my error. I should have used standard paper and set up at least a crude file system. Harness your Bible studies! What a treat to glance over things you wrote a year ago, five years, or longer, and realize how God has been at work.

The rest of this book is a plan to help you focus on the God of the Scriptures by studying His characteristics. Our prayers, when we make our requests and when we receive God's answers, are intricately woven into God's nature. We don't just pray—we pray to God through Jesus Christ.

The first chart is a four-week prayer plan. Each day, you begin by focusing in on one characteristic of God. There are many other characteristics of God! I've chosen seven to help you remember a specific characteristic each day of the week. When I'm praying according to this plan, I know immediately when I wake up Monday morning I can praise God for his goodness. As I wait for the bus on Thursday, I can think about God's presence with me at the bus stop. All day Sunday I can concentrate on God's kindness, his *hesed* (lovingkindness) that never fails.

The next chart lists "refills" for your characteristics listed in the four-week prayer plan. I've added other characteristics and listed Scripture for them. You can build your own lists as you study through the Bible. Try to make the charts work for you. Don't wait for a perfect prayer system. Pray.

Begin your quiet time by focusing on God and praising Him. Read the Bible verses and thank God for His power, kindness, love. Consider how Jesus revealed Himself on earth. What does this passage teach you about your Heavenly Father? Think about that characteristic as you pray for your family, friends, yourself, your church. If you are concentrating on God's love, ask God to show His love to your mom today. Or pray that your son would believe God's love. Or ask God to love your next-door neighbor through you.

Go ahead and make all your regular requests. Talk to God; have fellowship with Him. I've made a space for recording any specific requests, then a blank to note God's answer; but you may want to begin your own prayer notebook. When you see if God answers yes or no, go back and fill in the blank, recording any insight God has given you into prayer.

Next, I've suggested an area of the world to pray for each day. Pray to the Lord of the Harvest to send our laborers into His harvest. Ask God to open their hearts to the gospel, to firmly establish new believers in the Word. There are some good books out about world needs that would help you pray more intelligently and specifically for international needs.

As you pray for the world, you will broaden your perspective on God's activity on earth. Have you ever noticed how, when your mind wanders during prayer, it almost always finds its way home again—home to thoughts about yourself? Planned prayer can help cut down mind wanderings.

This prayer plan is not exhaustive. We need daily confession. As we focus on God, the Spirit should begin to convict us of how far we fall short of God's standard—His love, His kindness, His mercy, His justice, His holiness. Confess sin when God's Spirit convicts you; and thank God for His forgiveness.

Try the prayer plan at the conclusion of this chapter. At the end of four weeks, look back prayerfully at God's answers to your prayers. What have you learned from God's dealings with you? Record the requests God has granted on the page marked: "YES ANSWERS." Praise God and thank Him.

Then, list your requests which God turned down on the page marked: "NO ANSWERS." What can you learn from those prayers? Do you understand why God said no? Can you trust Him for his answers? Thank God for His no answers.

On the last page, "WAITING ROOM," list any requests God has kept in a holding pattern. Check this list again in another four weeks. Has your desire increased or decreased?

If this plan has helped you pray more effectively, draw up another four-week chart, using "refill" verses and characteristics.

The way to take God's no for an answer is to know God, to focus on Him, and to let Him teach you in His special laboratory of prayer.

4-WEEK PRAYER PLAN

	Monday	Tuesday	Wednesday	Thursday	Friday	Saturday	Sunday
Week 1	GOODNESS Ps. 145 Date:___ Answer:___ Latin America	OMNIPOTENCE Ps. 8 Date:___ Answer:___ W. Europe	OMNISCIENCE Ps. 139:1-6 Date:___ Answer:___ E. Europe	OMNIPRESENCE Ps. 139:7-24 Date:___ Answer:___ Middle East	JUSTICE/HOLINESS Ps. 75 Date:___ Answer:___ Africa	LOVE Ps. 146 Date:___ Answer:___ Asia	KINDNESS Ps. 89 Date:___ Answer:___ N. America
Week 2	GOODNESS Ps. 73 Date:___ Answer:___ Latin America	OMNIPOTENCE Ps. 6 Date:___ Answer:___ W. Europe	OMNISCIENCE John 4:1-26 Date:___ Answer:___ E. Europe	OMNIPRESENCE Ps. 46 Date:___ Answer:___ Middle East	JUSTICE/HOLINESS Ps. 50 Date:___ Answer:___ Africa	LOVE 1 John 15:9-17 Rom. 8:31-9 Date:___ Answer:___ Asia	KINDNESS Ps. 63 Date:___ Answer:___ N. America
Week 3	GOODNESS Ps. 92 Date:___ Answer:___ Latin America	OMNIPOTENCE Ps. 104 Date:___ Answer:___ W. Europe	OMNISCIENCE John 2:24-25 Isa. 48:3-5 Date:___ Answer:___ E. Europe	OMNIPRESENCE Ps. 23 Date:___ Answer:___ Middle East	JUSTICE/HOLINESS Ps. 96 Date:___ Answer:___ Africa	LOVE Ps. 25 Date:___ Answer:___ Asia	KINDNESS Ps. 40 Date:___ Answer:___ N. America
Week 4	GOODNESS Ps. 100 Date:___ Answer:___ Latin America	OMNIPOTENCE Ps. 148 Date:___ Answer:___ W. Europe	OMNISCIENCE Rom. 16:25-7 Date:___ Answer:___ E. Europe	OMNIPRESENCE Ps. 46 Date:___ Answer:___ Middle East	JUSTICE/HOLINESS Ps. 99 Date:___ Answer:___ Africa	LOVE Eph. 3:14-9 Date:___ Answer:___ Asia	KINDNESS Ps. 136 Date:___ Answer:___ N. America

"REFILLS"

Goodness	Omnipotence	Justice	Holiness	Kindness	Love	Grace,Mercy	Immutability	Savior
Jer. 31:14	Ps. 6	Ps. 1	Ps. 2	Ps. 13	Ps. 86	Ps. 4	Rom. 6:26	Ps. 3
Ps. 25	Ps. 16	Ps. 7	Ps. 5	Ps. 52	Ps. 89	Ps. 6	Ps. 42	Ps. 11
Ps. 31	Ps. 19	Ps. 9	Ps. 15	Ps. 98	Ps. 112	Ps. 21	Ps. 45	Ps. 12
Ps. 118	Ps. 24	Ps. 10	Ps. 22	Ps. 106	John 3:16	Ps. 32	Ps. 46	Ps. 14
Ps. 125	Ps. 47	Ps. 43	Ps. 26	Ps. 107	Eph. 5:1-2	Ps. 38	Ps. 90	Ps. 16
	Ps. 48	Ps. 53	Ps. 29	Ps. 108	1 Cor. 13	Ps. 41	Ps. 93	Ps. 17
	Ps. 49	Ps. 54	Ps. 76	Ps. 117	John 13:1	Ps. 51	Ps. 110	Ps. 18
	Ps. 50	Ps. 67	Mark 1:24	Ps. 136	1 John 4:7-21	Ps. 56	Ps. 121	Ps. 20
	Ps. 66	Ps. 75	Rev. 4	Ps. 138		Ps. 57		Ps. 22
	Ps. 77	Ps. 82	Rev. 15	Ps. 30		Ps. 65		Ps. 27
	Ps. 95	Ps. 94		Ps. 33		Ps. 78		Ps. 28
	Ps. 96	Ps. 101		Ps. 36		Ps. 84		Ps. 31
	Ps. 97	Ps. 140				Ps. 85		Ps. 34
	Ps. 99					Ps. 86		Ps. 35
	Ps. 103					Ps. 103		Ps. 37
	Ps. 104					Ps. 111		Ps. 54
	Ps. 113					Ps. 116		Ps. 55
	Ps. 114					Ps. 123		Ps. 61
	Ps. 115					Ps. 126		Ps. 68
	Ps. 124					Ps. 127		Ps. 69
	Ps. 135							Ps. 70
	Ps. 144							Ps. 71
	Ps. 147							Ps. 81
	Ps. 148							Ps. 94
	Ps. 156							Ps. 142
	Rom. 4:21							
	Rom. 5:6							
	Rom. 16:25							

YES ANSWERS

Request   *Date Made*   *Date Answered*

NO ANSWERS

Request	Date Made	Date Answered	Any Insights

WAITING ROOM

Request   *Date Made*   *Any Insights*

THE BIBLE IN A YEAR

	Month 1			Month 2			Month 3	
1	Gen. 1—2	Matt. 1	1	Ex. 17—18	Rom. 3	1	Num. 18—19	Ps. 17
2	3—5	2	2	19—20	4	2	20—22	18
3	6—7	3	3	21—22	5	3	23—24	19
4	8—9	4	4	23—24	6	4	25—26	20
5	10—11	5	5	25—27	7	5	27—30	21
6	12—13	6	6	28—29	8	6	31—32	22
7	14—15	7	7	30—31	9	7	33—34	23
8	16—18	8	8	32—34	10	8	35—36	24
9	19—20	9	9	35—36	11	9	Deut. 1—3	25
10	21—22	10	10	37—38	12	10	4—5	1 Cor. 1
11	23—24	11	11	39—40	13	11	6—7	2
12	25—27	12	12	Lev. 1—3	14	12	8—10	3
13	28—29	13	13	4—5	15	13	11—12	4
14	30—32	14	14	6—8	16	14	13—14	5
15	33—34	15	15	9—10	Ps. 1	15	15—16	6
16	35—36	16	16	11—12	2	16	17—19	7
17	37—38	17	17	13—15	3	17	20—21	8
18	39—40	18	18	16—17	4	18	22—24	9
19	41—42	19	19	18—19	5	19	25—26	10
20	43—44	20	20	20—21	6	20	27—28	11
21	45—47	21	21	22—23	7	21	29—31	12
22	48—50	22	22	24—25	8	22	32—34	13
23	Ex. 1—2	23	23	26—27	9	23	Josh. 1—2	14
24	3—4	24	24	Num. 1—3	10	24	3—4	15
25	5—6	25	25	4—6	11	25	5—6	16
26	7—8	26	26	7—9	12	26	7—8	2 Cor. 1
27	9—10	27	27	10—11	13	27	9—10	2
28	11—12	28	28	12—13	14	28	11—12	3
29	13—14	Rom. 1	29	14—15	15	29	13—14	4
30	15—16	2	30	16—17	16	30	15—16	5

THE BIBLE IN A YEAR

	Month 4				Month 5				Month 6	
1	Josh. 17—18	2 Cor. 6	1	2 Sam. 5—6	Ps. 32	1	1 Chron. 5—6	Phil. 1
2	19—20	7	2	7—9	33	2	7—8	2
3	21—22	8	3	10—11	34	3	9—10	3
4	23—24	9	4	12—13	35	4	11—13	4
5	Judg. 1—3	10	5	14—15	36	5	14—15	Col. 1
6	4—5	11	6	16—18	37	6	16—17	2
7	6—8	12	7	19—21	38	7	18—19	3
8	9—10	13	8	22—24	39	8	20—22	4
9	11—13	Mark 1	9	1 Kings 1—2	40	9	23—24	1 Thess. 1
10	14—15	2	10	3—4	41	10	25—26	2
11	16—17	3	11	5—6	42	11	27—29	3
12	18—19	4	12	7—9	43	12	2 Chron. 1—2	4
13	20—21	5	13	10—11	44	13	3—5	5
14	Ruth 1—2	6	14	12—13	45	14	6—8	2 Thess. 1
15	3—4	7	15	14—16	46	15	9—10	2
16	1 Sam. 1—3	8	16	17—18	47	16	11—13	3
17	4—5	9	17	19—20	48	17	14—15	Luke 1
18	6—8	10	18	21—22	49	18	16—17	2
19	9—10	11	19	2 Kings 1—3	50	19	18—19	3
20	11—13	12	20	4—5	Gal. 1	20	20—21	4
21	14—15	13	21	6—8	2	21	22—24	5
22	16—18	14	22	9—10	3	22	25—26	6
23	19—20	15	23	11—12	4	23	27—28	7
24	21—22	16	24	13—14	5—6	24	29—31	8
25	23—24	Ps. 26	25	15—17	Eph. 1	25	32—33	9
26	25—26	27	26	18—19	2	26	34—36	10
27	27—28	28	27	20—22	3	27	Ezra 1—2	11
28	29—31	29	28	23—25	4	28	3—4	12
29	2 Sam. 1—2	30	29	1 Chron. 1—2	5	29	5—6	13
30	3—4	31	30	3—4	6	30	7—8	14

Why Am I a Missionary?

Why Should You Be a Missionary?

by
Jonathan Dietrich

To order additional copies of this book, please visit
http://deserttreeministry.org/book.html
or email volunteer@deserttreeministry.org

ISBN-13: 978-0-9888278-0-6

Printed by College Press
Collegedale, TN

COLLEGE PRESS

Contents

Preface

Have you ever wondered why certain people decide to become missionaries? What motivates them to leave behind a promising career and work in relative obscurity? Why do some choose to move to a foreign country where danger and risk are high compared to their home country? Why do some people feel compelled to minister to prison inhabitants or street dwellers? I get asked occasionally why I have chosen to move to Africa. Some people think that I am crazy for not pursuing a professional career in computer science after graduating with my degree. Others have given me advice to start my own business. Some comment, "Isn't the political situation over there unstable? Aren't there safer places to go? Won't you be risking your life?" It has even been offered, "If what you need to do is to get it out of your system, I'll pay for your round-trip ticket for a short mission trip. Just do it and get it over with."

In some churches, if missionaries are ever mentioned, the idea is indirectly conveyed that being a missionary is reserved for a select few qualified individuals specially called by God to do a special work. The idea is that missionaries were those from a generation or two back who traveled to an exciting place and converted the heathen. We read about "the old times" in mission story books, but many of us are disconnected from the concept of missions in our lives.

In an attempt to answer some of these questions and to encourage people to think again about the purpose of missions, I decided to write out a thorough answer that clearly shows strong Biblical support for missions. Missions is not only about sending others to the mission field; it involves *you*. Missions is not only about distant locations; it involves you, *here*. Missions is not only about something that happens next year; it involves you, here, *now*. Missions is not what some Christians do part time as a hobby; it involves you, here, now, *completely.*

Many great missionaries have lived and died, and their stories are definitely inspiring and worth reading. David Livingstone's work in Africa, George Mueller's labors for orphans, Hudson Taylor's ministry to the Chinese, Nate Saint and his colleagues' work in South America, and John Andrews' evangelizing in Europe are all good examples to consider. And many other missionaries have left behind inspiring examples of courage and faith in action. Becoming familiar with the lives and ministries of these missionaries can bring encouragement to anybody considering or involved in mission work.

While we may learn much from the lives of these people, our focus here will be on the life and ministry of Christ as a role model for missions. He is the greatest missionary that Earth will ever have, and His mission story is the best one from which to gain insight. He demonstrated the qualities of a genuine missionary far better than any human has. He showed us what missionary life is all about. The logical place to begin a story is at the beginning of the story, so let us go there now.

Notes

Texts are quoted from the New King James Version and are *italic* and indented. When you see a verse quoted, please slow down a little bit and take time to let God's Word sink in.

▮▮ Sentences or paragraphs marked with this pause symbol are to remind you to pause and take some time to think about the question or statement, not just passing over it quickly. "Let these words sink down into your ears." Luke 9:44.

The term "missionary" can refer to anybody who attempts to convert others to a certain doctrine or program. Everyone is a missionary. Some missionaries represent Satan's character and bring others to Satan. Other missionaries represent God's character and bring others to God. In this book, I use the term "missionary" in its commonly understood meaning of missionary for God.

War in the Universe

"And war broke out in heaven."
Revelation 12:7

I am a missionary because...

- I live in time of war.
- I love my King, and I know that He is going to win this war.
- I want others to defect Satan's ranks and join God's army.

...What about you?

"Oh, that I had a thousand lives and a thousand bodies! All of them should be devoted to no other employment but to preach Christ to these degraded, despised, yet beloved mortals."
Robert Moffat

Long, long ago, before God created man or woman, the universe was perfect. All of God's creation was sinless, and all the angels delighted in worshiping and honoring God. No conflict, no grumbling, no pain, no trouble existed. God had created an angel to be the group leader of all the other angels. We know from Isaiah 14:12 that this angel's name was Lucifer. He was a perfectly impressive angel. Just listen to a description of him that we find directly out of the mouth of the Lord.

> *"You were the seal of perfection, full of wisdom and perfect in beauty. You were in Eden, the garden of God; every precious stone was your covering: the sardius, topaz, and diamond, beryl, onyx, and jasper, sapphire, turquoise, and emerald with gold. The workmanship of your timbrels and pipes was prepared for you on the day you were created. You were the anointed cherub who covers; I established you; you were on the holy mountain of God; you walked back and forth in the midst of fiery stones. You were perfect in your ways from the day you were created." Ezekiel 28:12–15*

How wonderful Lucifer must have been, full of wisdom and perfect in beauty! His wisdom exceeded that of Daniel (Ezekiel 28:3; Daniel 1:20).

This state of perfection did not last forever, however. God wants His creation to love Him because they want to love Him, not because they are forced to love Him. Thus God gives each of His created beings a choice of whom they will love and worship. Forced love cannot exist, for love cannot be forced. If forced, love would cease to be love. God says about Lucifer,

> *"You were perfect in your ways from the day you were created, till iniquity was found in you." Ezekiel 28:15*

God does not sin, and He did not create iniquity in Lucifer. God does not tempt anybody (James 1:13). But somehow, and we do not know how or why, sin was found in Lucifer after he was created.

"You became filled with violence within, and you sinned; ... Your heart was lifted up because of your beauty." Ezekiel 28:16–17

How amazing, how mysterious, that in this perfect environment, Lucifer desired more honor and riches than he already had! Was he not the wisest and most beautiful of all angels? Had God not placed him in an honored position already? How could Lucifer desire something more than the perfect beauty God had blessed him with? Pride is terrible. It was then, and it is now. While we do not understand the origin of pride and cannot explain why sin arose in a perfect environment, Scripture is clear that Lucifer cultivated pride in his heart, and this contagious disease destroyed the perfect atmosphere in heaven.

Now God was faced with a terrible problem. Should He allow this new, terrible thing called pride to continue spreading to other angels, or should He lovingly separate them from the others to quarantine them? This choice must have torn God's heart, but the decision was clear. Sin and God cannot mix, for God is perfect. Sin cannot exist in His presence. Either God would have to destroy sin then, or He would have to separate the sinner from Himself.

"Behold, the Lord's hand is not shortened, that it cannot save; ... but **your** *iniquities have separated you from your God; and your sins have hidden His face from you."* (emphasis supplied) Isaiah 59:1–2

The Lord is powerful and was able to save Lucifer, but not without his consent. Lucifer's personal choice was to continue in sin. It was *his* sin that separated him from God, and it was *his* sin that hid God's face from him.

God said of Lucifer,

"therefore I cast you as a profane thing out of the mountain of God; ... I cast you to the ground." Ezekiel 28:16–17

Rebellious Lucifer could not have remained alive in heaven unless he repented,

"for our God is a consuming fire." Hebrews 12:29

Had God instantly destroyed Lucifer there, questions would have arisen in the minds of the angels about the fairness of God. Try to imagine yourself as one of the angels in heaven as we read John's account of Lucifer's rebellion in Revelation 12.

"And war broke out in heaven; Michael and his angels fought with the dragon; and the dragon and his angels fought, but they did not prevail, nor was a place found for them in heaven any longer. So the great dragon was cast out, that serpent of old, called the Devil and Satan, who deceives the whole world; he was cast to the earth, and his angels were cast out with him."
Revelation 12:7–9

Not only Lucifer, but one third of the angels yielded to pride in their hearts and were evicted from heaven (Revelation 12:4). Indeed, Lucifer's arguments must have been very attractive, convincing, and believable. Had God destroyed all sinners immediately, He would risk losing the loyalty of the other two thirds of the angels. Questions about the validity of Lucifer's arguments would have lingered. They had previously looked up to Lucifer as their friend and leader. "Could he have been right?" some might have wondered had God destroyed Lucifer. "Was God right in what He did? Is He fair?"

In order to clear up such questions forever, the Godhead gathered their infinite wisdom to construct a master plan. While allowing Lucifer to clearly demonstrate the results of his plan of rebellion for all to see, the Godhead would carry out Their plan of redemption. What began as "war in heaven" would continue as "war on earth." Lucifer, now known as Satan, would continue his activities of opposing the work of God. Simultaneously, God would continue His work. Satan would always be trying to gain control, but God would always remain in control.

Join me in listening to an imaginary conversation among the Godhead.

"We have already lost one third of our close angel friends to Lucifer. We certainly do not want to lose any more. I love each angel infinitely. Loss hurts awfully."

"How can we show the remaining angels that Lucifer's claim is false and that Our character is truly perfect and loving?"

"You know, I can hardly bear the thought of it, but Adam and Eve are going to make the same decision that Satan made. They will base their decision on selfish motives, not on love for their Father. That means there will eventually be a world full of people who will be confused about Our character. Satan will continually attempt to convince as many as possible that We are self-centered and tyrannical, and will attempt to gather as many people as he can to join him in warfare against Us."

"What will be the most effective means of communicating what We are really like?"

"I cannot bear to have all of Our children separated from Us by sin. We must arrange a plan to get them out of their mess."

"I think that one of Us should go live with them and demonstrate that We love them."

"As the Son of God, I am willing to go. Yes, I see what is involved, but I believe the mission trip is worth the trouble and risk.
Yes, resources required are immense.
It will consume a lot of Our time.
And I will not have access to all the comforts of Our heavenly home.
I will be born in a barn, and will not even own a home to live in.
Life there on Earth will be full of hardships.
Living there is dangerous—I will be living among enemies that are trying to kill Me; they oppose truth and desire to rid Earth

of opposition to their belief system. People will not always be friendly.

The risk involved is enormous. If I fail in My mission, I lose My life as well as the lives of every human being. They will no longer have an opportunity for an eternal, loving relationship with Us.

This mission trip is going to be very expensive; it will cost everything, ultimately even My own life.

And what about failure? What if Satan influences Me to yield to him even once? If I fail, infinite loss is the result. Infinite loss! Satan wins the conflict and can claim that God's claims are false.

But just think about success—infinite gain! Success in this mission means an opportunity for every human being that ever lives to live eternally. Even if only one person chooses to follow God completely, his eternal life is of infinite value and is worth the risk. The amount of time, trouble, resources, discomfort, danger, risk, or pain is incomparable to the value of the successful outcome of this plan."

"You are right, Son. As the Father, I will miss You immensely on Your missionary experience. But I will be intensely interested in what happens. I will always be just a call away. If You ever need help or encouragement, just talk to Me; I am always available for a conversation with You. In fact, just like We talk throughout the day here, We will still be able to have a continuous dialog while You are on Earth. I am willing to give You, My Son, to the world so that the entire universe will understand forevermore Our love for those We have created."

"As the Holy Spirit, I will encourage and comfort You, Son of God. You will be God, but You will also be a human with human feelings. You will not be able to depend on Yourself to live a godly life. Listen to Me when I speak, because I will be happy to act as Your early warning alarm system to alert You of temptations and to encourage You to rely fully on Your Father for strength to resist them. I am going to miss You, too, but I believe the plan is worth it because I love people so much. I will be ever present to encourage You."

Thus, in infinite love and wisdom, plans were made for the first missionary trip. It would become the most expensive, most dangerous, most risky, and most distant mission trip ever organized in history.

This incomprehensibly amazing plan for our salvation was devised and set into place long before sin entered heaven. When fully carried out, it would clearly and fully answer any accusations against God and His character forever. Time passed. God created the world and Adam and Eve. They sinned and humans began multiplying on Earth. Despite one extensive cleansing act of washing the world with the Flood, sin and sinners continued to increase. Then, when the time in Earth's history was right,

"the Word became flesh and dwelt among us, and we beheld His glory, the glory as of the only begotten of the Father, full of grace and truth." John 1:14

By choosing to live and die among us, Jesus showed by comparison and contrast the difference between the character of God and the character of Satan. The day that Jesus died on the cross, Satan lost the long conflict that he started back in heaven. His claims are now clearly proven to be false, while God's claims are plainly demonstrated to be true. Jesus showed the love of God and the extent to which He is willing to go to save even one person. And now for us, instead of a theory or an idea up in heaven, God's love has become real in a visible, human form.

▌▌ Is God fair?

"You say, 'The way of the Lord is not fair.' Hear now, O house of Israel, is it not My way which is fair, and your ways which are not fair?" Ezekiel 18:25

▌▌ Is there anything more God could have done to make His character more clear to us and to the universe?

*"He who did not spare His own Son but gave Him up for us all,
how will He not also with him graciously give us all things?"
Romans 8:32*

God has already provided everything possible to encourage us
to make the decision to follow Him. One day soon, every
person will recognize that He could not possibly have done
more than to make an infinite sacrifice at infinite risk. Even
though one may not accept Jesus' sacrifice of love for himself,
he is forced to recognize God's fairness.

*"As I live, says the Lord, every knee shall bow to Me, and every
tongue shall confess to God." Romans 14:11*

The angels loudly proclaim in front of God's throne,

*"Worthy is the Lamb who was slain to receive power and riches
and wisdom, and strength and honor and glory and blessing!"
Revelation 5:12*

Ultimately, after the rebellion is finished, every living being
in the entire universe will proclaim,

*"Blessing and honor and glory and power be to Him who sits on
the throne, and to the Lamb, forever and ever!" Revelation 5:13*

The unanimous answer throughout the entire universe is a
resounding, "Yes, God is fair!"

Although we know that Satan has been overcome, he will
become more intense and angry as we progress through the
final moments of earth's history. He hates God and tries his
best to deprive God of as many subjects as he can.

*"The devil has come down to you in great wrath, because he
knows that his time is short!" Revelation 12:12*

Satan knows that he is doomed. He believes the Bible
prophecies about himself.

*"Yet you shall be brought down to Sheol, to the lowest depths of
the Pit." Isaiah 14:15*

"Therefore I brought fire from your midst; it devoured you, and I turned you to ashes upon the earth.... You ... shall be no more forever." Ezekiel 28:18-19

Satan desires to bring as many people as possible with him to eternal destruction in hell. Not only Satan, but all sin and unrepentant sinners will cease to exist someday.

The Lord says to the wicked,

"For behold, the day is coming, burning like an oven, and all the proud, yes, all who do wickedly will be stubble. And the day which is coming shall burn them up." Malachi 4:1

And to the righteous, He says,

"You shall trample the wicked, for they shall be ashes under the soles of your feet." Malachi 4:3

"Now salvation, and strength, and the kingdom of our God, and the power of His Christ have come, for the accuser of our brethren, who accused them before our God day and night, has been cast down. And they overcame him by the blood of the Lamb and by the word of their testimony." Revelation 12:10-11

▌▌ What is my response when I consider the price in which God's love and fairness was demonstrated? Do I sit back and merely say, Thanks, that's nice? Would not such a response be the height of ingratitude? Or does the love of Jesus for me motivate me to action?

When I see what Jesus did for me, when I see what sacrifice and risk He accepted, when I try to understand the infinite value and love of what Jesus did, I cannot help but choose to accept what He has done for me. Jesus' life of sacrifice inspires me. It inspires me not only with love and adoration for Him, but it inspires me to action.

We are not left as mere observers in this story; we have a role to play. Although the outcome of the conflict between God and Satan has been determined, Satan stubbornly continues fighting. As he intensifies his anger in the short time he has remaining, why should we not intensify our devotion and

Christian warfare? Each soul lost is felt in an incredible way in God's heart, and Satan wishes to hurt God to the maximum.

Do we feel enough—do we feel anything—in our hearts for souls that are lost? The battles continue, and right now, you are a participant in this great controversy. Not only are you engaged in this warfare, but people all around you are struggling as well. Each day there are casualties, and people are buried to await their award. We cannot be indifferent to the eternal well-being of these people. We must take an interest in sharing the gospel with those who do not understand. We cannot be neutral in this conflict. We are either actively supporting Satan, or we are actively supporting God.

Why would you choose to work for the losing side? We already know the outcome of the war. Are you involved in active warfare in God's army? If not, there is only one other side. Which side are you on?

> "*Choose for yourselves this day whom you will serve.... But as for me and my house, we will serve the Lord.*" Joshua 24:15

Understanding the controversy between Christ and Satan gives us a context on which to base all of life's decisions. Whether we know it or not, whether we like it or not, whether we want to or not, we are involved in this conflict. We are participants. We are combatants. There is no neutrality. Our choices in life, whether small or large, evidence which side we are on. Knowing with certainty from God's unchanging, eternal Word that God is victorious in this conflict, which side have you chosen to be on?

▋▋ Which side have you been helping? Which side will you choose now? Is it clear to people here and to the watching universe that you are on Christ's side?

To neglect making a conscious decision to be on God's side is to choose the losing side.

As you choose to join God's side and become a part of His army, you are given a specific task to accomplish. You are given a mission. God has made His army's work clear. In fact, Jesus' missionary life on earth is an example for us to follow. Our mission is the same as Christ's mission. To understand our work and our mission better, we need to study Jesus' life and example.

CHRIST OUR MISSIONARY

"God had an only Son and He made Him a missionary."
David Livingstone

Christ's missionary life is the Pattern from which we should model our lives. To His disciples He said, "Follow Me."
"If anyone desires to come after Me, let him deny himself, and take up his cross, and follow Me." Matthew 16:24

God does not merely say "Do this, and figure out how you are going to do it." He always enables us to do the things He asks us to do. By journeying to Earth as a missionary, Jesus left us a clear example, and expects us to follow in His steps.
"Christ also suffered for us, leaving us an example, that you should follow in His steps." 1 Peter 2:21

Christ is our example Missionary, sent from heaven to earth to show us more clearly God's character. In the chapters that follow, we will study His example and how we can imitate it.

The more we study the life of Christ and His character and His mission, the more clearly we will understand it. Every time we study, we will find something new to learn. This topic is infinite, inexhaustible, unending.

Recognize this as you read the material that follows and understand that this book is not intended to be a complete defense and description of missions or missionary work. It is a non-comprehensive summary study intended to help launch you into deeper study on this topic.

Take time to meditate on the questions. Look up the texts in your Bible and mark them. Pray for God to teach you His will as you read.

Commission

"Go therefore and make disciples of all nations."
Matthew 28:19

I am a missionary because...

o   I want to be obedient to God's command.

o   It is my duty.

o   God has assigned me this task.

o   God led us here.

...What about you?

"If you don't have a definite call to stay here,
you are called to go."
Keith Green

We are not left in the dark to wonder what our work is or how we are to do our work. Our commission is clear, and we have Jesus as our Example to follow.

Think with me about the meaning of the word "commission." Break it up into the two parts "co" and "mission." "Co" means "with." "Mission" in this case means a special assignment. We can think about the following commissions as special assignments given from God where He works "with" the one given the assignment.

The word "missionary" is for those who accomplish the mission. A definition of "missionary" is "one who is sent or appointed by authority to perform a service."

- O Somebody is sent:
  Jesus was sent.
- O Somebody is appointed:
  God appointed Him by His own authority.
- O A service is being performed:
  Jesus was to do the will of His Father in heaven.

Christ's Commission

Before we study about our Great Commission, we need to look at Jesus' commission and the surrounding events. It is important that we understand how Jesus was sent because we, as modern disciples, are sent as He was sent.

Talking to His Father, Jesus said,
"As You sent Me into the world, I also have sent them into the world." John 17:18

And later, talking to His disciples, Jesus said,
"Peace to you! As the Father has sent Me, I also send you." John 20:21

Unless we understand Jesus' commission, we will not grasp the significance of His mission, and we will not be effective missionaries. So what was Jesus' commission, and how was He sent?

- At a specific time in history, and
- in a strategic geographical region,
- Jesus was anointed, and
- was filled with the Holy Spirit to begin His ministry.

TIME

First of all, the work of Jesus' commission was set to begin at a precise time in history. This had been planned for thousands of years, and even before Creation (Revelation 13:8). His official ministry was to begin at His anointing, predicted in the seventy-week prophecy (Daniel 9:24). Jesus was to minister for the first half of the last week in this time period, or for three and a half years. Jesus came exactly on time.

PLACE

Secondly, Jesus' ministry was designed to take place in a certain geographic region. Long before, Micah predicted that Jesus would be born in a small town in Judah, called Bethlehem, and that He would minister to and feed His flock who would be the remnant of Jacob,

"among the Gentiles, in the midst of many peoples." Micah 5:2, 4, 7

Daniel also foretold that Jesus would minister to God's special people in Jerusalem. (Daniel 9:24) Indeed, Jesus ministered to the Jews in Jerusalem and in the immediate surrounding area of Palestine. Jerusalem, the center for trade for much of the world, was indeed "in the midst of many peoples."

BAPTISM

A third observation is that Jesus' mission officially began with His anointing service, or baptism. (Luke 3:23) We often associate anointing with pouring oil onto somebody's head. Jesus' anointing did not involve oil, but it did involve the Holy

Spirit represented by a dove. In Scripture, oil often refers to the Holy Spirit.

> *"John bore witness saying, 'I saw the Spirit descending from heaven like a dove, and He remained on Him.'" John 1:32*

God the Father was very pleased by this public demonstration of a full surrender to Him. Jesus realized the significance of this anointing relative to the tasks of His ministry here. He became "filled with the Holy Spirit," and was "led by the Spirit." (Luke 4:1) The Spirit immediately led Him into the wilderness where He was tempted by Satan. He suffered severely for us there. Wild beasts were around Him, but angels from heaven ministered to Him. (Mark 1:12–13)

HOLY SPIRIT

Fourthly, Jesus understood His important work of helping us to better understand the character of God, and that He had received the Holy Spirit for accomplishing this work. One day He was teaching in the synagogue in Nazareth and decided to read the following passage from Isaiah 61:

> *"The Spirit of the Lord is upon Me, because He has anointed Me to preach the gospel to the poor; He has sent Me to heal the brokenhearted, to proclaim liberty to the captives and recovery of sight to the blind, to set at liberty those who are oppressed; to proclaim the acceptable year of the Lord."*

Then He remarked,

> *"Today this Scripture is fulfilled in your hearing." Luke 4:18–21*

Why did He receive the Holy Spirit? It was to enable Him to do the work that God had for Him to do. It was a multi-faceted work involving all areas of human need. And toward the end of His earthly ministry He said,

> *"I have glorified You on the earth. I have finished the work which You have given Me to do.... I have manifested Your name."*
> *John 17:4, 6*

By relying on the Holy Spirit, Jesus lived a life of complete surrender to the Father's will.

ACTION

By becoming human, Jesus chose to be as helpless as we are to do God's will. But He accomplished much by relying on His Father's gifts and infinite resources. Speaking of Himself, Jesus said,

"The Son can do nothing of Himself, but what He sees the Father do; for whatever He does, the Son also does in like manner.... I can of Myself do nothing." John 5:19, 30

By reflecting His Father, Jesus showed that His success was the result of His dependence on God. He lacked nothing He needed for His work. Look at this amazing list of things that were given to Jesus.

o Power to forgive sins...............................Matthew 9:6, 8

o All authority in heaven and earth...........Matthew 28:18

o Authority to execute judgment.........................John 5:27

o All things...................................John 13:3, 5; 17:7

o Wisdom to do mighty works..............................Mark 6:2

o Life in the Father..John 5:26

o Works...John 5:36

o People to give everlasting life...................John 6:38–40;
                                                        John 17:11, 24

o Words for salvation of people...................John 17:8–9

o Glory..John 17:22, 24

o A cup to drink..John 18:11

Jesus' commission is indeed amazing to study. His mission was to commence at a certain time in history and in a specific geographical region. The beginning of His official ministry was marked by His being anointed by the Holy Spirit. His life was filled with the Holy Spirit, and He was given whatever resources He needed to carry out the works specified in His commission.

Our Commission

" 'You are My witnesses,' says the Lord." *Isaiah 43:10*

Just before Jesus returned to heaven at the end of His mission trip to Earth, He left His disciples with instructions. This Great Commission applies to us as much as it applied to them. Jesus said,

"All authority has been given to Me in heaven and on earth. Go therefore and make disciples of all the nations, baptizing them in the name of the Father and of the Son and of the Holy Spirit, teaching them to observe all things that I have commanded you; and lo, I am with you always, even to the end of the age."
Matthew 28:18–20

As we look at this Scripture and others, we will discover similarities to Jesus' commission. Each of us is to take part in fulfilling this commission at a specific time and in a certain region. Just as Jesus did, we will need to depend completely on the Holy Spirit to successfully carry out the details of this commission.

Remember the definition of "missionary" we read earlier: "one who is sent or appointed by authority to perform a service."

- O Somebody is sent:
  We are sent.
- O Somebody is appointed:
  God appointed *us* by His own authority.
- O A service is being performed:
  We are to do the will of *our* Father in heaven.

Time

God's plan for each person is to be fulfilled on a precise time line, and Jesus is not the only person to be born exactly on time. Take for example the prophet Jeremiah. God told him,

> *"Before I formed you in the womb I knew you; before you were*
> *born I sanctified you; I ordained you a prophet to the nations."*
> *Jeremiah 1:5*

God had a plan for Jeremiah and designed that he would be
born when the nations needed a prophet. God sees the future
and every soul to be born.

> *"Whom He foreknew, He also predestined to be conformed to the*
> *image of His Son." Romans 8:29*
> *"He chose us in Him before the foundation of the world."*
> *Ephesians 1:4*
> *"[God] has saved us and called us with a holy calling ... before*
> *time began." 2 Timothy 1:9*

Wow! God may not have put a time in the Bible about you or
me as individuals, but He knew when you would live as surely
as He knew when Jesus' mission trip would happen. God has
you on this Earth for a specific purpose. When He says "Go
therefore," do not question His command. Simply obey. Now
is the time to obey His command because now is when you
have been given the gift of life.

PLACE

While Jesus' ministry took place in the area surrounding
Jerusalem, He planned for His disciples to extend their circle
of influence.

> *"But you shall receive power when the Holy Spirit has come upon*
> *you; and you shall be witnesses to Me in Jerusalem, and in all*
> *Judea and Samaria, and to the end of the earth." Acts 1:8*

A quick geographical analysis of this statement enables us to
observe concentric circles. Jerusalem was nearby, Judea and
Samaria were bordering, and the end of the earth was
everything else.

Perhaps here lies a principle of starting to be a missionary
where you are. Do not wait for a special call to travel to some
far land, but begin to be a missionary now where you are.
Minister to your family and close friends. Branch out to your

neighbors. And as God leads, increase your circle of influence to areas farther from home.

The Great Commission tells us to go and make disciples of *all* the nations. It does not include only the ones that are the easiest to access. It does not include only those that are politically stable. It does not include only the most popular or glamorous. It does not include only those places with a comfortable climate. It includes all inhabited regions of the world. Do we not have missionaries in most of the countries in the world? Are we not doing very well as a church in our mission work? If that is what you are thinking, it is time to get a more realistic view of our responsibility to God. The special end-time messages carried by the three angels of Revelation 14 have an associated domain. Look here at verse 6.

> *"Then I saw another angel flying in the midst of heaven, having the everlasting gospel to preach to those who dwell on the earth—to every nation, tribe, tongue, and people."*

Jesus did not die for the salvation of nations—He died for the salvation of individuals from those nations.

> *"You are worthy ... for You were slain, and have redeemed us to God by Your blood out of every tribe and tongue and people and nation." Revelation 5:9*

God died for every person in every nation, tribe, language, and people group. Our job in general as Christians is to carry the message of salvation to *everybody*. The work may be easy or hard, fun or boring, safe or dangerous, cheap or expensive, cold or hot, highlands or lowlands, social or solitary, but we have a duty to spread the gospel.

God knows where He wants you to work, and He knows how to enable you to be most effective in that area. Jesus' place of labor was Palestine, far from His heavenly home. Your place to be a missionary may be in your home town. Or, God may be calling you to work for Him in a more distant area. Do not quickly dismiss that thought. Perhaps if you are too old to travel, or if you have some other physical limitation, God's work for you is in a nearby region. However, if you are younger and physically capable, seriously consider God's command to "Go." It is a command that few people seem impressed with, despite its universal applicability.

BAPTISM

The third similarity between Jesus' commission and ours is baptism. The baptism of Jesus, our Example, at the official beginning of His ministry is significant to us as missionaries. Jesus gave us an example of complete commitment. Baptism is a publicly performed symbol of a person's decision to completely surrender their will to God. They decide to leave behind the life run by their natural selves, and to bury it completely by immersion in the water of baptism. The new person who comes up out of the water is one who will let God control their will completely. (Romans 6:4–6) While Jesus was not a sinner, and thus did not leave a life of sin, He did, through baptism, show His 100% commitment to follow God's will for His life. As missionaries for God, we must dedicate more than a fraction of our lives to God. He wishes for us to surrender to Him everything that He has loaned us—possessions, money, time, health, the power of thought, and even life. Another word for this 100% commitment and surrender is conversion.

We find another example of an anointing at the beginning of ministry with the story of King David. He was anointed by Samuel at God's command.

> "And the Lord said, 'Arise, anoint him; for this is the one.' Then Samuel took the horn of oil and anointed him in the midst of his brothers; and the Spirit of the Lord came upon David from that day forward." 1 Samuel 16:13-14

David was anointed and became possessed by the Spirit of the Lord. His anointing prefaced his official labors as a servant to the people he ruled.

HOLY SPIRIT

Closely connected with baptism is receiving the Holy Spirit. When John the Baptist saw the dove descend on Jesus at His baptism, he recalled what God had told him:

"Upon whom you see the Spirit descending, and remaining on Him, this is He who baptizes with the Holy Spirit." John 1:33

"Be baptized ... and you shall receive the gift of the Holy Spirit." Acts 2:38

We should

"be filled with the Spirit." Ephesians 5:18

We cannot maintain a 100% commitment to follow Jesus on our own. We have to rely on continuous help, and that is one role the Holy Spirit is ready to fill. He will gladly help us to maintain our commitment to God, if we ask for His help and are ready to accept it.

Jesus says,

"Behold, I send the Promise of My Father upon you." Luke 24:49

What is this promise?

"But the Helper, the Holy Spirit, whom the Father will send in My name, He will teach you all things, and bring to your remembrance all things that I said to you." John 14:26 (see also John 15:26; 16:7)

How are we sent?

"As the Father has sent Me, I also send you.... Receive the Holy Spirit." John 20:21-22

"Workers are needed now. As a people, we are not doing one fiftieth of what we might do as active missionaries. If we were only vitalized by the Holy Spirit, there would be a hundred missionaries where there is now one. But where are the missionaries? Has not the truth for this time power to stir the souls of those who claim to believe it? When there is a call to labor, why should there be so many voices to say, 'I pray thee, have me excused?' " *Counsels on Health* p. 507

ACTION

Lastly, we are sent to do the same things that Jesus did while He was here. Look again at this passage from Isaiah 61:

> *"The Spirit of the Lord is upon Me, because He has anointed Me to preach the gospel to the poor; He has sent Me to heal the brokenhearted, to proclaim liberty to the captives and recovery of sight to the blind, to set at liberty those who are oppressed; to proclaim the acceptable year of the Lord."*

Because we are sent as He was sent, we have similar tasks to perform in our ministry. Before we go into more detail on the actions of our ministry, we will take a look at Jesus' ministry in the next chapter.

MY EXPERIENCE

I believe that God has had a special commission for my life from long ago. As I have matured and learned to recognize God working out His plan for my life, I have been amazed. My life is not perfect, and I sadly have not followed His plan every time. But I strive to follow it more and more.

Over and over again I have experienced wonder and joy in recognizing and accepting God's commission and its elements of time, place, baptism, Holy Spirit, and action. Let me explain with a brief illustration.

Little by little, God led me to the conclusion that He was calling me to foreign missions. At first, I did not know when or how it would ever happen, as there seemed to be too many complicated factors to come together to make it happen. But as I listened to the voice of the Holy Spirit and followed His promptings to action, and as I committed my life to Him each day, I found that God took care of the obstacles.

I decided that I would not wait for an opportunity in a foreign land to share the gospel with others. I would start with the people around me. I shared with others experiences and Bible studies from my walk with God.

Because I had committed my life 100% to God and was willing to go wherever He sent, I eventually found myself in Chad, Africa. It is not the most pleasant place on earth, and life here is full of challenges. I came unmarried, but with a desire to get married sometime. But God brought another person to Chad, also committed to following Him. She is a wonderful and lovely lady and I eventually married her.

What if I had said "no" to God's choice of timing? What if I had said, "I'm not ready to go to Chad yet. I'm not comfortable with the idea." Or what if I had decided to wait until I had life more figured out?

What if I had said "no" to God's choice of location? What if I had said, "Chad is a hard place. I'd rather go to an easier place where there is better food or a nicer climate."

Or what if I had not committed my life 100% to God? Or what if I had not listened to the Holy Spirit's promptings in many areas?

What if I believed that God was indeed leading me, but decided not to act on my convictions because of some excuse?

I could not see the future before coming to Chad. But I trusted in God's wisdom and that He knew what He was doing. I regret no part of following God's plan. I still do not know the future. But I know how God has led in the past and this encourages me to remain faithful to God's calling. Accepting His commission for me is the best thing I have done and has given me fulfillment and joy in life.

WHAT IS YOUR RESPONSE?

"The call to place all on the altar of service comes to each one. We are not all asked to serve as Elisha served, nor are we all bidden to sell everything we have; but God asks us to give His service the first place in our lives, to allow no day to pass without doing something to advance His work in the earth. He does not expect from all the same kind of service. One may be called to ministry in a foreign land; another may be asked to give of his means for the support of gospel work. God accepts the offering of each. It is the consecration of the life and all its interests, that is necessary. Those who make this consecration, will hear and obey the call of Heaven." *Prophets and Kings* p. 221

God, since You have a plan laid out for my life, I want to follow it rather than devise my own plan. I am willing to go to whatever geographic region I am called. I will commit my life 100% to You, my Father, now and every day, and will rely on the Holy Spirit for help to maintain Christ-like thoughts and actions. Thank you for giving me the strength and ability to fulfill my commission.

So Send I You

by E. Margaret Clarkson

So send I you, to labor unrewarded
To serve unpaid, unloved, unsought, unknown,
To bear rebuke, to suffer scorn and scoffing,
So send I you, to toil for Me alone.

So send I you, to bind the bruised and broken,
O'er wandering souls, to work, to weep, to wake,
To bear the burdens of a world aweary,
So send I you, to suffer for My sake.

So send I you, to loneliness and longing,
With heart a hung'ring for the loved and known,
Forsaking home and kindred, friend and dear one,
So send I you, to know My love alone.

So send I you, to leave your life's ambition
To die to dear desire, self-will resign,
To labor long and love where men revile you,
So send I you, to lose your life in Mine.

So send I you, to hearts made hard by hated,
To eyes made blind because they will not see,
To spend—tho it be blood—to spend and spare not
So send I you, to taste of Calvary.

So send I you, by grace made strong to triumph
O'er hosts of hell, o'er darkness, death, and sin,
My name to bear, and in that name to conquer,
So send I you, My victory to win.

So send I you, to take to souls in bondage,
The word of truth that sets the captive free,
To break the bonds of sin, to loose death's fetters.
So send I you, to bring the lost to Me.

So send I you, my strength to know in weakness,
My joy in grief, My perfect peace in pain,
To prove My power, My grace, My promised presence.
So send I you, eternal fruit to gain.

So send I you, to bear My cross with patience,
And then one day with joy to lay it down,
To hear My voice, "Well done, My faithful servant,
Come share My throne, My kingdom, and My crown!"

"As the Father hath sent Me,
So send I you."

Ministry

"As each one has received a gift, minister it to one another,
as good stewards of the manifold grace of God.
If anyone speaks, let him speak as the oracles of God.
If anyone ministers, let him do it as with the ability
which God supplies,
that in all things God may be glorified through Jesus Christ,
to whom belong the glory and the dominion forever and ever.
Amen."
1 Peter 4:10–11

I am a missionary because...

○ Jesus' work is the work of all His followers.

○ I see a world that is in great need.

○ I wish to follow Jesus' example of ministry.

...What about you?

"Someone asked, 'Will the heathen who have never heard the Gospel
be saved?' It is more a question with me whether we — who have the
Gospel and fail to give it to those who have not — can be saved."
Charles Spurgeon

We are sent on a mission. But what is our work in this mission? How do we minister to other people?

CHRIST'S MINISTRY

Jesus' ministry basically consisted of actions that show us a representation of God and His character. He often demonstrated His Father's character both through the medical ministry and through the ministry of teaching truth. He came to relieve any type of suffering He encountered, whether it was physical or spiritual. The great Medical Missionary fulfilled His mission perfectly.

> *"I have glorified You on the earth. I have finished the work which You have given Me to do.... I have manifested Your name." John 17:4, 6*

DEPENDENCE ON GOD

Jesus relied on God for the direction and power for His mission work. He recognized that He was helpless without His Father.

> *"The Son can do nothing of Himself, but what He sees the Father do; for whatever He does, the Son also does in like manner." John 5:19*

> *"I can of Myself do nothing. As I hear, I judge; and My judgment is righteous, because I do not seek My own will but the will of the Father who sent Me." John 5:30*

> *"I do nothing of Myself; but as My Father taught Me, I speak these things." John 8:28*

UNIVERSALITY

Jesus' ministry was not exclusive; He ministered to people based on their need of a Savior, not based on some superficial categorization system. Jesus taught so that all His listeners could benefit from His teaching, whether they were the children on His lap or the youth or the adults. Gender did not matter to Him. Even though women were thought of as inferior in the culture of the time, Jesus spent considerable time ministering to women. Jesus saw past class or wealth as He ministered both to the rich young ruler and to the poor widow who brought her offering. Knowing that all cultures are in need of a Savior, Jesus spent time with Jews, Samaritans, Romans, and others. He talked with the liberals and with the conservatives of His day. The church people hated the tax collectors and anybody associated with them. But if you lived then and were a dishonest businessman like Zaccheus, Jesus would have eaten in your home and tried to help you understand God's love. If you were sexually immoral like those in the story of the woman caught in adultery, Jesus would have ministered to you. If you were a murderer or a thief, He would have offered you forgiveness and died in your place. If you were a leper, clothed in rags and surrounded in stench, Jesus would have touched you and ministered to you. Jesus treated each person not in relation to their current status in society, but in relation to their need and their eternal potential should they accept His sacrifice and gain salvation.

AFFECT ON HIS REPUTATION

Associating with these "ignorant" and "worthless" people sometimes affected Jesus' reputation negatively. The church leaders of the day did not appreciate His outreach ministry to these sinners and hopeless people; they mocked Him. When they confronted His disciples about eating meals with "sinners," Jesus responded that He came to call sinners to repentance; that was His work (Matthew 9:13).

> "The Son of Man came eating and drinking, and they say, 'Look, a glutton and a winebibber, a friend of tax collectors and sinners!' But wisdom is justified by her children." Matthew 11:19

"There was never one who walked among men more cruelly slandered than the Son of man. He was derided and mocked because of His unswerving obedience to the principles of God's holy law. They hated Him without a cause. Yet He stood calmly before His enemies, declaring that reproach is a part of the Christian's legacy, counseling His followers how to meet the arrows of malice, bidding them not to faint under persecution." *Thoughts from the Mount of Blessing* p. 32

TEMPTATIONS

Satan tried his hardest to mess up Christ's ministry right at the beginning by sending fierce temptations. When that failed, he determined to vigilantly bombard Christ with temptations throughout His ministry.

Temptations that Jesus faced are far greater than those we will ever face. Proportional to the potential eternal results of a ministry are Satan's attempts to interfere with that ministry.

OUR MINISTRY

"God sends you into the world as His representatives. In every act of life you are to make manifest the name of God. This petition calls upon you to possess His character. You cannot hallow His name, you cannot represent Him to the world, unless in life and character you represent the very life and character of God. This you can do only through the acceptance of the grace and righteousness of Christ." *God's Amazing Grace* p. 94

Notice how our mission affects us to our very core. *Every* action in our lives is an opportunity to show others what God is like. Representing God requires a deep and complete change in character from the way we naturally are. This change is only possible through the power of God.

DEPENDENCE ON GOD

By myself, I can do nothing. My best plans and ideas are useless without God. Paul, a great preacher and teacher, recognized that while he was doing a great work together with God, it was God who was giving his work success.

> *"Not that we are sufficient of ourselves to think of anything as being from ourselves, but our sufficiency is from God."*
> *2 Corinthians 3:5*

> *"So then neither he who plants is anything, nor he who waters, but God who gives the increase. Now he who plants and he who waters are one, and each one will receive his own reward according to his own labor. For we are God's fellow workers."*
> *1 Corinthians 3:7-9*

As we see success in our work, we will be tempted to think more highly of ourselves. We may think that our personality or our technique or our great ideas are bringing success. But we must always remember that we are only the tool in God's hand. It is God who brings success to our work. We must not trust in anything else.

> *" 'Not by might nor by power, but by My Spirit,' says the Lord of hosts." Zechariah 4:6*

> *"Some trust in chariots, and some in horses; but we will remember the name of the Lord our God." Psalm 20:7*

UNIVERSALITY

As Jesus' ministry was not exclusive, nor should ours be. He ministered to all people; so should we. Missionary work is not just for the few who travel to some foreign country. Our missionary work is defined by God's universal command and the people's need of a Savior, even when it crosses cultural boundaries, and even when it affects our reputation negatively.

> *"Go into all the world and preach the gospel to every creature."*
> Mark 16:15

This is our command. This command reaches across all cultures, all classes.

■■ Think for a moment how this command might change your life if you took its personal application seriously.

Does it include representing God's character to:
...that annoying, bratty child who runs around the halls at church? Yes.
...the old neighbor lady who is grumpy and stubborn? Yes.
...your son or daughter who has a rebellious spirit? Yes.
...the old man who lives by himself in a messy house and uses bad language? Yes.
...your "liberal" friend who frustrates you by listening to worldly music or who eats food you would not eat or has strange theology? Yes.
...your "conservative" friend who is more focused on God's law than God's love and who doesn't accept others who believe differently? Yes.
...your business competitor who deceptively got the bigger end of the contract? Yes.
...the young woman who dresses immodestly and acts inappropriately toward guys? Yes.
...the man with huge, smelly sores, sick with AIDS, and destined to die soon? Yes.
...the uneducated, stone-age people in the African bush? Yes.
...the person who killed your dog? Yes.
...your spouse or family member who has cherished bitterness against you for a long time? Yes.

■■ If some of these examples bring annoying feelings to you, think about how you might have annoyed God with your similar attitudes. How much trouble have you been to Him? How much pain and sorrow have you brought to His heart by your selfishness and stubborn rebellion? When you are challenged to minister patiently and gently, reflect on God's mercy toward you. That will help put things into perspective.

All are in need of a Savior, because all have sinned. As our characters are changed by a miracle of God, others will begin to see more of God's character demonstrated in our lives. If we live our lives within the will of God, we will be an uplifting example to everybody, no matter what gender, race, culture, language, class, status in society, or age they are.

The universality of this command is clear. But do we really believe in its universality? What do our actions show? For many, their actions show an extremely limited understanding of the word "all." Some act as if it means "all in my church." Others act as if it means "all my friends." Still others act as if self were all the world. But remember how Jesus acted toward sinners.

Isn't it God's desire for His people to make it their goal
> *"to loose the bonds of wickedness, to undo the heavy burdens, to let the oppressed go free, and that you break every yoke? Is it not to share your bread with the hungry, and that you bring to your house the poor who are cast out; when you see the naked, that you cover him, and not hide yourself from your own flesh? Then your light shall break forth like the morning, your healing shall spring forth speedily, and your righteousness shall go before you; the glory of the Lord shall be your rear guard." Isaiah 58:6–8*

If our relationship with God is current and growing, our actions will overflow from our thoughts. Our deeds will be evidence of a commitment to God. Our actions will not be defined by the immediate circumstances but by God's purpose for our lives. People will see God's character beaming out through our lives just as the Israelites saw the glory of God shining from Moses' face after his encounter with God.

"Christ's method alone will give true success in reaching the people. The Saviour mingled with men as one who desired their good. He showed His sympathy for them, ministered to their needs, and won their confidence. Then He bade them, 'Follow Me.' " *The Ministry of Healing* p. 143

Jesus' example showed us practical Christianity that causes us to take a genuine interest in ministering to the complete needs of people, both physical needs and spiritual needs. Jesus did not approach people with the sole purpose of converting them by talking to them about religion; He showed us how to take a personal interest first in people's physical needs. Referring to judgment events at His second coming, Jesus explained the differences between the sheep and the goats in Matthew 25:34–46. The sheep are welcomed into His kingdom while the goats are not. The actions of these sheep revealed their genuine love for God and their commitment to following the example of their Shepherd who ministered to people's needs. Their ministry to the hungry, the thirsty, the stranger, the naked, the sick, and the prisoner was viewed by God as ministry done to God Himself!

> *"Assuredly, I say to you, inasmuch as you did it to one of the least of these My brethren, you did it to Me." Matthew 25:45*

❚❚ How will you treat others as you imagine Jesus behind each person you interact with?

AFFECT ON OUR REPUTATION

Sometimes we try to protect our reputation at the expense of fulfilling God's call to missions in our lives. Are you afraid of what your secular friends and coworkers will think if you bring up spiritual topics in the conversation? Are you afraid of what others will think if you quit your good job to work overseas? Do you fear what your family will say? Or do you fear that your Christian friends at church will think you are strange or fanatical?

> "While slander may blacken the reputation, it cannot stain the character. That is in God's keeping. So long as we do not consent to sin, there is no power, whether human or

satanic, that can bring a stain upon the soul.... His words, his motives, his actions, may be misrepresented and falsified, but he does not mind it, because he has greater interests at stake. Like Moses, he endures as 'seeing Him who is invisible' (Hebrews 11:27); looking 'not at the things which are seen, but at the things which are not seen' (2 Corinthians 4:18).

"Christ is acquainted with all that is misunderstood and misrepresented by men. His children can afford to wait in calm patience and trust, no matter how much maligned and despised; for nothing is secret that shall not be made manifest, and those who honor God shall be honored by Him in the presence of men and angels." *Thoughts from the Mount of Blessing* p. 32

TEMPTATIONS

As we decide to do our assigned work wholeheartedly, Satan gets nervous. He knows what we can accomplish through God's power when we are committed and surrendered to Him. The more active we are in spreading truth and winning souls, and the more firm we are in our decision to be a faithful missionary, the more active and firm Satan becomes against us and our work.

Therefore, we become special targets for his attacks of troubles, opposition, doubts, and other temptations. If he could only get us to react to stress in our life in a natural human way, he would be successful in greatly diminishing our influence as ministers of God.

This day, commit to be faithful, but prepare for the attacks of the Devil. The stronger your commitment to God, the stronger Satan will attack you. This is why Jesus was so strongly attacked and tempted by the Devil throughout His life. But we have His example to encourage us through temptation and trial.

My Experience

The older I get, the more I realize how little or nothing I can do on my own and how much I need Divine aid. But when I make the choice to depend on God instead of myself, I avoid much stress and worry. God does not want me to become discouraged with challenges in ministry, but wants me to trust in Him for everything I need.

Fairly soon after I first arrived in Chad, I began Bible studies with some of the local people. Not knowing French, I enlisted the help of a short-term volunteer to help translate for me. Before that translator left, I prayed earnestly to God for help and depended on Him to provide a solution. Either I would receive the gift of tongues, or God would provide another translator, or I would have to stop giving Bible studies for a time until I learned more French. I told God that as far as I knew, those were my options and that I was leaving the problem in His hands. Then one of my students invited his friend to attend Bible study. His friend then eagerly volunteered to translate for me. I depended on God and He beautifully arranged for me to continue with this part of my ministry.

Another challenge I faced in my decision to be a missionary was the affect on my reputation at the university I was attending. Near the end of my studies for my Computer Science degree, some people could not understand why I would ignore well-paying job offers or invitations for interviews. Why would I not want to continue with my masters degree? They questioned the wisdom of my choices and thought I was foolishly wasting my degree.

I had to simply ask myself, "What is God asking me to do?" and leave my reputation for Him to protect. I must obey God rather than man when the two conflict. My reputation with God is more important to me than my reputation with man. I want to make decisions that are wise in God's estimation.

WHAT IS YOUR RESPONSE?

"He who came from heaven to be our example spent
nearly thirty years of His life in common, mechanical
labor; but during this time He was studying the word and
the works of God, and helping, teaching, all whom His
influence could reach. When His public ministry began, He
went about healing the sick, comforting the sorrowful, and
preaching the gospel to the poor. This is the work of all His
followers." *Education* p. 267–268

▌▌ To whom have I been a missionary this week? How have I
represented Jesus to somebody else today? What kind of
missionary does my family think I am? Am I willing to follow
Christ's example and leave my comfort zone and minister to
others even if it is culturally inappropriate? Perhaps I attend
prayer meeting and Bible study at my church each week. But
how often did I pray and study with somebody outside my
church this week?

*With Your help, God, I will show a genuine interest in helping people
in need. This means building friendships with them, genuinely
caring about them, and ultimately sharing the good news of the
gospel with them. Please make Your leading clear to me and help me
to be alert to Satan's interference.*

Motivation

I am a missionary because...

- I am learning to value souls more and more.
- I wish to bring joy to God.
- Life is more fulfilling when I am making a difference in people's lives.
- Time is short; the work is urgent.
- I want to invest in eternity, not just for this life.

...What about you?

▌▌ What motivates you to do what you do? Why do you have the job that you do? Why do you spend time the way you do?

To help us think through this topic, imagine that you are preparing for a mission trip to another country. What is your underlying motivation for being a missionary? Are you looking for adventure? Do you enjoy traveling and exploring unfamiliar parts of the world? Are you one who enjoys visiting the little shops, purchasing various hand-made crafts, and tasting local foods? Do you want to experience miracles of God's protection and provision like those you hear about in mission stories? Maybe you want to teach a group of natives a better way of life and lead them to baptism. Perhaps an organization is paying you to help them out. Or perhaps you expect to be really popular at your school when you return from your trip. Yes, these are sometimes bonuses included with life in the mission field, and certainly can be part of the motivation for mission work.

However, if any of these is as far as your motivation goes, why not just go on a vacation? It is not wrong to be motivated in part by these things, but our primary motivation must grow from something that is not transient. In many cases, the sense of adventure wears off quickly as the daily routine sets in. Unfamiliar places become familiar after living there for a time. New foods become the norm. What we need is a stable motivation that we can depend on. I would like to suggest one motivation that may seem overly simplistic at first, but is fundamental to the idea of being a missionary. That motivation comes from a study of the life and ministry of Jesus, and by understanding His character more and more.

The more I study God's character in Scripture, the more I realize how opposite my natural character is from God's and how much I want it to be changed. As I study the life of Jesus and see His love for me as shown by His incomprehensible self-sacrifice, my heart is bound by strong ties of love to His. My interests become one with His. His desires become mine.

My will is joyfully surrendered to Him. I am motivated to do works of service by a response of love toward Him for the example He has given.

CHRIST'S MOTIVATION

Money did not motivate Him, for He left heaven full of riches to live in poverty. And even after that, He quit His carpentry job prior to entering full-time, volunteer ministry.

Popularity did not motivate Him, for He left His home as God, the most popular Being in all the universe. Yes, at times during His life here, large crowds gathered around Him; but sometimes those same crowds turned against Him. Very few followed Him from good motives.

The thought of taking a vacation did not motivate Him, for He left the most perfect vacation land of happiness. In Paradise, He did not get weary; as God, He is the source of energy and rest. On Earth, Jesus worked long days ministering to people's needs, spent entire nights in prayer, and often became weary.

Prospects of climbing the ladder of power to take a position as an earthly ruler did not motivate Him; He was humble, ultimately humble, yet King of the universe. He was King of an everlasting kingdom.

LOVE AND VALUE OF THE LOST

Jesus' ministry was motivated by a desire to save lost people and by the joy found in saving them. He was motivated by a love for people. His desire for all of them to be saved was strong, for He understood the value of even one soul.

"For the Son of Man has come to seek and to save that which was lost." Luke 19:10

"Behold! The Lamb of God who takes away the sin of the world!" John 1:29

" 'Come now, and let us reason together,' says the Lord. 'Though your sins are like scarlet, they shall be as white as snow.' "
Isaiah 1:18

"I say to you that likewise there will be more joy in heaven over one sinner who repents than over ninety-nine just persons who need no repentance." *Luke 15:7*

"The soul that has given himself to Christ is more precious in His sight than the whole world. The Saviour would have passed through the agony of Calvary that one might be saved in His kingdom. He will never abandon one for whom He has died. Unless His followers choose to leave Him, He will hold them fast." *The Desire of Ages* p. 483

"By this we know love, because He laid down His life for us. And we also ought to lay down our lives for the brethren." *1 John 3:16*

"In this the love of God was manifested toward us, that God has sent His only begotten Son into the world, that we might live through Him. In this is love, not that we loved God, but that He loved us and sent His Son to be the propitiation for our sins."
1 John 4:9–10

"For when we were still without strength, in due time Christ died for the ungodly. For scarcely for a righteous man will one die; yet perhaps for a good man someone would even dare to die. But God demonstrates His own love toward us, in that while we were still sinners, Christ died for us." *Romans 5:6–8*

COMMISSION

Jesus was also motivated by His commission. Throughout His life as recorded in the gospels, Jesus always kept in mind that He was on a mission to do the will of His father who had sent Him.

"For I have come down from heaven, not to do My own will, but the will of Him who sent Me." *John 6:38*

Jesus remembered that He had been sent, and this helped Him to keep focused on His mission, even through the darkest times.

GREAT CONTROVERSY

Jesus was motivated by the Great Controversy. He understands this terrible conflict fully. Satan used to be Lucifer, His top angel. Jesus and Lucifer used to be close friends. But now Lucifer has rebelled and taken the name Satan. Because of Jesus' solid commitment to God while He was on earth as our Example, Satan attacked Him more than he will ever attack any of us. Yet Jesus resisted and defeated Satan and his demons again and again throughout His life. Jesus gained 100% victory because He understood the importance of this battle.

OUR MOTIVATION

Our motivation for service must not be mixed with selfishness. It is good and right to support your family. But if your only motivation to work is to find money, a vast area of your life is unfulfilled. It is good and right to enjoy what you do. But if your only motivation is enjoyment and fun, realize that this life is only temporary. What does it matter if you have fun and then die?

▌▌ What work are you doing for eternity? How will you lead others to Jesus?

As you continue reading, ask God to help you change and refine your motives for service to Him.

LOVE AND VALUE OF THE LOST

As we learn to abide in Christ and appreciate His love for us more, our values will change to become His values. Our feelings will change to become His feelings. Our goals change to become His goals. Our character changes and becomes more like His character. We will be motivated by His love for the lost, an understanding of how He values them, and a sense of the urgency of the work He has commanded us to do.

> *"Go out quickly into the streets and lanes.... Go out into the highways and hedges, and compel them to come in, that my house may be filled." Luke 14:21, 23*

A shepherd who owns one hundred sheep will leave the ninety-nine and go out into the night to search for one if it becomes lost. (Luke 15:4) The saving of one soul is worth any risk and danger.

▌▌ Do you want to bring happiness and joy to heaven? Go out in search of those people who need to be led to Jesus. Teach them about God's forgiveness and encourage them to repent of their sins.

> *"Likewise, I say to you, there is joy in the presence of the angels of God over one sinner who repents." Luke 15:10*

▌▌ How much is your love for souls?

> *"Beloved, if God so loved us, we also ought to love one another." 1 John 4:11*

> *"Greater love has no one than this, than to lay down one's life for his friends." John 15:13*

> *"By this we know love, because He laid down His life for us. And we also ought to lay down our lives for the brethren." 1 John 3:16*

"Love for souls for whom Christ died means crucifixion of self. He who is a child of God should henceforth look upon himself as a link in the chain let down to save the world, one with Christ in His plan of mercy, going forth with Him to seek and save the lost. The Christian is ever to realize that he has consecrated himself to God, and that in character he is to reveal Christ to the world. The self-sacrifice, the sympathy, the love, manifested in the life of Christ are to reappear in the life of the worker for God." *The Desire of Ages* p. 417

BRING JOY TO GOD

Motivation for service should also come from a desire to help relieve God's suffering in His own heart. "I can hardly wait for Jesus to return and end all this sin and suffering," I hear some say. I often have the same desire for the day when there will be

"no more death, nor sorrow, nor crying." Revelation 21:4

We should long for that day, yet this could be a selfish motive. Do not forget that God observes all sin and suffering and feels the pain of every hurting person. While we see an extremely limited view of sin and suffering around us, God must take in the horrible sight simultaneously over all the world. We cannot imagine what it is like to see all of this at once, yet God does every day. And because God's heart is infinitely good and pure and holy, He is infinitely more sensitive to the pain of sin and suffering.

"For we know that the whole creation groans and labors with birth pangs together until now.... Likewise the Spirit also helps in our weaknesses. For we do not know what we should pray for as we ought, but the Spirit Himself makes intercession for us with groanings which cannot be uttered." Romans 8:22, 26

While we cannot comprehend the extent and magnitude of sin, we can try to begin to understand what God must experience every day. And as we love Him, we will desire to work with Him in ending the misery of sin. Love for God should be the primary motivation for works of service. That will motivate us to fight on His side of the war that began in heaven and continues here today.

COMMISSION

We are also motivated by our commission, our duty, to
"Go therefore and make disciples of all the nations."
Matthew 28:19

This command is for everybody. It is for you. It is for me. Throughout our lives, we must keep in mind that

> *"we are ambassadors for Christ, as though God were pleading through us."* 2 Corinthians 5:20

Motivation for service should come from a desire to accurately and appropriately represent God's character to those within our sphere of influence. A life lived like Christ's will not go unnoticed, and will bring glory to God.

> *"Let your light shine before others, so that they may see your good works and give glory to your Father who is in heaven."* Matthew 5:16

God has commanded. Let's be busy with His work!

Study Ezekiel 33:1–20 carefully. Our responsibility is serious. Our eternal destiny is affected by our response to our duty.

TIME IS SHORT

People have been looking for Jesus to come for hundreds and thousands of years now. Adam and Eve looked forward to the day when the Savior would come. So did Noah, and Abraham, and David. Jesus did come, but most people were not ready for Him.

Now, we are still looking for Him to come, but this time we are looking for His second appearing. Signs all around us show that this earth's history is almost expired. We say that Jesus is coming soon. Well, He is! Do not relax. Do not be discouraged. Do not lose your motivation. Jesus will not be late, whether you are ready or not.

> *"And this gospel of the kingdom will be preached in all the world as a witness to all the nations, and then the end will come."* Matthew 24:14

What are we waiting for? We have no time to waste. Our time is limited. Doing our work of spreading the gospel will not be easier in the future than it is now. Now is the easiest time for the gospel to spread. As the end gets nearer and as the battle gets more fierce, our task will become more and more difficult. The devil is becoming increasingly angry with God's people because he knows that his time is short. (Revelation 12:12) Use your God-given talents to bring the good news to others before it is too late for you and for them!

GREAT CONTROVERSY

We find motivation in our understanding of the Great Controversy between Christ and Satan. No one can remain neutral in this battle.

Like the fishermen long ago whom Jesus called, our work today is to connect with Jesus and become
"the means of taking men out of the service of Satan, and placing them in the service of God." *Gospel Workers* p. 24

"Could our eyes be opened, and could each see the conflict of angelic agencies with the Satanic confederacy, who are combined with evil human agencies, what astonishment would come upon the soul. The holy angels are working with terrible intensity for the salvation of men, because the destroyer of souls is seeking to make of no effect the salvation which has been purchased at infinite cost. Could our spiritual vision be opened, we should see that which would never be effaced from the memory as long as life should last. We should see souls bowed down under oppression, loaded with grief and pressed down as a cart beneath the sheaves, and ready to die in discouragement. We should see angels flying swiftly to aid the tempted ones who stand as on the brink of a precipice. These tempted souls are unable to help themselves, and avoid the ruin which threatens them; but the angels of God are forcing back the evil angels, and guiding the souls away from the dangerous places, to plant their feet on a sure foundation. We should see battles going on between the two armies, as real as those fought by opposing forces on earth. When the power of Satan over souls is broken, we see men binding their will to the cross, and crucifying the flesh with the affections and lusts. It is indeed a crucifixion of self; for the will is surrendered to Christ. The will of man is none too strong when it is sanctified and put on the side of Christ. The will is a power, and as many triumphs are to be won in spiritual warfare, and many points of progress to be made in the spiritual journey, and many lessons to be learned from Christ, the great Teacher, it is necessary that the will should be sanctified. In surrendering the will, the root of the matter is reached. When the will is surrendered, the streams that flow from the fountain will not be bitter, but will be as pure as crystal. The flowers and fruit of Christian life will bloom and ripen to perfection." *The Signs of the Times*, October 29, 1894

ETERNAL INVESTMENT

Our decisions are affected by how we think we will be benefited in the future. Hope of gaining an advantage from an investment motivates people to take many a risk. For example, some people choose to buy the cheapest shoes, only to find out that those shoes fall apart within a month. Depending on the price of the shoes, this might be a good investment or a bad one. Some people invest in the stock market not knowing the future, whether they will gain or lose. But since they believe the likelihood of gaining is high, they invest their money in stocks. Others buy land in hopes that the value of the land will increase and they will gain from it.

In general, it is wise planning to think ahead and invest in things that are good quality. Even if they cost a bit more, they will serve their purpose longer. But why then do missionaries often make choices that appear to be bad investments? Why would you sell your hobby collection now instead of waiting for it to increase in value? Why would you sell your big house and move into a smaller one? Why would you turn down multiple lucrative job offers and accept the call to be a volunteer worker?

It is when we catch a glimpse of the value of eternity that we begin to change our thinking about what is truly valuable. Instead of thinking only how we can be benefited in the next few years, shouldn't we think about how we and others can be benefited for eternity? Is this not a great motivation? Every material thing on earth is temporary and will have an end someday. So Jesus says,

> *"Do not lay up for yourselves treasures on earth, where moth and rust destroy and where thieves break in and steal; but lay up for yourselves treasures in heaven, where neither moth nor rust destroys and where thieves do not break in and steal. For where your treasure is, there your heart will be also." Matthew 6:19-21*

No other career choice will make a more lasting effect than choosing to be a missionary wherever God calls you. No other investment decision will bring such spectacular returns on so small a relative investment. Our life and our will is such a small sacrifice to make in comparison with the incomprehensible returns of spending eternity with God and His other children.

This takes faith—faith in God. It requires taking God at His word. It means believing that God will do what He says. It means looking past our own wisdom and relying on His wisdom for making decisions. When we really believe what God says, we will base our decisions on unseen, but substantial eternal realities.

GENUINE EXPERIENCE IS UNCONTAINABLE

Motivation for missionary work comes from a genuine experience with God.

Imagine with me that you are an African living in your village and your neighbor comes up to you to get some travel advice. He wants to look at some land for sale in another village, but he has never been there before. He asks you which direction this village is and if it is possible to reach there by motorbike during this wet season. Your neighbor on the other side is eavesdropping and replies over the grass fence, "My dad traveled there several times last year. I heard him say that the best way to that village is via the south road by the river and that the road has been passable for many years."

But you reply, "I tried going down that south road just recently and it has been washed out. But just yesterday, I traveled to the village via the north road through the bush and although there is a lot of water in certain areas, it is passable by moto fine enough if you stay on the middle of the trail."

Which statement is your neighbor more likely to believe in? Will he trust in the hear-say statement of your other neighbor or will he likely put confidence in your personal-experience statement? Knowing that your neighbor has just a little fuel in his motorcycle tank, you will strongly advise him to follow your instructions, or he will end up stranded in the bush at night.

Do you have to try really hard to pass on the good advice to your neighbor? It is not something you have to try to do. It comes naturally. You want to. You have recent experience and can explain to him the best route. It will be this way when we are truly converted. We will naturally desire to share what we know with others. And even when we don't try, it just shows. We will not want to see their life go down in ruin.

Think about the life of a plant. It does not grow by trying to grow, or bear fruit by trying to bear fruit. It grows and bears fruit as a result of daily growing under the power and supervision of Jesus. The fruit is a natural result of growth.

Jesus compared this concept to a city on a hill.
"You are the light of the world. A city that is set on a hill cannot be hidden. Nor do they light a lamp and put it under a basket, but

on a lampstand, and it gives light to all who are in the house. Let
your light so shine before men, that they may see your good
works and glorify your Father in heaven." Matthew 5:14-16

We are motivated as missionaries because our experience
with God is a genuine experience and we cannot help but
share that experience with others. Even by observation,
others can see this in us, and our example is a powerful
influence. Arguments may be unbeatable and logically sound,
but these may only irritate and provoke the person on the
other side. But a godly life and example is irresistible, and it
will leave an impression on the observer.

When our experience in knowing and obeying God is genuine,
we cannot hold it to ourselves. We just can't help but be
missionaries! In Peter's and John's day, the council saw that
although they were not well-educated, they were bold
missionaries. The council determined to stop Peter's and
John's work. But their genuine experience with Jesus was
uncontainable. They replied to the council,
"Whether it is right in the sight of God to listen to you more than
to God, you judge. For we cannot but speak the things which we
have seen and heard." Acts 4:19-20

The Gospel is real. It is genuine. I know it to be true from
personal experience. My experience cannot remain genuine
without sharing it with others. It is uncontainable.

Promise of Success

Are you motivated by promises of success? Do you want to be
successful in what you do? Then, be a missionary. Search for
lost souls and bring them to Jesus. He promises true
missionaries success.

We sometimes make business partnerships with other people
without knowing whether or not we will meet with success at
the end. But a partnership with God cannot fail. Yes, we work,
but it is the Holy Spirit who works through us. Power for

work comes from God. We are responsible for using this power under the direction of the Holy Spirit. If we do not ask for and look for this power, we will be failures. Of ourselves, we cannot bring somebody closer to God. But when we partner with Him, relying on His power, our work will be a sure success.

> "The lesson of persevering faith and labor Christ Himself has taught us. In the parable of the lost sheep He has presented to our imagination no picture of a sorrowful shepherd returning without the sheep. The shepherd's search ceases not until the lost is brought back to the fold. The woman whose coin is lost searches till she finds it. These parables do not speak of failure but of success and joy in the recovery of the lost. Here is the divine guarantee that not one lost soul is overlooked, not one is left unsuccored. With all our efforts in seeking for the lost, Christ will cooperate." *Pastoral Ministry* p. 117–118

FULFILLMENT AND SATISFACTION

❚❚ Do you want to be happy, fulfilled, and satisfied in your work and in your life?

Then be a missionary.

In my own life, obeying God's call to be a missionary as a life-calling has brought me great joy and fulfillment. Nothing else brings more satisfaction. No other job, no amount of money, no number of things can bring more peace than knowing that I am where God wants me to be doing what God wants me to do. I am highly motivated by knowing that in doing God's work is great joy and peace.

MY EXPERIENCE

I am motivated in a number of ways. But one compelling motivation is an understanding of the great controversy between Christ and Satan. I know that this battle is real.

One day, my wife and I and some friends set out to erect a church building in a nearby village. Although we had made proper arrangements for land, and although the chief of the village was present, a mob led by some drunk men appeared on the scene to oppose the work and to threaten and disturb us. Normally, this sort of situation would motivate me to leave the scene.

But knowing that God was in control, we were motivated to persist. God had provided the land as a gift from the village. God was working in the hearts of our small congregation. And the location of the land is strategically located to reach several villages. Why would God start something and not finish it?

In prayer, I felt convicted that we should not back down but move forward in prayer and faith. I felt as though demons were raging around us. Even though the man's eyes were bulging as he yelled at me, I felt a strange sense of peace knowing that holy angels were also present. God's work was moving forward, and Satan was not happy.

One of the drunk leaders started picking a fight with the chief and called him off into the bush to fight. My newly baptized friend got between them and called the drunk man away for a talk. Upon returning, the drunk man's attitude had completely changed. He was now apologetic and allowed us to continue with the construction of the church. The mob dispersed and we completed the basic structure and roof without further disturbance. A small group of people continues to meet in that church today.

Experiences like this motivate me to be faithful in God's work. The devil is not happy, but God knows how to move His work along. I can have confidence in my work because I know I am working with God and on the winning side of this conflict.

WHAT IS YOUR RESPONSE?

My motivation for being a missionary springs from a love for God and is fundamentally twofold: 1) I want to become more like Jesus, 2) and I want to help others become more like Him. With new motivation, I will with increased energy and intensity search out souls to win. No matter what my occupation, I will look for ways to share truth with those around me. God, please deepen my love, give me a desire to be more like Jesus, and make me motivated to serve You.

My Brother

from *Missionary Leader* Vol. 20, No. 9, September 1932

I was up near the city road one day:
Some men were digging a drain;
The sky was dark, and the streets were gray
With a misty, drizzling rain.
I had done my work and was hurrying by,
But a man is bound to know
What's up when he hears a frightened cry,
And a crowd begins to grow.

Ill news flies fast. The word was passed,
"The drain," "the props," and "save!"
The earth had slipped, and the men were fast—
Three souls in a living grave.
They had mates at hand, by luck, poor chaps,
Who hurried with pick and rope.
Thought I, they'll dig them out quick, perhaps,
But little the worse, let's hope.

So I stood and watched them for a while,
As I'd nothing else to do;
They threw the earth in a goodly pile
And one of the lads got through.
"Hurrah!" went up from the watching throng,
And rang through the misty air,
A girl I knew came running along,
And sighted me standing there.

"O Jim!" she gasped, "Can't you help? Go, go!"
And she seized and shook my arm;
"It is your brother, lad, that is down below,
And you standing here so calm!"
"My brother!" Then in a second's space
I was digging away like mad,

Fearing to light on his poor, dead face—
The only brother I had!

And I got him out, with a bruise or two,
But nothing of harm beside.
You'd scarcely think what I say is true,
But I there broke down and cried
To think that I'd been standing there
When my kin was like to die,
Letting the others do all my share,
Out of sheer stupidity.

It seems to me, when I come to think,
That our life on earth goes so;
Some standing safely on the brink,
Some sunk in the depths below.
And I am sure, if men only knew
That their brothers were like to die,
They'd hasten to see what they could do,
Instead of just standing by.

Prayer

"Pray without ceasing."
1 Thessalonians 5:17

I am a missionary because...

O As I open my heart to God in prayer, He makes His will known to me.

O Prayer has increased my desire to serve God.

O Without prayer, my spiritual life would die.

...What about you?

"In our lifetime, wouldn't it be sad if we spent more time washing dishes or swatting flies or mowing the yard or watching television than praying for world missions?"
Dave Davidson

The topic of prayer is worthy of an entire book. I do not attempt to adequately cover the topic of prayer in this book. Here we will focus primarily on John 17.

Prayer is one of the basic necessities of a missionary. It is where we receive power in our spiritual life. Without prayer, the living Christian experience dies and we lose our connection with God.

Jesus showed us by example how important prayer is. He often prayed to His Father. Finding a quiet place to pray was important to Him, and He often found that night was the only possible time for uninterrupted prayer.

CHRIST'S PRAYER LIFE

Christ's prayer life was centered around what God could do through Him and involved three directions: prayer for Himself, prayer for His followers, and prayer for the lost. We will take a quick look at John 17 as an example of part of Jesus' prayer life.

> "The instruction given me by One of authority is that we are to learn to answer the prayer recorded in the seventeenth chapter of John. We are to make this prayer our first study. Every gospel minister, every medical missionary, is to learn the science of this prayer...."
> *Testimonies for the Church Volume 8* p. 239

> "Let us make Christ's prayer the rule of our life, that we may form characters that will reveal to the world the power of the grace of God. Let there be less talk about petty differences, and a more diligent study of what the prayer of Christ means to those who believe on His name. We are to pray for union, and then live in such a way that God can answer our prayers.
> "Perfect oneness—a union as close as the union existing between the Father and the Son—this is what will give

success to the efforts of God's workers." *Reflecting Christ* p. 200

PRAYER FOR HIMSELF

"Father, the hour has come. Glorify Your Son, that Your Son also may glorify You." John 17:1

PRAYER FOR BELIEVERS

"They have believed that You sent Me. I pray for them. I do not pray for the world but for those whom You have given Me, for they are Yours." John 17:8-9

PRAYER FOR THOSE NOT YET SAVED

"I do not pray for these alone, but also for those who will believe in Me through their word." John 17:20

OUR PRAYER LIFE

"Prayer is the breath of the soul. It is the secret of spiritual power. No other means of grace can be substituted and the health of the soul be preserved. Prayer brings the heart into immediate contact with the Wellspring of life, and strengthens the sinew and muscle of the religious experience. Neglect the exercise of prayer, or engage in prayer spasmodically, now and then, as seems convenient, and you lose your hold on God. The spiritual faculties lose their vitality, the religious experience lacks health and vigor." *Messages to Young People* p. 249–250

Below are a collection of texts illustrating three directions to focus our prayers: for ourselves, for believers, and for the lost. You will find it encouraging to look up these texts in your own Bible and to study the context. Pray through each text, one at a time, asking God to guide you as you apply it.

For Ourselves

○ Pray for the Holy Spirit.
  What will be the result of asking God for the Holy
  Spirit?
  God is eager to give us the Holy Spirit if we ask.
  (Luke 11:13)

○ Pray for heart conversion.
  What will be the result of asking God for a new, clean
  heart?
  *"Create in me a clean heart, O God, And renew a steadfast
  spirit within me."* Psalm 51:10

○ Pray for revival.
  What will be the result of asking God for revival?
  "Revive me according to Your Word." Psalm 119:25, 107, 154
  "Revive me in Your way." Psalm 119:37
  "Revive me in Your righteousness." Psalm 119:40
  "Revive me according to Your lovingkindness." Psalm 119:88
  "Revive me according to Your justice." Psalm 119:149
  "Revive me according to Your judgments." Psalm 119:156

○ Pray that your character and life will be pleasing to
  God.
  *"Let the words of my mouth and the meditation of my heart
  be acceptable in Your sight, O Lord, my strength and my
  Redeemer."* Psalm 19:14

○ Pray that your life will glorify God.
  *"Everyone who is called by My name, whom I have created
  for My glory; I have formed him, yes, I have made him."*
  Isaiah 43:7

For Believers

It is important to maintain our own personal relationship
with God through prayer. But He wants us to unselfishly pray
for others, too. Take a moment and think about Bible stories
that tell of believers praying for other believers.

■■ What types of things were they praying for? What were the results of those prayers?

- o Pray for the Holy Spirit
  - o Peter and John prayed that those who had accepted the Word of God would also receive the Holy Spirit. (Acts 8:14–15)
- o Pray for God's workers in time of crisis or difficulty.
  - o The believers prayed for Peter in prison. (Acts 12:5)
  - o Paul asked for prayers for an open door to preach the Word. (Colossians 4:3; 2 Thessalonians 3:1)
- o Pray for revival in our church.
  - o Daniel prayed for forgiveness for Israel. (Daniel 9)
- o Pray for more missionaries.
  - o Ask the Lord of the harvest to send more laborers. (Matthew 9:38)
- o Pray for their salvation.
  - o Paul desired and prayed that Israel would be saved. (Romans 10:1)
  - o Moses sincerely prayed for Israel's salvation. (Exodus 32:32)
- o Pray for spiritual growth.
  - o Paul prayed that they would have wisdom, a knowledge of God, enlightened understanding, and experience the power of God. (Ephesians 1:15–21; Philippians 1:9; Colossians 1:9)

FOR THE LOST

We must pray for those who do not know God. We should even pray for the people who hassle us and give us troubles. Who irritates you the most in your life? Whom do you dislike the most? Who does not know how to live a Christ-like life? Pray for them.

- O Pray for your enemies and those who are against you.
  - º *"But I say to you, love your enemies, bless those who curse you, do good to those who hate you, and pray for those who spitefully use you and persecute you."* Matthew 5:44
- O Pray that God will pardon their sins and hold back His judgment. How interested are you in other's salvation?
  - º Samuel saw it as a sin not to pray for the people. *"Moreover, as for me, far be it from me that I should sin against the Lord in ceasing to pray for you; but I will teach you the good and the right way."* 1 Samuel 12:23
  - º Moses was even willing to give up his eternal life if God would forgive Israel's sin. *"Yet now, if You will forgive their sin—but if not, I pray, blot me out of Your book which You have written."* Exodus 32:32
  - º *"Pardon the iniquity of this people, I pray, according to the greatness of Your mercy, just as You have forgiven this people, from Egypt even until now."* Numbers 14:19
  - º *"And the Lord was very angry with Aaron and would have destroyed him; so I prayed for Aaron also at the same time."* Deuteronomy 9:20

INFINITE PROMISES

When we pray, we often do not comprehend the potential results of prayer. We might think of the biggest plan we think is possible and then ask God to answer that request. But we are missing out on a much bigger experience. Read this passage:

> *"If you abide in Me, and My words abide in you, you will ask what you desire, and it shall be done for you."* John 15:7

▌▌ Do you believe it? Do you really believe it? Do you really believe that God gives you anything you ask for? Is this promise real?

Think about it. If we desire something small, and we ask for it, the promise tells us that God will give it to us. If we desire something big, and we ask for it, the promise tells us that God will give it to us. There is no size limit here! In fact, this is an infinite promise! Grab your Bible and read these other infinite promises.

Mark 11:24; John 14:12-14; John 15:7-8, 16; John 16:23-24, 26

So why do our prayers seem to be unanswered sometimes? One key to understanding these promises is to understand the conditions:

- ○ Ask in Jesus' name
- ○ Believe that your prayer will be answered

To pray in Jesus' name is asking God to do the things He promises, the things Jesus wants to have happen.

> "To pray in the name of Jesus is something more than a mere mention of that name at the beginning and the ending of a prayer. It is to pray in the mind and spirit of Jesus, while we believe His promises, rely upon His grace, and work His works." *A Call to Stand Apart* p. 27

> "We must not only pray in Christ's name, but by the inspiration of the Holy Spirit. This explains what is meant when it is said that the Spirit 'maketh intercession for us, with groanings which cannot be uttered.' Romans 8:26 Such prayer God delights to answer. When with earnestness and intensity we breathe a prayer in the name of Christ, there is in that very intensity a pledge from God that He is about to answer our prayer 'exceeding abundantly above all that we ask or think.' Ephesians 3:20" *Christ's Object Lessons* p. 147

"To pray in Christ's name means much. It means that we are to accept His character, manifest His spirit, and work His works. The Saviour's promise is given on condition. 'If ye love Me,' He says, 'keep My commandments.' He saves men, not in sin, but from sin; and those who love Him will show their love by obedience." *The Desire of Ages* p. 668

"Delight yourself also in the Lord, and He shall give you the desires of your heart." Psalm 37:4

What we need to do now is to delight ourselves in the Lord. We need to learn to love the things that God loves, and shun the things that God shuns. Pray for the love of sinners that Jesus had. Pray that God will lay on you a burden for souls. Then ask Him, claiming these infinite promises, and get to work. God has promised. He will fulfill. Go search out souls. Pray with them. Pray for them.

My Experience

Without prayer, I would not be a missionary.

I find that maintaining a Christ-like attitude throughout the day is much easier on days when I take sufficient time to talk with God in prayer in the morning, than on days when I choose not to take as much time with Him in the morning. I have also found that prayer is much more than a morning activity. It is an attitude of recognizing His presence and our need of Him throughout the day.

Prayer helps me to be Christ-like. When I remember that Jesus is my constant Companion, I do not want to do something that will displease Him. It is only when I forget Him that I fall under temptation.

Prayer helps me to be others-centered. When I pray for others, I realize that my needs are often not nearly as great as their needs. Praying for others throughout the day helps to cheer me and to remind me of God's abundant blessings in my life.

When I first moved to Africa as a single young man, I had a tendency to become lonely at times. But Jesus became a closer Friend than ever to me. I would talk with Him and tell Him my joys and my frustrations and my challenges. He became my ever-present Companion. I felt that He was the only Friend of mine who could even come close to understanding my life.

At the end of each day I have learned a secret of sweet sleep: give my burdens and challenges to God to guard for me during the night. Talking to God and giving Him my burdens is relieving and comforting and I sleep in peace knowing that God is in control.

Without prayer, without a means of communicating to God my trials and difficulties and blessings, I could not remain a missionary. I am a missionary and remain so because of prayer.

WHAT IS YOUR RESPONSE?

God, first of all I pray that my heart will be transformed so that my witness will be clear and bold. Please encourage and strengthen other believers and fellow workers, that they will remain courageous and strong as we work together. I will pray also for those who will become believers through our work. Help me to grasp the infinite prayer promises, acting on them by faith, remembering that You can do impossible things.

OTHER EXAMPLES

Continue studying Christ's prayer life, and your prayer life will grow. But there are many other encouraging examples of prayer worthy of study. The following list is a summary from the book *Prayer*, chapter 13, "Men and Women of Prayer." If you have access to the book, please read through that chapter. Even if you don't, you can look up these stories in your Bible and meditate on them.

▌▌ Think about the subject of their prayer. What were they praying for? How did they pray? What was the result of their prayer? What does their prayer teach me about my prayer life? How can I change how I pray? How will these examples help me to become a better missionary?

- ○ Enoch walked with God. Prayer was the breath of his soul. (Genesis 5:24)

- ○ Abraham built an altar wherever he pitched his tent. He was not embarrassed to show that he was a friend of God. (Genesis 12:8; 13:18; James 2:23)

- ○ Jacob showed us the importance of prevailing prayer and unyielding faith. (Genesis 32:26)

- ○ Moses interceded for the Israelites and often brought his challenges before God. (Exodus 32:32)

- ○ Hannah prayed faithfully for a child and God answered her. Her son Samuel became a prophet of God. (1 Samuel 1:27)

- ○ David showed us how to pray for repentance. (Psalm 51)

- ○ Solomon showed humility in his prayer. (1 Kings 3)

- ○ Hezekiah prayed for Israel and was healed. (2 Chronicles 32:20–26)

- ○ Daniel prayed effectually and fervently for his people. (Daniel 9) He also continued praying during persecution. (Daniel 6)

- ○ Nehemiah prayed with faith and courage. (Nehemiah 1)

- ○ Peter prayed and God resurrected a dead woman. (Acts 9:36–43)

- ○ The church prayed constantly for Peter. (Acts 12)

Immanuel

"And the Word became flesh
and dwelt among us."
John 1:14

I am a missionary because...

○ I want to minister to people on their level.

○ I want people to better understand God's character.

...What about you?

"It will not do to say that you have no special call to go to China.
With these facts before you and with the command of the Lord Jesus
to go and preach the gospel to every creature, you need rather to
ascertain whether you have a special call to stay at home."
Hudson Taylor

GOD WITH US

Ever since Adam and Eve sinned, God has missed direct communion with His people. In Eden, God would walk with Adam and talk with him and spend time with him. But after Adam and Eve chose to disobey God, they had to be separated from Him. Sin separates us from God. God missed His walks with Adam, and wished for a closer relationship not only with him, but with all Adam's descendants.

Many people began separating themselves from God more and more as they disobeyed and chose their own way. But Enoch did not forget God. The Bible says that he walked with God, and this pleased God so much that God took him to heaven even before he died!

As time went on, people continued drifting farther away from God. The Israelites eventually became slaves in Egypt and nearly forgot God altogether. But God's desire to be with His people did not diminish. He said:

> *"Let them make Me a sanctuary, that I may dwell among them."*
> *Exodus 25:8*

The Godhead decided that Their plan of salvation would be most effective if Jesus would live with and be with the people. One of Jesus' names is "Immanuel," which means "God with us." In one of the most amazing but perhaps least understood moves, He decided to not only live with humans, but to become a human!

> *"[Jesus] made Himself of no reputation, taking the form of a bondservant, and coming in the likeness of men. And being found in appearance as a man, He humbled Himself and became obedient to the point of death, even the death of the cross."*
> *Philippians 2:7–8*

> *"And the Word became flesh and dwelt among us, and we beheld His glory, the glory as of the only begotten of the Father, full of grace and truth." John 1:14*

By becoming like us and living and working among us, Jesus left an example worthy of imitating.

Us With Them

> "Christ's method alone will give true success in reaching the people. The Saviour mingled with men as one who desired their good. He showed His sympathy for them, ministered to their needs, and won their confidence. Then He bade them, 'Follow Me.' " *The Ministry of Healing* p. 143

How can we be effective missionaries? In summary, be a friend to the people around you. Be willing to mingle with the people. Show an interest in them. Try to identify yourself with their lives, their struggles, their challenges, and their joys.

> "There is need of coming close to the people by personal effort." *The Ministry of Healing* p. 143

> "Christ was sent of the Father to represent His character and will. Let us follow His example in laboring to reach the people where they are." *Medical Ministry* p. 79

> *"Let this mind be in you which was also in Christ Jesus."* Philippians 2:5

As we allow our minds to be shaped more closely to the mind of Jesus, our lives will be stronger and stronger witnesses to His love and power. As we come in contact with our neighbors, as we live "with them," and care about them and their eternal destiny, they will see and understand more about what God is like.

> "The love of Christ mellows the heart and smooths all roughness from the disposition. Let us learn from Him how to combine a high sense of purity and integrity with sunniness of temperament. A kind, courteous Christian is the most powerful argument in favor of the gospel that can be produced." *Selected Messages Book 3* p. 238

> *"How then shall they call on Him in whom they have not believed? And how shall they believe in Him of whom they have not heard? And how shall they hear without a preacher?"*
> Romans 10:14

▌▌ Are you a kind, courteous Christian? How are you representing His character?

"A picture is worth a thousand words." To show and describe something is much more effective than just describing something. Merely reading a description is far less effective than seeing a living Christian. I can tell you that mangoes taste good, but you will not be as fully convinced as when you see and smell and hold and feel and taste a real, fresh mango. Be a real, fresh Christian for people to see and smell and hold and feel and taste. Your life will convince people of the power of the gospel faster and more effectively than any sermon or study can.

God has assigned each one of us to be His ambassadors (2 Corinthians 5:12). That means we can no longer ignore our responsibility and sit comfortably in our homes or churches, relaxing comfortably in the false security of the thought that "I have the truth. I'm safe."

▌▌ How will people see a kind courteous Christian if there are none to observe? You may be the last or only opportunity somebody has to learn about God.

God has commanded us to "Go." God knows that we humans are sometimes challenged with trying to grasp concepts that we cannot verify with our senses. As Jesus came to show us an example of what God is like, so we are sent to show to others an example of what God is like.

The deeper a person knows Jesus personally, the more his life shines out in contrast to others. People notice a genuine difference in his life. Whether we are pumping gas at the fuel station, waiting in the doctor's office, working on the engine, or preparing food, people will notice. Our countenances speak volumes. People will notice if we are patient and happy. They will notice if Jesus is our Friend and if the Holy Spirit lives in us.

▌▌ How interested are you in other people's salvation? Are you concerned that some may not know God and may suffer the second death? Are you willing to reach the people where they are, not condemning them but leading them gently to Jesus? Lost sheep do not generally search after their shepherd; they must be searched for.

Perhaps God is calling you to minister more to your neighbors. Or perhaps He is calling you to move to another city, or state, or country. What will you do about those hundreds of people groups who do not have a knowledge of God? Who will "go" and "dwell among them?"

Jesus left His heavenly home and came to our planet to show us a clearer picture of God. Why are we afraid to follow His example on a much smaller scale? He has shown us the way and has promised us success as we follow in His footsteps.

You might say, "But those people there are so dumb and ignorant. They've been living their lives for this long without me and they won't ever miss me if I don't show my face. I'll leave them alone. There is no need for me to live with them and show an interest in them."

▌▌ What if Jesus had said that about us?

▌▌ What if Jesus had decided that the human race had gone too far out of reach to recover?

▌▌ What if He had said, "Those humans are so deeply rooted in custom that they will not want to change their ways?"

Many people didn't even want Jesus to be near them or in their village. But Jesus valued them and loved them more than any of us ever could. Thank God that He came to bring us salvation!

It is true that some people are dumb and ignorant and that generations have come and gone without a knowledge of Christ. It is also true that they are just as valuable in God's sight as is the most intelligent brain surgeon or rocket scientist on the planet. God is not prejudiced against a certain people group, whether they are great or small, smart or dumb, educated or ignorant. Neither should we be prejudiced.

"There is no partiality with God." Romans 2:11

"If you show partiality, you commit sin, and are convicted by the law as transgressors." James 2:9

Be willing to follow God's leading no matter where He calls you. Choose to see each person as God sees them. Wherever you live, let your light shine so that others may become acquainted with God and His character.

MY EXPERIENCE

Living among Africans in Chad has given me a new understanding of Jesus' mission that I could not get while trying to reach them from a distance. It is one thing to feel sorry for those in need and be willing to send money or supplies to help. But it is a different thing to actually go and live and be among them.

I do not mean to be derogatory toward the people here in Chad. But from the perspective of a person who has lived in a more developed country, life here contrasts sharply from what he is used to. Many people do not bathe regularly and do not wash their clothes very often. Very few people brush their teeth. Some enjoy eating rats and lizards. People cannot afford tissue or toilet paper, so they use their hand to take care of those needs. And they often do not have soap to use. There is no deodorant. They drink muddy water because there is no good water source. Many people do not know how to read or write. And the list goes on.

But wait! God could easily have written a list like that about me in comparison to the perfect life and environment in heaven. Compared to where I could be spiritually, I am illiterate in the things of God. Compared to what my life should be, my life history is stained and spotted with mistakes. Compared to what I should have fed my brain, I have seen and consumed material that is not the best or the purest for me. My righteousness is as filthy rags. The difference is almost unimaginable. Yet Jesus lived among us and became one of us. He experienced life as a human. And He loves each of us as if there were not another soul on earth. No matter what a person's past or present circumstances are, He forgives anyone, anywhere.

Jesus' example has been inspiring to me. I have prayed that God will give me a love for the people here, and He has answered my prayer. I love the people here. I want to continue deepening my value of people as He values them. Though sometimes I fail, I choose to see each person as one for whom Jesus has paid an infinite price. Each person is infinitely valuable. I want to love them as God loves them. If I did not have this perspective, following Immanuel's example would not be easy.

What is Your Response?

I choose to follow Immanuel's example and desire to mingle with people and meet them where they are on their level. A Christ-like life is a powerful witness, and I want to place myself where my witness will be seen by those who need to see it. Jesus, You lived among humans and came close to them. I desire to follow Your example and be willing to be among whomever You call me to minister.

Further Reading for You

"When Christ left His high command, He might have taken upon Him any condition in life that He chose. But greatness and rank were nothing to Him, and He chose the most humble walk of life. No luxury, ease, or self-gratification came into His experience. The truth of heavenly origin was to be His theme; He was to sow the world with truth, and He lived in such a way as to be accessible to all." *Lift Him Up* p. 166

Sacrifice

"The sacrifices of God are a broken spirit,
A broken and a contrite heart—
These, O God, You will not despise."
Psalm 51:17

I am a missionary because...

- O   I appreciate how much Jesus has sacrificed for me.
- O   I recognize that God is the owner of everything and that I am the steward of what He has given me.
- O   I love God more than my possessions.
- O   "We are never called upon to make a real sacrifice for God." *The Ministry of Healing* p. 473

...What about you?

"He is no fool who gives up what he cannot keep
to gain that which he cannot lose."
Jim Elliot

Many people, when they think about the sacrifice involved in being a missionary, reject their responsibility. They fear that it will be too painful or too risky to sacrifice everything.

▌▌ Have you had any of these thoughts when considering obedience to God?

"I might lose my job."
"My friends and family will think I am crazy."
"What will I do when I am old?"
"How will I ever find a spouse?"
"I'll have to sell my big house and my other things."
"I won't have as much time for my hobbies."
"I can't leave my friends."
"How will I educate my children?"

When we worry about these things, we demonstrate our misunderstanding of what sacrifice God is asking from us. Sometimes we apparently do not even know what sacrifice means. When we study Jesus' example of sacrifice, we will better understand how we are to sacrifice.

CHRIST'S SACRIFICE

What was Jesus' attitude toward sacrifice? Did He naturally shrink back from it? How much did He sacrifice for us? Take some time to go through this section. Think about each point and meditate on it and ask God to impress you deeply with a better understanding of what Jesus was willing to sacrifice in order to bring us salvation.

HOME

Jesus left behind His beautiful, perfect, comfortable home in heaven, a home so wonderful that we cannot even begin to comprehend it. Here, on Earth, His first place to stay was in the Bethlehem animal shelter. What a contrast! The King of the universe came from His palace and shared His first bedroom with smelly, dirty animals! Throughout His life, Jesus lived as though His time here was temporary. He was more interested in eternal investment than in establishing a comfortable place to live temporarily.

"And Jesus said to him, 'Foxes have holes and birds of the air have nests, but the Son of Man has nowhere to lay His head.' "
Luke 9:58

Use your imagination. Try to picture what Jesus' home was like in heaven and how different His earthly home was.

"I saw the beauty of heaven. I heard the angels sing their rapturous songs, ascribing praise, honor, and glory to Jesus. I could then realize something of the wondrous love of the Son of God. He left all the glory, all the honor which He had in heaven, and was so interested for our salvation that He patiently and meekly bore every indignity and slight which man could heap upon Him. He was wounded, smitten, and bruised; He was stretched on Calvary's cross and suffered the most agonizing death to save us from death, that we might be washed in His blood and be raised up to live with Him in the mansions He is preparing for us, to enjoy the light and glory of heaven, to hear the angels sing, and to sing with them." *Testimonies for the Church Volume 1* p. 123–124

FAMILIAR, SAFE ENVIRONMENT

There are no criminals in heaven. Nobody there thinks about self or personal pleasure, but everybody is looking out for the happiness of others. Perfect peace exists throughout heaven. We cannot comprehend what it is like to live in such an environment.

But Jesus chose to move to a very selfish environment that was not safe. This was a risky venture. Satan was bombarding Him with temptations. Evil men were continually trying to trap Him or to kill Him. People were not looking out for the happiness of others. Jesus patiently endured much hostility because His mission to seek and save the lost was of utmost importance to Him.

> *"For consider Him who endured such hostility from sinners against Himself, lest you become weary and discouraged in your souls." Hebrews 12:3*

> "Never can the cost of our redemption be realized until the redeemed shall stand with the Redeemer before the throne of God. Then as the glories of the eternal home burst upon our enraptured senses we shall remember that Jesus left all this for us, that He not only became an exile from the heavenly courts, but for us took the risk of failure and eternal loss. Then we shall cast our crowns at His feet, and raise the song, 'Worthy is the Lamb that was slain to receive power, and riches, and wisdom, and strength, and honor, and glory, and blessing.' Revelation 5:12." *The Desire of Ages* p. 131

FAMILY

Jesus left behind His family—His Father, Holy Spirit, and all the angels who worshiped and adored Him. Jesus loved His heavenly family and was bonded far more closely with a love far more pure than we can know. Yet, when Jesus lived here for more than thirty years, He gave up the face-to-face conversations with His Dad that He had before leaving heaven. Through prayer, of course, Jesus talked directly to His Dad continually, though it was not the same as talking directly face to face. And we even have examples of other humans speaking face to face with God (Genesis 32:30; Exodus 33:11; Deuteronomy 5:4), but these were still scaled-down versions to preserve human life. While Jesus kept direct communication open with His Father, He still missed being with His family physically.

Power and Glory

"When Jesus left heaven, and there left His power and glory, Satan exulted. He thought that the Son of God was placed in his power.... If he could tempt Jesus to depart from the will of God, as he had done in his temptation with Adam and Eve, then his object would be gained." *Confrontation* p. 54

Became Human

Jesus is God. He ever has been and He ever will be. Yet, in a way we cannot fully explain or understand, He became a human to help us understand God better. We cannot see God, but now we better understand Him through Jesus' human example. And He will remain human for the rest of eternity!

"Who, being in very nature God, did not consider equality with God something to be grasped, but made Himself nothing, taking the very nature of a servant, being made in human likeness." Philippians 2:6-7

"Since the children have flesh and blood, He too shared in their humanity so that by His death He might destroy him who holds the power of death—that is, the devil—and free those who all their lives were held in slavery by their fear of death." Hebrews 2:14-15

"Christ has carried His humanity into eternity. He stands before God as the representative of our race." *S.D.A. Bible Commentary Volume 7* p. 925

"[God] gave His only-begotten Son to come to earth, to take the nature of man, not only for the brief years of life, but to retain his nature in the heavenly courts, an everlasting pledge of the faithfulness of God. O the depth of the riches both of the wisdom and love of God! 'Behold, what manner of love the Father hath bestowed upon us, that we should be called the sons of God' (1 John 3:1)." *Selected Messages Book 1* p. 258

"Christ left His position in the heavenly courts, and came to this earth to live the life of human beings. This sacrifice He made in order to show that Satan's charge against God is false—that it is possible for man to obey the laws of God's kingdom. Equal with the Father, honored and adored by the angels, in our behalf Christ humbled Himself, and came to this earth to live a life of lowliness and poverty—to be a man of sorrows and acquainted with grief. Yet the stamp of divinity was upon His humanity. He came as a divine Teacher, to uplift human beings, to increase their physical, mental, and spiritual efficiency." *Lift Him Up* p. 235

OUR SACRIFICE

Are you motivated to sacrifice something for God? After studying Jesus' attitude of sacrifice, our desire should be to follow His example.

"The foundation of the plan of salvation was laid in sacrifice. Jesus left the royal courts, and became poor, that we through His poverty might be made rich. All who share this salvation, purchased for them at such an infinite sacrifice by the Son of God, will follow the example of the True Pattern. Christ was the chief cornerstone, and we must build upon this foundation. Each must have a spirit of self-denial and self-sacrifice." *Testimonies for the Church Volume 3* p. 387

Being a missionary does indeed require sacrifice—self-sacrifice and self-denial. Perhaps this is why so many people ignore their calling to be a missionary. They do not want to live a life like Jesus did. They are afraid that it will be painful or uncomfortable or risky. To follow the example of Jesus would be too much of a sacrifice. If that is how you feel, it is time to promptly wake up and begin to think not just for the moment, but for eternity.

"Your attitude should be the same as that of Christ Jesus."
Philippians 2:5

Study again Jesus' life and example. We can <u>never</u> sacrifice as much as He did.

It may be helpful to view yourself as a tool in God's hand. A shovel by itself can do nothing. It might rest "safely" in the shed, enjoying the "easy" life, but accomplishing nothing of value. But if the shovel is "willing" to be used, it becomes useful. Does a tool experience stress? Does a tool have a difficult life at times? Does a tool sometimes get sharpened or bent back into shape? Yes, our characters are not perfect and sometimes need trimming and pruning through trials. But as we faithfully commit to being used by God, relying on His strength, we will find that sacrifice is not a bad thing. In fact, it brings us a happiness that nothing else can. Sacrifice is the opposite of selfishness, and selfishness never brings true happiness.

> *"Come to Me, all you who labor and are heavy laden, and I will give you rest. Take My yoke upon you and learn from Me, for I am gentle and lowly in heart, and you will find rest for your souls. For My yoke is easy and My burden is light."*
> Matthew 11:28-30

God will not ask us to do something impossible. In fact, He wants to make our life easier and more restful! When we accept His calling, we are yoked with Him. A yoke attaches two animals together so that they share the load. Jesus shares the load with us. In fact, He takes most of it because He says that His yoke is easy and light!

GOD OWNS EVERYTHING

▌▌ What is God asking you to sacrifice?

Think over the things that you own. Think about the resources available to you. Think of how God has blessed you with intelligence and life. What does God ask for? To understand this, we need to understand the Biblical concept of ownership. That is a topic for deeper study at another time, but we will briefly look at it here. God says,

> *"Every animal of the forest is mine, and the cattle on a thousand hills.... If I were hungry I would not tell you, for the world is mine, and all that is in it." Psalm 50:10, 12*

Understanding the real nature of our sacrifices is helpful. Try to follow this logic. For us to sacrifice something, we must have something to sacrifice. I cannot give something I do not have. For us to have something to sacrifice, God has provided us with that something. That something is therefore God's, and He has only placed us in temporal possession of it as stewards. Is it then sacrifice to give back to God that which He has loaned us? The idea of sacrifice takes on a whole new meaning when we think about it this way. We only return to God what He has blessed us with!

Suggested reading: Deuteronomy 8. This chapter encourages us to remember that all gifts come from God, and that sometimes things are taken away from us to remind us of this fact.

The perceived severity of sacrifice often is more connected with our conception of sacrifice than with actual sacrifice. It is more about the condition of our hearts and the level of our understanding of eternal things than about giving up possessions. For example, if God calls you to a new place where your house will be much smaller, you might be tempted to think you are sacrificing "your" big, comfortable home to live in a smaller, less-nice home. But remember who enabled you to live in the big home? Why not praise Him for the time you had in the big home and trust that He knows how to provide for your needs and make you happy in a small home? Or perhaps the Holy Spirit is asking you to sacrifice "your" money for the work of God. Whose money is it? Who is the source of wealth? It is God who blessed you with money and when He sees it best to move the money along, He is not limited in His ability to continue providing for your needs.

Possessions, a Test of the Heart

If God owns everything, why does He loan us things? Why does He bless us with possessions? He gives us things as a means of developing our character and of helping others. It is a test for us and our character to see if we are willing to trust God no matter what. God expects us to use whatever we have, little or much, to glorify Him. The more possessions of which God has made us stewards, the more responsibility we have before God for our use of those possessions. God wants us to use and develop our talents and our resources, not hoard them. See Matthew 25:14–30.

As David recognized long ago, sacrifice costs us something. Sacrifice is not giving a drop out of our bucket of resources. It means we will respond by giving substantially in proportion to how God has blessed us. David said,

"nor will I offer burnt offerings to the Lord my God with that which costs me nothing." 2 Samuel 24:24

But we would have nothing to give were it not for God blessing us with something to give. Why then are we hesitant to give back to God what came from Him?

Look at the example of a young man who was very rich. Jesus told him:

" 'If you want to be perfect, go, sell what you have and give to the poor, and you will have treasure in heaven; and come, follow Me.' But when the young man heard that saying, he went away sorrowful, because he had great possessions." Matthew 19:21–22

▌▌ How would you respond if Jesus gave you the same command?

▌▌ Have you gone away sad after God asked you to sacrifice something for Him?

▌▌ Is there something in your life that is more important to you than following God? What do you value more than God or treasure in heaven?

It was God who had blessed the rich man with many possessions. But once he was rich, he lacked the incentive to wisely manage his possessions for God's work. He became spoiled and was in danger of losing out on heaven. God was asking for the very thing that was keeping him from eternal life, yet he preferred his temporary possessions.

> "Christ did not ask a greater sacrifice than He Himself had made. 'He was rich, yet for your sakes He became poor, that ye through His poverty might be rich.'
> 2 Corinthians 8:9. The young man had only to follow where Christ led the way.
> "...But he was not ready to accept the Saviour's principle of self-sacrifice. He chose his riches before Jesus. He wanted eternal life, but would not receive into the soul that unselfish love which alone is life, and with a sorrowful heart he turned away from Christ." *Christ's Object Lessons* p. 393

Possessions do not bring true happiness. God had given this young man many blessings, yet he failed to recognize God as the owner and went away sad. When Jesus asked him to sell what he had and use it to bless others, he realized that his heart was more attached to his possessions and comforts of life than to God. But God wants our hearts to be attached to eternal things. To His disciples, Jesus gave this instruction:

> *"Sell what you have and give alms; provide yourselves money bags which do not grow old, a treasure in the heavens that does not fail, where no thief approaches nor moth destroys. For where your treasure is, there your heart will be also." Luke 12:33-34*

When called to sacrifice, realize that possessions and even life itself are temporary. All gifts are from God. Without Him, we would have nothing. And, we do not know the future. Our barn may burn down. The bank may close. Our car might be destroyed in a hail storm. A loved one may suddenly die.

▌▌ Why are we often so attached to things that we are unwilling to invest in something eternal, something that is guaranteed forever? Is it because we really do not believe God? Do we trust our eyes, our plans, the opinions of men, and the customs of society more than the promises of God? Why do we not place more worth on something genuinely valuable such as developing a Christ-like character or leading a soul to Christ?

For our own good, God desires a complete sacrifice, complete loyalty, complete surrender to Him. Our commitment to God surpasses even our commitment to our family. It is priority number one.

> *"If anyone comes to Me and does not hate his father and mother, wife and children, brothers and sisters, yes, and his own life also, he cannot be My disciple. And whoever does not bear his cross and come after Me cannot be My disciple." Luke 14:26–27*

"What?" you might be thinking, "Am I to hate my family?" Hate here cannot mean to literally hate our family in anger because Jesus Himself said to love even our enemies. (Matthew 5:44) Scripture is clear that we should love each other and our families deeply. Husbands are to love their wives with Christ's love. (Ephesians 5:25) We should certainly love our families, and we should never think that God is calling us to leave our wife or our children, sacrificing them to do His work. If you are married when God calls you, He is calling your spouse with you. Family units can be powerful witnesses.

Yet in comparison to supreme love for God, love for family is inferior. Jesus is pointing out that if we love our family so much that we would rather be in their favor than to obey God, we are not worthy to be His disciple. We cannot depend on any human more than we depend on Jesus; our love for Him must be greater than our love for anybody or anything else. The following verse clarifies this more.

"He who loves father or mother more than Me is not worthy of Me. And he who loves son or daughter more than Me is not worthy of Me. And he who does not take his cross and follow after Me is not worthy of Me." Matthew 10:37-38

"So likewise, whoever of you does not forsake all that he has cannot be My disciple." Luke 14:33

Serving God involves sacrifice—sacrifice of anybody or anything that we value more than we love God. Do we have to give away or sell all our possessions? Not unless God tells us to, but we must be willing to receive or give as God asks, even when He asks us to give all.

Let us clarify two things before we move on. The first is the importance of family. Since we are studying only the topic of sacrifice in this chapter, we could easily arrive at an unbalanced conclusion about our obligation to our families. Clearly, family is our first mission field, and it is in the home that family members are prepared for work in the church and the world. Some fathers or mothers or husbands or wives are away from home so much that they are not fulfilling their home obligations to their spouse or children.

"Better sacrifice any and every worldly consideration than to imperil the precious souls committed to your care. They will be assailed by temptations and should be taught to meet them; but it is your duty to cut off every influence, to break up every habit, to sunder every tie, that keeps you from the most free, open, and hearty committal of yourselves and your family to God." *The Adventist Home* p. 138

The second clarification is related and addresses the motive of sacrifice. Sacrifice from the wrong motives is not pleasing to God. If you sacrifice everything, perhaps including your life, but do not surrender your heart to Him completely, it is not acceptable to Him.

▌▌ Is it possible to love our mission work so much that we neglect proper time with God or family? Are we so focused on being viewed by others as successful missionaries that we forget how God views success? Be careful that your motives originate from love to God and a heart that is 100% surrendered to Him.

> *"And though I bestow all my goods to feed the poor, and though I give my body to be burned, but have not love, it profits me nothing." 1 Corinthians 13:3*

ENABLE OTHER'S MINISTRY

The believers during the time of the apostles responded well to the call to sacrifice. They viewed their possessions as means to further the work of the gospel. (Acts 4:32–37) The believers' sacrifice enabled the apostles to commit their lives more fully to ministry. Generosity among the believers made a big difference. Because they realized that their possessions were blessings from God without whom they would have nothing, they were willing to make sacrifices to help spread the gospel. This generosity enabled some missionaries like Paul to continue their full-time ministry. Paul wrote to the Philippians,

> *"Indeed I have all and abound. I am full, having received from Epaphroditus the things sent from you, a sweet-smelling aroma, an acceptable sacrifice, well pleasing to God. And my God shall supply all your need according to His riches in glory by Christ Jesus." Philippians 4:18–19*

Likewise, God calls people today to give generously of their resources to support people in full time ministry. As Paul reminds us, God will supply all the needs of those who give. He supplies us from His riches. God's riches are unlimited, which means that His capability to supply all our needs is unlimited!

YOUR HEART

▌ Does God need my things? Is He poor and short on resources so that He has to ask me to give things to Him? Certainly not.

▌ Is God capable of paying His workers directly? Certainly.

But God asks us to sacrifice for our benefit as this gives us an opportunity to search our hearts and recognize our selfishness, leading us to Him and salvation. It gives us an opportunity to participate in His work and cooperate with Him.

> *"Sacrifice thank offerings to God. He who sacrifices thank offerings honors me, and he prepares the way so that I may show him the salvation of God." Psalm 50:14, 23*

> *"The sacrifices of God are a broken spirit, a broken and a contrite heart—these, O God, You will not despise." Psalm 51:17*

God is not interested in money or other things. He is asking for your heart, your will.

▌ Are you willing to give God a sacrifice of a broken spirit and a contrite heart?

All that you are and all that you have are His. When you give Him your heart, He will use you to accomplish a wonderful work of distributing His blessings to others. When your heart is one with His, you will be happy and willing to sacrifice anything He asks.

> "God requires us to yield our own will to His; but He does not ask us to give up anything that it would be for our good to retain. No one can be happy while he devotes his life to selfish gratification. A course of obedience to God is the wisest course for us to pursue; for it brings peace, content, and happiness as the sure result." *The Review and Herald*, October 16, 1883

My Experience

I hope the following experiences do not come across as being proud or boastful. My intent in sharing the following experiences is to encourage you to think about your own life and what God is asking of you.

One of my favorite hobbies is photography, especially nature photography. I could happily spend hours at a time alone with my camera in the field or in the mountains photographing God's nature. After college, I invested in some nice equipment. In total, I spent close to $2000. I used my camera frequently, and the pictures I took were rewarding to me.

Then came my call to Africa. I did not know what my living situation would be like. How would I keep my camera equipment safe in a mud hut? How would I protect it from being stolen? I began to realize that perhaps God was calling me to sell my camera and nice Canon professional lens to invest the money in my work in Africa. Although it was a hard decision for me, I did sell the camera and lenses. Would I rather worry about my camera getting ruined or stolen or would I rather invest the money in eternal interests? (I am not saying that owning camera equipment is wrong; I am just sharing my personal experience.)

Now that several years have passed, I still miss my camera. But I am content with our little point-and-shoot camera. Somebody did donate a better quality point-and-shoot camera, and I have enjoyed using that. But I recognize that it is God who blessed me with the money to buy the equipment in the first place. Why should I complain or be sad when He asked me to give it up? People might comment, "You surely sacrificed when you left your camera behind." But it was really God's camera. And if He wants it back, He can have it. I am happier without it. If God had asked me to sell it and I had kept it, my happiness would be diminished.

Melody and I have sacrificed many other things. We have moved away from our dear families and now see them rarely. We miss them a lot. We miss some of the delicious food available in our home country and wish there was not so much sand and so many bugs in the local food. We miss a good Internet connection. Sometimes we wish for air-conditioning in hot weather. We miss warm showers; cold bucket showers are not always pleasant. Life here is not as comfortable or convenient. We have given up a lot to live here.

But we are happy. Nowhere else could we be happier. Sacrifice for God brings happiness. And in reality, we have sacrificed so little compared to what Jesus has sacrificed for us.

WHAT IS YOUR RESPONSE?

God's work requires sacrifice, but not from a grudging heart. He wants free-will offerings—those made because we want to give, not because we have to give. In order to work for Him, we must have a spirit of self-sacrifice. How is your heart? Pray now that God will give you more of a spirit of self-sacrifice as you read the following paragraphs.

> "Our divine Master has given us an example of how we are to work. And to those whom He bade, 'Follow me, and I will make you fishers of men,' He offered no stated sum as a reward for their services. They were to share with Him His self-denial and sacrifice....
>
> "And now, as in that time and as in the days of Christ's earthly ministry, devotion to God and a spirit of sacrifice should be regarded as the first requisites of acceptable service. God designs that not one thread of selfishness shall be woven into his work." *The Review and Herald*, January 4, 1906

"Jesus left heaven, and came to our world to save souls. You must come close to those for whom you labor, that they may not only hear your voice, but shake your hand, learn your principles, feel your sympathy." *Gospel Workers* p. 192

"How easy would be the way to heaven if there was no self-denial or cross! How worldlings would rush in the way, and hypocrites would travel in it without number! Thank God for the cross, the self-denial. The ignominy and shame our Saviour endured for us is none too humiliating for those saved by the purchase of His blood. Heaven will indeed be cheap enough." *Our Father Cares* p. 110

"If Christ left the ninety and nine, that he might seek and save the one lost sheep, shall we be justified in doing less? God himself set an example of self-sacrifice in giving up his Son to a shameful death. Is not a neglect to work even as Christ worked, to sacrifice as he sacrificed, a betrayal of sacred trusts, an insult to God? The lost sheep is to be found at any peril, any cost." *An Appeal for Missions* p. 15

"Everyone who accepts Christ as his personal Saviour will long for the privilege of serving God. Contemplating what heaven has done for him, his heart is moved with boundless love and adoring gratitude. He is eager to signalize his gratitude by devoting his abilities to God's service. He longs to show his love for Christ and for His purchased possession. He covets toil, hardship, sacrifice." *The Ministry of Healing* p. 502

I choose to be willing to sacrifice anything that God asks me to give up. I ask Him to change my heart. God, please detach my affections from the things of this world and attach them to eternal things—things that really matter. Help me to accept a spirit of self-sacrifice and to remember what Jesus has done for me.

FURTHER READING FOR YOU

Our use of possessions in relation to our responsibility for the salvation of souls. *Early Writings* p. 48–50
The Review and Herald, January 4, 1906 "The Spirit of Sacrifice"
An Appeal for Missions

I Gave My Life for Thee
by Frances Havergal

I gave my life for thee.
My precious blood I shed,
That thou mightest ransomed be,
And quickened from the dead.
I gave, I gave My life for thee,
What has thou given for Me?
I gave I gave my life for thee,
What has thou given for Me?

My Father's house of light
My glory circled throne
I left for earthly night
For wandering sad, and lone.
I left, I left it all for thee.
Has thou left aught for me?
I left, I left it all for thee.
Has thou left aught for me?

I suffered much for thee
More than any tongue can tell
Of bitterest agony to rescue thee from hell
I've borne, I've borne it all for thee.
What has thou borne for me?
I've borne, I've borne it all for thee.
What has thou borne for me?

Proof of Love
Robert Whitaker[1]

God is not so deceived
With selfish thrift
As to forget
That sacrifice alone
Is proof of love;
The Master made the test
The all-ness
Not the small-ness
Of the gift

---

1 *The Youth's Instructor* 12 Oct, 1899. Web. 4 Dec. 2012
<www.adventistarchives.org/docs/YI/YI18991012-V47-40__C.pdf>

God's Provision

"My God shall supply all your need
according to His riches in glory by Christ Jesus."
Philippians 4:19

I am a missionary because...

o God has provided me with strength and a desire to obey Him.
o As I have put my trust in God to provide for my needs, He has always provided.
o God has given me life, and I wish to use my time for His purposes.

...What about you?

"God's work done in God's way will never lack God's supply."
Hudson Taylor, missionary to China

Many people feel a calling to do more for God, but feel restricted by various obstacles. Some people have car or house payments. Others have children near college age or perhaps in college already. Some have a good paying job with insurance benefits and paid vacation time. Various other commitments to work or family hold some back. Some feel unqualified to give Bible studies. Perhaps some do not have enough money to travel. Feeling not talented enough is another excuse.

▐▌ But will God ever call us to do something unwise or impossible?

▐▌ Should we reject God's calling only because we think it is impossible?

God knows how to provide for all of our needs. If God calls me to do something, He will enable me to do it. If He calls me to organize and present a series of evangelistic meetings, He will bless me as I do my best and move forward in prayer. If God is calling me to move somewhere, He can easily arrange for somebody to rent or buy my house. Even if the house doesn't sell, I can move forward confident in God's calling. There is no difficulty or need that is too great for God to supply. That means there is no excuse big enough to cause us to evade God's call.

> *"My God shall supply all your need according to His riches in glory by Christ Jesus." Philippians 4:19*

Let's break that verse up into a few pieces:

- ○ *"My God"* God is a personal God. He is interested in you and wants the best for you. Is He *your* God, or merely the God of your family or pastor or church?

- ○ *"shall"* This is not "maybe," or "possibly," but certain and solid. This is a promise we can count on. Do you believe that God keeps His promises? Have you experienced this for yourself?

○ *"supply all your need"* God will not call you to a place and then only supply you with half of what you need. He will not assign you a job and then only bless you with half of the ability to complete that job.

○ *"according to His riches in glory by Christ Jesus."* How big are God's riches compared to our needs? The riches of heaven far exceed the total sum of all the riches on earth. God wants to bless us abundantly.

"As the will of man co-operates with the will of God, it becomes omnipotent. Whatever is to be done at His command may be accomplished in His strength. All His biddings are enablings." *Christ's Object Lessons* p. 333

When God calls you to do something, obediently follow His leading without worry. Providing for your needs is not hard for God.

THOSE WHO GIVE AND THOSE WHO GO

God provides for mission work in various ways. For some, God blesses them with a job and an income and expects them to use their money in His work. For a time, Paul made tents to provide some income for his work. For others, God calls them away from their job and income and asks them to devote their life full time to direct ministry. Paul also received offerings from people who wanted to support mission work. Let us look at how God provides for those who give and for those who go.

PROVISION FOR THOSE WHO GIVE

Those who are accustomed to giving probably already know about an amazing cycle sometimes referred to as the "circuit of beneficence." As Jesus worked to glorify His Father, His Father blessed Him with the ability to continue His work. As Jesus did not seek His own glory but to glorify His Father, so Christians will use their gifts from God to glorify Him, and not themselves. And as we glorify our Father in heaven, He blesses us with the ability to continue His work.

If you have the books, take the time to read in *The Desire of Ages* chapter 1 and *Education* chapter 11 about the law of life. We understand that everything Jesus received, He received from God. And everything He received, He took to give. If we understand this law of life, we will not hesitate to give when God asks us to give. We will become like a pipe with a faucet. As long as the faucet remains open, the water keeps flowing. As long as we are open to sharing God's blessings, they will keep flowing and flowing.

Nature illustrates this lesson in a multitude of ways. A flowing stream contains fresh, clean water. It takes water, but gives it as it flows along, nourishing flowers and trees and grass along its banks. The Dead Sea is a different story. It is a body of water with an inlet, but with no outlet. It is a stinky, dead place. The sun *takes* energy *to give* light. The tree *takes* water *to give* fruit. The birds *take* air and food *to offer* their songs.

The problem with us humans is that we are sometimes like the Dead Sea. We take to hoard. We take to glorify ourselves, not to glorify God. How are you managing the talents God has given you? Are you giving or hoarding? Are you afraid of losing out on something or becoming poor if you give? There is no need to worry. Make a decision now to claim God's promise to supply your needs.

There is no set amount a person should give. He should give according to his capability. A small plant does not give off as much oxygen as a large tree, but it does its work in proportion to its ability. God asks no more from us.

If God gives you the talent of public preaching, don't keep it to yourself; use it for His glory. If He gives you the talent of kind words spoken in private, don't keep it to yourself; use it for His glory. As you use your talents, they will grow and develop. Do not worry about how big or how small they are, only use what you have.

"For if there is first a willing mind, it is accepted according to what one has, and not according to what he does not have."
2 Corinthians 8:12

You might complain to God, "I do not have much. My offering will not go very far. The need is great and I only have a tiny amount to offer." But do you remember how God viewed the widow's tiny offering?

"Now Jesus sat opposite the treasury and saw how the people put money into the treasury. And many who were rich put in much. Then one poor widow came and threw in two mites, which make a quadrans. So He called His disciples to Himself and said to them, 'Assuredly, I say to you that this poor widow has put in more than all those who have given to the treasury; for they all put in out of their abundance, but she out of her poverty put in all that she had, her whole livelihood.'" Mark 12:41-44

Some rich people were making large donations. This very poor widow put in two tiny coins—all that she had. Yet in God's sight, her gift was massive in comparison to the gifts of the rich. Why? God measures our offerings not by the amount, but proportionately to our ability to give. The large gifts of the rich were only a small percentage of what they owned and were not true sacrifices. They gave because they were proud and wanted people to notice them. The widow gave because she loved God and His work. She gave 100%—all that she had! In God's eyes, hers was the more significant offering.

"Let each one give as he purposes in his heart, not grudgingly or of necessity; for God loves a cheerful giver." 2 Corinthians 9:7

Let's break this verse up into a few pieces:
   o *"Let each one"* Everybody should give.

○ *"as he purposes in his heart"* The choice to give is a personal choice.

○ *"not grudgingly or of necessity; for God loves a cheerful giver."* God wants us to give because we want to and are happy to give, not because we have to or feel like we have to "pay up."

"Give, and it will be given to you: good measure, pressed down, shaken together, and running over will be put into your bosom. For with the same measure that you use, it will be measured back to you." Luke 6:38

"For everyone to whom much is given, from him much will be required; and to whom much has been committed, of him they will ask the more." Luke 12:48

"Whenever God's people, in any period of the world, have cheerfully and willingly carried out His plan in systematic benevolence and in gifts and offerings, they have realized the standing promise that prosperity should attend all their labors just in proportion as they obeyed His requirements. When they acknowledged the claims of God and complied with His requirements, honoring Him with their substance, their barns were filled with plenty. But when they robbed God in tithes and in offerings they were made to realize that they were not only robbing Him but themselves, for He limited His blessings to them just in proportion as they limited their offerings to Him.

"Some will pronounce this one of the rigorous laws binding upon the Hebrews. But this was not a burden to the willing heart that loved God. It was only when their selfish natures were strengthened by withholding that men lost sight of eternal considerations and valued their earthly treasures above souls. There are even more urgent necessities upon the Israel of God in these last days than were upon ancient Israel. There is a great and important work to be accomplished in a very short time. God never designed that the law of the tithing system should be of no account among His people; but, instead of this, He designed that the spirit of sacrifice should widen and deepen for the closing work." *Testimonies for the Church Volume 3* p. 395–396

When God asks us to give, He is not asking us to hurt ourselves or to bring us to ruin. God knows how to provide for our needs far better than we do.

We cannot out-give God.

The Israelites gave a significant portion of their income back to God, and God provided for their needs always.

"No less than one third of their income was devoted to sacred and religious purposes." *Testimonies for the Church Volume 3* p. 395

PROVISION FOR THOSE WHO GO

While God asks some people to contribute their money to support God's work, He asks other people to give up their jobs and be supported by others in full-time mission work. Either way, God always provides for His work, and we should not hesitate to follow His leading.

Matthew responded promptly to Jesus' call "Follow Me." He left a lucrative job and a comfortable home to follow Jesus.

"So he left all, rose up, and followed Him." Luke 5:28

Peter and Andrew responded to Jesus' call to "Follow Me," even though they were poor fishermen:
"They immediately left their nets and followed Him." Matthew 4:20
"Do not be afraid. From now on you will catch men." Luke 5:10

James and John responded similarly to the same call:
"Immediately they left the boat and their father, and followed Him." Matthew 4:22

"When they received the Saviour's invitation, they did not hesitate, and inquire, How shall I live, and sustain my family? They were obedient to the call." *The Desire of Ages* p. 273

God calls the rich and poor alike.

▌▌ How do you react when God calls you to follow Him? Perhaps you think, "I can't, I have house payments," or "Wait, I'd like to get married first." Or do you think of any number of other excuses? (Please don't misunderstand me. We should not neglect our obligations to pay a debt. And it is not wrong to get married. But there is no obstacle too big for God.)

▌▌ Are you more interested in temporary things or eternal things?

When God calls us, the first response should be that we are honored to work with Him and for Him. The thought of reward or salary will not be our primary question.

When Jesus first sent out the twelve disciples two by two,
"He commanded them to take nothing for the journey except a staff—no bag, no bread, no copper in their money belts—but to wear sandals, and not to put on two tunics." Mark 6:8-9
Jesus gave the seventy other missionaries the same command in Luke 10—to go without carrying provisions. In obedience to Jesus' command, they went and did a mighty work of preaching and healing.

▌▌ Why did Jesus instruct His workers to travel without provisions?

It certainly is not wrong to plan ahead for a trip or carry provisions on a trip. But He wanted to teach them lessons of complete reliance on God. Their source of success was not their planning but God's power.

"And He said to them, 'When I sent you without money bag, knapsack, and sandals, did you lack anything?' So they said, 'Nothing.' " Luke 22:35

"By faith Abraham obeyed when he was called to go out to the place which he would receive as an inheritance. And he went out, not knowing where he was going." Hebrews 11:8

God is able to provide for your needs. He cares about your temporal needs, and He cares about your eternal life. Deciding to follow Jesus and leave everything behind is not dangerous or foolish if that is what He calls you to do.

Peter was convicted to follow Jesus. But he got distracted with thoughts about wages and payment in exchange for service to God.

"Then Peter answered and said to Him, 'See, we have left all and followed You. Therefore what shall we have?' " Matthew 19:27

He was still self-focused and wanted to know what benefit he would receive from his labors for God. He thought that the better he was and the better he worked, the better his payment or reward would be. We need to remember the same thing that Peter needed to remember:

"You are not your own. For you were bought at a price."
1 Corinthians 6:19–20

"But what things were gain to me, these I have counted loss for Christ. Yet indeed I also count all things loss for the excellence of the knowledge of Christ Jesus my Lord, for whom I have suffered the loss of all things, and count them as rubbish, that I may gain Christ." Philippians 3:7–8

Jesus did not respond harshly to Peter. He wanted to assure him that his needs would be taken care of, but that the reward in this life was incomparable to the ultimate reward of eternal life. He also reminded Peter that persecutions would come—not that God would forsake or forget His people, but that He would recognize their need and provide for it.

> *"Jesus answered and said, 'Assuredly, I say to you, there is no one who has left house or brothers or sisters or father or mother or wife or children or lands, for My sake and the gospel's, who shall not receive a hundredfold now in this time—houses and brothers and sisters and mothers and children and lands, with persecutions—and in the age to come, eternal life. But many who are first will be last, and the last first.' "* Mark 10:28–31

Trust in God. Do not be afraid to trust fully in Him. Surrender your heart 100% to Him. Do not worry about the cost of obedience; rather, worry about the cost of disobedience! Eternal life with God is of infinitely more value than anything else on this earth. Think of the gain of eternal happiness with people you were influential in leading to Jesus! Why are our minds so stuck on earthly things so often? Why not trust God and follow Him when He calls?

> *"He who did not spare His own Son, but delivered Him up for us all, how shall He not with Him also freely give us all things?"* Romans 8:32

> "Our heavenly Father has a thousand ways to provide for us of which we know nothing. Those who accept the one principle of making the service of God supreme, will find perplexities vanish and a plain path before their feet." *The Ministry of Healing* p. 481

> "In this work [of winning souls] all the angels of heaven are ready to co-operate. All the resources of heaven are at the command of those who are seeking to save the lost. Angels will help you to reach the most careless and the most hardened. And when one is brought back to God, all heaven is made glad; seraphs and cherubs touch their golden harps, and sing praises to God and the Lamb for their mercy and loving-kindness to the children of men." *Christ's Object Lessons* p. 197

My Experience

My dad was a literature evangelist for the first twenty years of my life. I am thankful for my parents' example during this time because I learned to trust God to provide for my needs.

There were times when the check was zero for the month. The dog ate pot scrapings and potato peelings (cooked on the wood stove) to survive for a while, but he lived. Four times we experienced a broken-down vehicle and not enough money to fix it, and God replaced each vehicle with another one through friends or relatives who were impressed to help us. Never did we lack something essential. My family could not pay for my university education. But when they did what they could, and I did what I could, God took care of the rest through scholarships and grants. I graduated owing the college nothing.

Over and over I saw God providing for the needs of me and my family, and each time I trusted Him more and more. This was an important foundation, for I would need to trust God fully for my own life experience.

After my university experience, I had a job with a monthly paycheck. I had enough to pay for life essentials, some to put in savings, and some to give as mission offerings. Yes, I worked to "earn" a living, but that doesn't change the fact that it was God who was providing for my needs.

Then the day came when God called me to give up my job and join a volunteer mission organization. Some would say that I made a foolish decision. But God made it clear. He provided for pilot training and aviation mechanic training and has been faithful to provide for my needs here in Africa.

Now I am married. We continue to trust in God to provide for our needs. God is faithful. Life is not all joy and ease, but we lack nothing essential.

WHAT IS YOUR RESPONSE?

Lord, I recognize that all of your commands are also promises. When You ask me to do something for You, I choose to respond promptly and cheerfully, trusting in You fully to provide for my needs. You will not ask me to do something and then neglect me. Help me to trust you fully.

Fear, Risk,
Safety, and Suffering

"For this reason I also suffer these things;
nevertheless I am not ashamed,
for I know whom I have believed
and am persuaded that He is able
to keep what I have committed to Him
until that Day."
2 Timothy 1:12

I am a missionary because...

- O   I know that God can be trusted.
- O   Nothing is able to separate me from God's love.

...What about you?

In this chapter and in the four following chapters we will briefly explain how a missionary should deal with fear, how he determines risk, how he can be safe, and how he views suffering. What fears are appropriate and which are not? How can a missionary live and work in safety? What risks are worth taking, and which risks are foolish? Is suffering something to avoid or to welcome?

The answer to these questions depends a lot on our understanding of these four things: fear, risk, safety, and suffering.

- Fear. We are sometimes held back from doing what we know to be right because we fear the outcome. We fear that the risk is too great or we fear that we will not be safe. By this, we demonstrate our misunderstanding of the concepts of risk and safety in God's work.

- Risk. We calculate risk by estimating the chance of loss or harm to something of ours if we expose it to certain circumstances. This calculation varies greatly upon our understanding of the concept of ownership and stewardship.

- Safety. We determine if someone or something is safe if we think that the chances of harm done are low enough during a certain time or at a certain location. Most often we calculate safety based on visible evidence and past life experience.

- Suffering. We sometimes make decisions based on what will give us less suffering. But suffering is not something to fear, and we can be safe in suffering.

My wife and I have chosen to live and work together in Chad, Africa. Here, we face many challenges and dangers that we did not face in America. People often do not understand why we risk our lives by living here and ask me or our families back in the States why we have chosen to live here. Chad is not a safe place, is it?

While some of these fears are imaginations, some are based on real dangers. What comes to your mind when you think of Africa? Do you think of "lions" or "danger" or "witch doctor" or "malaria" or "tribal warfare" or "famine" or "AIDS" or "poisonous snakes" or "unstable governments"? Of course, Africa can be a scary place. It's the "dark continent." It's a place of ignorance and death. It's a place where people live much the way they have for hundreds of years.

But this is where we have made our home. Until God leads elsewhere, this will remain our home. Yes, all those scary things are here, even in Chad (thankfully, at least the lions don't live close to our home). The temperature in the shade sometimes reaches above 120 degrees F during the hot part of the year. During the dry season the air is usually very dusty. It is no wonder then, that people find it hard to understand why we are here. For example, here are some typical comments we sometimes receive from outside our family.

"Why do you live in Chad, of all places?"

"It is dangerous there. It is not safe. Come back home, or you may lose your life needlessly."

"You are sick with malaria. If I were you, I would get a flight home as soon as possible. It's just not safe for you to be there anymore if you are going to get sick like this. And by staying, you are risking getting typhoid fever."

"You should work in the States where you will be more comfortable."

"People have been trying to help those Africans for a long time and it hasn't worked. They are just a bunch of poor people and will never change. Just leave them alone in peace."

"You have had too many close calls with those vipers. What if one bites you and you die?"

"The political situation is not guaranteed to be stable. What will you do if the rebels invade?"

"What if you have a medical emergency? The medical care there is minimal. It would be safer if you lived in the States where there is a developed emergency response system." "Fruit and vegetables are scarce at times. Wouldn't you be more healthy if you lived where there is an abundance of fruit and vegetables?"

■■ While you are trying to avoid "needless" danger or pain or suffering, how many people are needlessly dying without knowing Jesus?

But step back a moment and think about your own environment. If you are honest, you will recognize a host of dangers in your own country. You are used to them, so you probably do not think about them very much. If we are real with ourselves, we will recognize that no matter where we are, we live in a world full of dangerous places, things, and situations. The details vary, but there are dangers everywhere. (To be frank, our life in Chad is easy and peaceful compared to what it could be in many other places. For example, we currently have religious freedom and relative peace in the country.)

Our bodies have built-in reactions to danger or perceived danger. Physically, adrenaline is released raising heart and respiration rates and giving us a burst of energy. Emotionally, we experience panic or fear. And our brains react by instantly forgetting our current line of thought and focusing on calculating a reaction or solution. These natural reactions help us to survive dangerous situations; that is good. But we need to learn how to control these natural reactions and feelings when they are not appropriate.

In the following four chapters, we will take a look at these four things that sometimes hinder us from obedience: fear, risk, safety, and suffering.

God encourages each one of us saying,

"Fear not, for I am with you; Be not dismayed, for I am your God. I will strengthen you, Yes, I will help you, I will uphold you with My righteous right hand." Isaiah 41:10

"The eternal God is your refuge, And underneath are the everlasting arms; He will thrust out the enemy from before you, And will say, 'Destroy!' " Deuteronomy 33:27

FURTHER READING FOR YOU

Psalm 91

A Recipe

from *Missionary Leader* Vol. 13, No. 7, July 1925

Woulds't thou be wretched? Tis an easy way:
Think but of self, and self alone all day;
Think of thy pain, thy grief, thy loss, thy care,—
All that thou hast to do, or feel, or bear.
Think of thy good, thy pleasure, or thy gain.
Think only of thyself—t'will not be vain.

Would'st thou be happy? Take an easy way:
Think of those round thee—live for them all day.
Think of their pain, their loss, their grief, their care
all that they have to do, or feel or bear.
Think of their pleasures, of their good, their gain;
Think of those round thee—it will not be vain.

Fear.
Do You?

I am a missionary because...

- I do not fear to be one.
- God has promised that I do not need to be afraid.
- I recognize that God will not forsake me and that He is with me.
- As I face new fears where life is different, God teaches me not to fear and my trust in Him grows even deeper than if I had remained sheltered from these fears.

...What about you?

"People who do not know the Lord ask why in the world we waste our lives as missionaries. They forget that they too are expending their lives ... and when the bubble has burst, they will have nothing of eternal significance to show for the years they have wasted."
Nate Saint, missionary martyr

Our level of fear in a situation is often determined by either how much we think we are in control or how much we think we know about something. Fear is "a painful emotion excited by an expectation of evil, or an apprehension of impending danger accompanied by a desire to avoid or ward off the expected evil."[2] To help us understand the source of fear, imagine the following situation.

When you and your friend are walking down the sidewalk in town and you see an angry dog running in your direction, you might be afraid. But your friend beside you is not afraid at all. He knows that there is an underground electric fence—invisible to you, but real—protecting you both from the angry dog. You are both on the sidewalk in the same situation; while you panic, your friend remains calm. He knows something that you do not. You are safe, even though you do not feel safe or know that you are safe. You fear simply because you do not understand the entire situation. You cannot see reality.

If I am a passenger in a small airplane and do not understand flight very well, I might panic when we hit mild turbulence and think that we will fall out of the sky. But if I am the experienced pilot in the same airplane, I will not (normally) feel afraid. I feel in control, and I feel safe. We are both in the same circumstances, but have very different feelings. The pilot has knowledge and experience that the passenger does not have.

▋▋ Is it possible that you are unnecessarily fearful in many life situations? Is it possible that you just lack some sort of experience or knowledge? Is it possible that sometimes when you are fearful, you are actually safe?

Angels are real and much more powerful than an underground electric fence. We often fear because we forget that angels are present. We cannot see them, but they are

---

2   "fear" Webster's 1828 Dictionary

most surely there. How does God view our fear and lack of trust?

■■ Where does fear originate?

> *"For God has not given us a spirit of fear, but of power and of love and of a sound mind." 2 Timothy 1:7*

When we recognize that it is not God who gives us a spirit of fear, we will think deeper the next time we are afraid. Often we are afraid because we forget about God's power. We forget that He is near. We forget that He loves and cares for us.

■■ Take some time to think about when or where you feel the safest in your life. Why do you not feel fearful at that time or at that place? What makes you feel safe and protected?

■■ Remember some times when you have felt fearful and unsafe.
Where were you? What were the circumstances that made you feel unsafe? Why did you feel that way?

We are sometimes afraid of obeying God because we fear the unknown. We feel Him calling us to do a work for Him, but we do not know Him well enough to be willing to trust Him. If your fears come from not knowing the future, learn how to trust God more. We cannot help the future by worrying and being afraid. If our fears come from feeling insufficient for God's calling, recognize His ability to provide.

Fear of the unknown can be cured by knowing better the One who knows the future.

Another source of fear is guilt. Some people are not willing to obey God's command to "Go" because they are not obeying another of God's commands. They live in fear originating from guilt. Look at the example of Adam. He knew God, yet became fearful because of guilt. Nothing about God or His character had changed. But when God came for their evening walk, Adam became afraid and said,

> *"I heard Your voice in the garden, and I was afraid because I was naked; and I hid myself." Genesis 3:10*

God does not want us to live in fear. He wants us to trust Him with the future. He wants us to live a guilt-free life. He wants us to "fear not" when He asks us to do something.

Do Not Be Afraid

Fear blocks our ability to think calmly and reasonably. It blocks our ability to listen intently to God's message for us. The command "fear not" is repeated in the Bible numerous times. When God or an angel visits a person, that person is sometimes fearful. To calm their fears, often the first thing said is, "Fear not!" At other times a person or group of people are given a task and they are fearful. They are told, "Do not be afraid."

> *"Do not be afraid, Abram. I am your shield, your exceedingly great reward." Genesis 15:1*

> *"What ails you, Hagar? Fear not." Genesis 21:17*

> *"[Isaac,] do not fear, for I am with you." Genesis 26:1*

> *"[Jacob,] do not fear to go down to Egypt." Genesis 46:3*

> *"You must not fear them, for the Lord your God Himself fights for you." Deuteronomy 3:22*

This "Fear not" message was delivered to many others including Zacharias, Mary, Joseph the husband of Mary, shepherds, Peter, a synagogue ruler, a multitude, women at Jesus' tomb, Paul, and John.

If you are tempted to be fearful, take time to read some Bible promises. Ask God to help you with your fear and make you willing to be obedient to Him.

> *"Be strong and of good courage, do not fear nor be afraid of them; for the Lord your God, He is the One who goes with you. He will*

not leave you nor forsake you.... And the Lord, He is the one who goes before you. He will be with you, He will not leave you nor forsake you; do not fear nor be dismayed." Deuteronomy 31:6, 8

"In God I have put my trust; I will not fear. What can flesh do to me?" Psalm 56:4

"Say to those who are fearful-hearted, 'Be strong, do not fear! Behold, your God will come with vengeance, With the recompense of God; He will come and save you.'" Isaiah 35:4

"For I, the Lord your God, will hold your right hand, Saying to you, 'Fear not, I will help you.'" Isaiah 41:13

"Thus says the Lord, who created you, O Jacob, And He who formed you, O Israel: 'Fear not, for I have redeemed you; I have called you by your name; You are Mine.'" Isaiah 43:1-2

"Thus says the Lord who made you And formed you from the womb, who will help you: 'Fear not.'" Isaiah 44:2

"The Lord is on my side; I will not fear. What can man do to me?" Psalm 118:6

My Experience

Only a short six weeks after I arrived in Chad, the four-year-old son of the missionary couple I was working with died. It was a difficult time, and a rough introduction to Chad. Before they left for a break and to recover, I remember the father pulled me aside and said, "Jonathan, what do you want to do? We may not be back before the other couple leaves, and you may be left here alone. Are you going to stay or do you want to pack up?"

It did not take me long to reply, for I had already made up my mind before this situation presented itself. My response was simple. "God has called me here, and I choose to stay."

The temptation to fear came from a number of directions. "How will I continue work without knowing the language?"

"What if something goes wrong and nobody is around to help me?" "What if I get sick and die?" My mind could have raced through many fearful "what-ifs." The future was unknown to me.

But I chose not to fear. I chose to trust that God has a master plan and that He was somehow going to use the present circumstances to His glory. Fear or worry would only be an indicator of mistrust in God. Trusting in God, I confidently remained. And the missionary couple whose son had died eventually returned to continue the work in Chad. God knows the future. He took care of my every need. Looking back on the situation a few years later, I see that I truly had nothing to fear.

What is Your Response?

Father in heaven, You will not call me to a job and leave me reason to fear. You are not the author of fear, and You repeatedly give the message "Fear not!" to us humans. You see the future and are all-powerful. What should I be afraid about? I choose to not fear and to trust You with all life situations.

Further Reading for You

"When Jesus was awakened to meet the storm, He was in perfect peace. There was no trace of fear in word or look, for no fear was in His heart. But He rested not in the possession of almighty power. It was not as the 'Master of earth and sea and sky' that He reposed in quiet. That power He had laid down, and He says, 'I can of Mine own self do nothing.' John 5:30. He trusted in the Father's might. It was in faith—faith in God's love and care—that Jesus rested, and the power of that word which stilled the storm was the power of God.

"As Jesus rested by faith in the Father's care, so we are to rest in the care of our Saviour. If the disciples had trusted in Him, they would have been kept in peace. Their fear in the time of danger revealed their unbelief. In their efforts to save themselves, they forgot Jesus; and it was only when, in despair of self-dependence, they turned to Him that He could give them help.

"How often the disciples' experience is ours! When the tempests of temptation gather, and the fierce lightnings flash, and the waves sweep over us, we battle with the storm alone, forgetting that there is One who can help us. We trust to our own strength till our hope is lost, and we are ready to perish. Then we remember Jesus, and if we call upon Him to save us, we shall not cry in vain. Though He sorrowfully reproves our unbelief and self-confidence, He never fails to give us the help we need. Whether on the land or on the sea, if we have the Saviour in our hearts, there is no need of fear. Living faith in the Redeemer will smooth the sea of life, and will deliver us from danger in the way that He knows to be best." *The Desire of Ages* p. 336

"Have God within and God overhead and you have nothing to fear." *This Day With God* p. 194

"Frequently the very best evidence that we can have that we are in the right way is that the least advance costs us effort and that darkness shrouds our pathway. It has been my experience that the loftiest heights of faith we can only reach through darkness and clouds....

"It is not safe for us to cherish doubts and fears, for these grow by looking upon and talking them. I feel to reach up my hand and grasp the hand of Christ as did the sinking disciple on the stormy sea. I want to do my work with fidelity that when I shall stand before the great white throne and am called to answer for the things done in the body, which are all written in the book, that I may see souls standing there to testify I warned them, I entreated them to behold the Lamb of God that taketh away the sins of the world." *This Day With God* p. 212

"For the disheartened there is a sure remedy—faith, prayer, work. Faith and activity will impart assurance and satisfaction that will increase day by day. Are you tempted to give way to feelings of anxious foreboding or utter despondency? In the darkest days, when appearances seem most forbidding, fear not. Have faith in God. He knows your need. He has all power. His infinite love and compassion never weary. Fear not that He will fail of fulfilling His promise. He is eternal truth. Never will He change the covenant He has made with those who love Him. And He will bestow upon His faithful servants the measure of efficiency that their need demands. The apostle Paul has testified: 'He said unto me, My grace is sufficient for thee: for My strength is made perfect in weakness.... Therefore I take pleasure in infirmities, in reproaches, in necessities, in persecutions, in distresses for Christ's sake: for when I am weak, then am I strong.' 2 Corinthians 12:9–10." *Prophets and Kings* p. 164

"Christ is our present, all-sufficient Saviour. In him all fullness dwells. It is the privilege of Christians to know indeed that Christ is in them of a truth. This is the victory that overcometh the world, even our faith. All things are possible to him that believeth; and whatsoever things we desire when we pray, if we believe that we receive them we shall have them. This faith will penetrate the darkest cloud and bring rays of light and hope to the drooping, desponding soul. It is the absence of this faith and trust which brings perplexity, distressing fears, and surmisings of evil. God will do great things for his people when they put their entire trust in him. Godliness with contentment is great gain. Pure and undefiled religion will be exemplified in the life. Christ will prove a never-failing source of strength, a present help in every time of trouble." *Testimony for the Church at Battle Creek* (1868)

"The fearful and unbelieving, who are punished with the second death, are of that class who are ashamed of Christ in this world. They are afraid to do right and follow Christ, lest they should meet with pecuniary [financial] loss. They neglect their duty, to avoid reproach and trials, and to escape dangers. Those who dare not do right because they will thus expose themselves to trials, persecution, loss, and suffering are cowards, and, with idolaters, liars, and all sinners, they are ripening for the second death."

Testimonies for the Church Volume 2 p. 630

Risk.
Will You?

"But what things were gain to me, these I have counted loss for Christ.
Yet indeed I also count all things loss for the excellence of the knowledge of Christ Jesus my Lord, for whom I have suffered the loss of all things,
and count them as rubbish, that I may gain Christ."
Philippians 3:7–8

I am a missionary because...

- O The magnitude of the value of souls saved far exceeds the magnitude of risk in achieving that goal.
- O Jesus risked everything for me and I want to risk something for Him.
- O I would rather risk in this temporary life than to risk losing my eternal life because I feared to risk.

...What about you?

"If we wait till we run no risk,
the gospel will never be introduced into the interior."
David Livingstone

Our minds like to process and evaluate situations to protect us from risk, or to protect us from "exposure to harm, injury, or loss." We identify risks and then attempt to "manage" that risk and protect ourselves from it. Often, this is a good thing. I risk injuring my eyes while using a grinder machine, so I wear eye protection. Many vehicle owners in America and other places choose to buy vehicle insurance to protect themselves against the risk of lawsuit after an accident. Those in civilized countries buy smoke alarms for their homes to reduce the risk of getting caught in a burning home and to possibly give an early warning in time to save their home. God expects us to be good stewards of what He gives us.

In other cases, we are more willing to accept a risk. If a person is trapped in an accident vehicle and smoke starts to rise, we are willing to risk our own safety in an attempt to save the life of the victim. Search and rescue teams will go to drastic measures and expense in order to save even one person from near death and the rescuers will sometimes risk their lives and spend large amounts of money to save one person. The benefit of a saved life is considered of sufficient value to risk other lives in order to save that one person.

Some people are willing to risk their health or even their life for no good reason. A tightrope walker will walk across a rope stretched 100 feet above the street below. A smoker invites disease and an early death for temporary pleasure. A person may weigh the risk of bungee jumping and decide that the benefit of a temporary burst of adrenaline is worth potential injury or death.

▉ How do we determine what risks are appropriate to take in God's work?

When Jesus was tempted to jump off the temple during His wilderness temptations, He would not take the risk. He would not jump, for to jump would be presumption. He had no command from God to jump. But there is no risk involved in perfect obedience to God's commands. He could trust himself completely in God's hands. He might die or live, but He perfectly trusted that God's will for him was best.

There are some who would risk their physical life for something foolish, yet are unwilling to risk anything for God. Some will risk their lives to rescue someone on the edge of a precipice, to give them a longer temporary life, but will not put forth any effort to save people for eternal life. Some wish to remain in a safe, risk-free place. Some wish to save their money rather than use it and risk losing it. For some, comfort is more important than obedience to God. We often try to manage our risks, especially when it involves God's work.

▌▌ Is the way you view risk the same as the way God would have us view risk? Do I trust myself or my judgment more than God's? Is there any exposure to true harm, injury, or loss in obedience to God?

One key to a correct understanding of risk is to understand the concept of God's ownership. God owns everything (Psalm 50:12). That means God owns "my" car, "my" house, "my" books, "my" land, "my" everything. We do not even own ourselves. God owns us (1 Corinthians 6:19–20). That means that God owns me and "my" family. Since all of "my" possessions are God's, I choose to glorify Him with my possessions and use them in a way that is pleasing to Him.

When I calculate risk with this understanding, my goals and perspectives change. Now, instead of trying to manage risks on "my" own things, I try to understand how God views the situation. Did God give me this possession or talent for me to hide it away from risk, or is He actually asking me to take a risk for Him?

Of course, God expects us to be wise and to minimize unnecessary risk. But let us be sure to define risk well before we disobey God. And let us remember that:

"Even mighty men are not delivered by their own strength. We wait on the Lord for our help and shield." Psalm 33:14–22

It is far more risky to trust our own judgment since we don't know the future, than to trust God's judgment, since He knows the future perfectly.

We must learn how to value souls. Meditate again on the risk Jesus took to give us the opportunity of enjoying everlasting life with Him. It was an infinite risk! Jesus came from a land where there are no criminals—He was born as a helpless baby in a land full of criminals. What amazing risk! Yet the benefit was so valuable to Him that Jesus decided to come and die for us. We are that valuable in His sight! Every person is that valuable to Him.

■■ How much are you willing to risk to save souls? Are you willing to risk comfort or health or even your life itself? What if winning souls is a dangerous and risky work?

"Do not fear those who kill the body but cannot kill the soul. But rather fear Him who is able to destroy both soul and body in hell. Are not two sparrows sold for a copper coin? And not one of them falls to the ground apart from your Father's will. But the very hairs of your head are all numbered. Do not fear therefore; you are of more value than many sparrows." Matthew 10:28–31

"God is putting burdens upon more inexperienced shoulders. He is fitting them to be care-taking, to venture, to run risks." *Life Sketches of Ellen G. White* p. 245

"Remember that Christ risked all. For our redemption, heaven itself was imperiled. At the foot of the cross, remembering that for one sinner Christ would have laid down His life, you may estimate the value of a soul." *Christ's Object Lessons* p. 196

"For the message of the cross is foolishness to those who are perishing, but to us who are being saved it is the power of God." 1 Corinthians 1:18

People may say you are risking too much to obey God. They say missionary work is too risky. You risk your health, your family, and life itself. But remember Jesus' example. He was not foolish, and nor is the Christian who follows His example.

MY EXPERIENCE

During my teenage years, I remember hiking up in the mountains with friends and family. We loved to explore. One day, someone discovered a series of waterfalls. To access the falls, we had to crawl along a narrow ledge while hanging on to roots and branches to keep from falling. Access to the bottom of the first falls was somewhat risky, but as I found sufficient roots and branches to cling to, I chose to take the risk and enjoyed a very beautiful and memorable experience there. The rest of our group decided to continue exploring the other falls downstream. I followed them to a certain point. From there they went around a corner on a small ledge with fewer hand holds. I decided that such a route was too risky for me and I stayed behind rather than take that risk. I am afraid of heights, and it scares me to be near the top of a cliff or waterfall with not much to grab nearby. I had weighed the risk and determined that I would visit the first falls, but not the second. In this case, I made my decision based on the facts and the evidence I had collected with my senses at the location. Weighing risk like this can be a good thing.

But in God's work, I am learning to weigh risk through His eyes. You might say that I have taken a huge risk by moving to Africa with my wife. If the political situation turns ugly, we could lose every physical thing we have invested in up to this point. The risk of personal infection and deadly diseases is higher than some other places. People around us might use powerful witchcraft against us. One or both of us might die. But I would rather die risking something for God than to live selfishly and lose out on eternity.

Late in 2011 my dear wife Melody became ill with malaria. The first treatment did not get rid of the malaria completely and she eventually had to get on IV Quinine. She was seriously ill, and we were beginning to wonder if she would survive.

Some people gave us advice to move back to the States where life is less risky. They implied that living here was taking a foolish risk. But, we thought, would it not be a foolish risk to move to a place where God has not called us? Would that not be more foolish?

Of course, God expects us to do our part to minimize unnecessary risk. We would temporarily evacuate if necessary. We use a treated mosquito net every night. Whenever possible, we minimize our time outside in the evenings when the mosquitoes come out; when we do go out in the evenings, we often use mosquito repellent. We try to maintain a healthful lifestyle to keep our immune system healthy. We do what is within our ability and the rest we leave to God.

God did answer our prayers and the prayers of hundreds of people around the world and Melody was healed. It didn't have to turn out that way, but this time God protected her from harm. We are not here on some grand adventure. We are here because God led us here and gave us a work to do. Until that work is done, or until He sends us elsewhere, we will work here.

Doing God's work is not taking a foolish risk. It is the best kind of risk we can take. What seems like a risk to us is really no risk at all when viewed in perspective with eternity. God knows how to keep His work going and how to protect His work and His workers. Obedience to God is the ultimate risk-free activity!

What is Your Response?

Help me, Lord, to be willing to risk anything for You. Please give me understanding to discern the difference between foolish risk for things of this world and wise risk for eternal things. Give me courage to move forward with Your work even when there are obstacles and challenges. Give me a vision of eternal things. I choose to place my value on eternal things and choose to be willing to risk anything to save souls.

Further Reading for You

"God calls for Christian families to go into communities that are in darkness and error, and work wisely and perseveringly for the Master. To answer this call requires self-sacrifice. While many are waiting to have every obstacle removed, souls are dying without hope and without God in the world. Many, very many, for the sake of worldly advantage, for the sake of acquiring scientific knowledge, will venture into pestilential regions and endure hardship and privation. Where are those who are willing to do this for the sake of telling others of the Saviour? Where are the men and women who will move into regions that are in need of the gospel, that they may point those in darkness to the Redeemer?" *Testimonies for the Church Volume 9* p. 33

"Here is true missionary work in which labor and means can be invested with the best results. There has been too great fear of running risks, and moving out by faith, and sowing beside all waters. Opportunities have been presented which have not been grasped and made the most of. There has been too great fear of venturing. True faith is not presumption, but it ventures much. Precious light and powerful truth need to be brought out in publications without delay." *Life Sketches of Ellen G. White* p. 217

"The history of the report of the twelve spies has an application to us as a people. The scenes of cowardly complaining and drawing back from action when there are risks to be encountered are re-enacted among us today. The same unwillingness is manifested to heed faithful reports and true counsel as in the days of Caleb and Joshua. The servants of God, who bear the burden of His cause, practicing strict self-denial and suffering privation for the sake of helping His people, are seldom better appreciated now than they were then." *Testimonies for the Church Volume 4* p. 154–155

"O, what gracious, full, complete assurances are given us, if we will only do what God requires us to do! Take hold of this matter as though you believed the Lord would do just as He has promised. Let us venture something upon God's word. In their zeal to be rich, many run great risks; eternal considerations are overlooked, and noble principles are sacrificed; yet they may lose all in the game. But in complying with the heavenly invitations we have no such risk to run. We must take God at His word, and in simplicity of faith walk out upon the promise, and give to the Lord His own." *Counsels on Stewardship* p. 90

"There is a fearfulness to venture out and to run risks in this great work, fearing that the expenditure of means would not bring returns. What if means are used, and yet we cannot see that souls have been saved by it? What if there is a dead loss of a portion of our means? Better work and keep at work than to do nothing. You know not which shall prosper, this or that. Men will invest in patent rights and meet with heavy losses, and it is taken as a matter of course. But in the work and cause of God, men are afraid to venture. Money seems to them to be a dead loss that does not bring immediate returns when invested in the work of saving souls. The very means that is now so sparingly invested in the cause of God, and that is selfishly retained, will, in a little while, be cast with all idols to the moles and to the bats. Money will soon depreciate in value very suddenly when the reality of eternal scenes opens to the senses of man.

"God will have men who will venture anything and everything to save souls. Those who will not move until they can see every step of the way clearly before them will not be of advantage at this time to forward the truth of God. There must be workers now who will push ahead in the dark as well as in the light, and who will hold up bravely under discouragements and disappointed hopes, and yet work on with faith, with tears and patient hope, sowing beside all waters, trusting the Lord to bring the increase. God calls for men of nerve, of hope, faith, and endurance, to work to the point." *Welfare Ministry* p. 266

FURTHER READING FOR YOU

Conflict and Courage, p. 244, "For Such a Time as This"
Mind, Character, and Personality Volume 2, chapter 51, "Fear"

Safe.
Are You?

"I will both lie down in peace, and sleep;
For You alone, O Lord, make me dwell in safety."
Psalm 4:8

I am a missionary because...

○ This is the safest occupation available. I am not safe
following anything other than God's calling for my
life.
○ I believe God's promises.

...What about you?

"If I settle on the far side of the sea,
even there your hand will guide me,
your right hand will hold me fast."
Psalm 139:9–10 (NIV)

Our definition of safety usually comes from our own evaluation of the situation and how well we think we can manage the risks involved. If we think the risk of harm is low, we call the situation safe. The problem is that we often do not evaluate safety in the context of God's work or eternity. Our minds are stuck on the here and now. We think, "How can I be the most safe and protect myself and my possessions?"

One definition of safety is "freedom from danger or hazard, exemption from hurt, injury or loss."[3] God defines safety in the context of eternal values, not temporary earthly ones. Christians are exposed to temporal danger, hazard, hurt, injury, loss, but gain eternal life and treasure. Real danger is defined in the context of eternity, not in a temporal context.

We can be forever grateful that Jesus did not share our typical attitude about safety. In the planning of our salvation, Jesus saw many things that were not "safe," but valued the outcome of His work so much that He was willing to be in "unsafe" conditions. Being born in the animal shelter was not "safe." From His earliest days, people tried to kill Him. He did not work in a "safe" environment. It was not "safe" for Jesus to touch the lepers. It would have been much "safer" for Jesus to remain in heaven, but He chose to come to earth and deal with human nature and the fiercest temptations of an angry Satan.

When we study Christ's example, we will find that true safety is not defined by the circumstances or physical danger involved but by maintaining a constant connection with God and being obedient to Him.

The key to rightly evaluating the safety of various situations is to keep our connection with God constant. Ignoring common-sense safety practices such as wearing a seat belt while driving on the highway, or using a mosquito net in a malaria zone would be foolish decisions. God expects us to

---

3   "safety" Webster's 1828 Dictionary

respect the laws of nature and not be foolish in our actions. But as soon as our decision to be "safe" blocks God's plan for our lives, we have made a mistake—one that leads us to disobedience.

Take for example Jesus' decision to return to Judea where the Jews wanted to stone Him.

> *"[Jesus] said to the disciples, 'Let us go to Judea again.' The disciples said to Him, 'Rabbi, lately the Jews sought to stone You, and are You going there again?' " John 11:7-8*

The disciples thought Jesus was crazy for wanting to go back to Judea. To them it seemed obvious that this was not a safe choice. Judea was where the Jews were trying to capture and kill Jesus—a certain death trap. But Jesus did not make His decision to return to Judea based on the apparent lack of physical safety.

> *"Jesus answered, 'Are there not twelve hours in the day? If anyone walks in the day, he does not stumble, because he sees the light of this world. But if one walks in the night, he stumbles, because the light is not in him.' " John 11:9-10*

Jesus knew that He was safe because He was:

- o "Walking"
  Walking implies action or doing. Jesus was doing, not idly ignoring God's work. He was moving forward.
- o "in the day"
  Jesus' actions were right. They were not the actions of darkness, but actions of obedience to God's revealed will.

He did not fear the threats of the Jews. As long as He was in God's will and walking in the light, He was perfectly safe.

Complete obedience to God is the only safe road to walk. Any time we ignore God's command, we are not safe.

▮▮ Are you safe? Are you walking in the light? Are you fully obeying God? How are you obeying the command to "Go"?

Walking in the light is contrary to the inclinations and tendencies of self. If we want to walk safely in the light as Jesus did, we must give up self and crucify it. The most common obstacle to walking in the light is self. We choose not to walk in the light when we choose not to obey. While following the desires of self may please us for a time, it is not a safe path to follow. True safety comes from trusting God completely. And by obeying God, we provide a good witness.

> *"Because you have made the Lord, who is my refuge, even the Most High, your dwelling place, no evil shall befall you, nor shall any plague come near your dwelling."* Psalm 91:9–10

▮▮ What would have been the result of Jesus' witness if He had chosen to remain at a "safe" distance from Judea? What if He had followed the advice of His disciples?

Below are a few more passages explaining true safety.

> *"The fear of man brings a snare, but whoever trusts in the Lord shall be safe."* Proverbs 29:25

> "Satan is ever seeking to impress and control the mind, and none of us are safe except as we have a constant connection with God. We must momentarily receive supplies from heaven, and if we would be kept by the power of God we must be obedient to all His requirements." *Testimonies for the Church Volume 4* p. 542

> *"So you shall observe My statutes and keep My judgments, and perform them; and you will dwell in the land in safety."* Leviticus 25:18

> *"Hold me up, and I shall be safe, and I shall observe Your statutes continually."* Psalm 119:117

We are safe as we maintain our connection with God and as we are obedient to Him.

"When Christ took human nature upon Him, He bound humanity to Himself by a tie of love that can never be broken by any power save the choice of man himself. Satan will constantly present allurements to induce us to break this tie—to choose to separate ourselves from Christ. Here is where we need to watch, to strive, to pray, that nothing may entice us to choose another master; for we are always free to do this. But let us keep our eyes fixed upon Christ, and He will preserve us. Looking unto Jesus, we are safe. Nothing can pluck us out of His hand. In constantly beholding Him, we 'are changed into the same image from glory to glory, even as by the Spirit of the Lord.' 2 Corinthians 3:18." *Steps to Christ* p. 72

"The Father's presence encircled Christ, and nothing befell Him but that which infinite love permitted for the blessing of the world. Here was His source of comfort, and it is for us. He who is imbued with the Spirit of Christ abides in Christ. Whatever comes to him comes from the Saviour, who surrounds him with His presence. Nothing can touch him except by the Lord's permission. All our sufferings and sorrows, all our temptations and trials, all our sadness and griefs, all our persecutions and privations, in short, all things work together for our good. All experiences and circumstances are God's workmen whereby good is brought to us." *The Ministry of Healing* p. 488–489

BIBLE EXAMPLES OF SAFE PLACES

❚❚ Are you in a safe place?

"The name of the Lord is a strong tower; the righteous run to it and are safe." Proverbs 18:10

"I will both lie down in peace, and sleep; for You alone, O Lord, make me dwell in safety." Psalm 4:8

The Bible is full of examples of people who lived or worked in risky, dangerous situations. When these people remained faithful to God, He protected them. When found in a dangerous situation, they trusted that God would deliver them. What would be perceived as a dangerous place by most people becomes the safest place if that is where God wants you. That is the key. Walking into battle without God's blessing (like the Israelites' first attack on Ai) is foolish. But as we follow God's direction, we are safe no matter what. Take some time to read some of the following stories. Ask yourself if they were in a safe place.

- ○ Elisha's servant was fearful because at first, he could only see the enemy surrounding him. The army of good angels was also there, but he did not see them until later. His fear left him only when he perceived what actually existed before. He was in a safe place. (2 Kings 6:15–17)

- ○ God said to spy out the land that was promised to them. Twelve spies returned, but ten of them said it was not safe. There were giants in the lands, and it was a dangerous place. Two remained faithful and said, "Let's go right away and enter the land as God has commanded." As a result of rejecting God and His command in an attempt to maintain "safety," the people died in the wilderness, except for the two faithful spies. (Numbers 13–14)

- ○ All the people of faith in Hebrews 11 were "safe." Abel was safe, though he died. Joseph was safe, though he was sold as a slave. Those who died in prison or who were sawed in two were safe, though their lives were difficult and trying. Through faith, they could see what others could not—the promise of an eternally safe home. (Hebrews 11)

- ○ The Israelites were protected while they were obedient but were in danger when disobedient. The story of the two attacks on Ai is one good example of this. (Joshua 7–8)

○ Baby Moses appeared to be in a dangerous situation. But God had a plan for Moses, and no power was great enough to prevent God's will. (Exodus 2)

○ Shadrach, Meshach, and Abed-Nego were safe in obedience to God's word. Even though threatened with a horrible, public death, they would not budge in their commitment to God. (Daniel 3)

○ Daniel was safe in obedience, even though he faced "sure death" in a den of hungry lions. When the law was passed to worship only the king, he could have thought, "I must protect my life. I have an important work to do for God. I'll just pray in my closet for now." But no, he continued worshiping God without shame. He knew that hungry lions might end his life here, but that his eternal life was safe in God's hands. (Daniel 6)

○ Stephen was full of the Holy Spirit the day he was stoned. He was in a safe place, and calmly trusted his life to God even during the moments of death. (Acts 7)

○ Abel was righteous and was safe, even though his brother Cain killed him. Abel considered obedience to God of more importance than even life. (Genesis 4:1–8; Hebrews 11:4)

○ Paul was told to not be afraid, even though the ship would run aground and be broken apart at sea. Paul, in the middle of the violent storm, was in a safe place. (Acts 27)

○ David was safe, even while facing a giant, an evil enemy of God. As David remained in God's will, God gave him strength, success, and safety. He did not fear. Had David feared a dangerous situation, he would not have accomplished such a mighty victory for God. David's past experience with the bear and lion had strengthened his faith for this experience. (1 Samuel 17)

○ Noah and his family were safe as they obeyed God. Noah obeyed God in everything. Those who disobeyed died in the flood. (Genesis 6–7)
"It was Christ who kept the ark safe amid the roaring, seething billows, because its inmates had faith in His power to preserve them." *The Review and Herald*, March 12, 1901

OTHER EXAMPLES OF SAFE PLACES

In more modern history, we find many other inspiring examples of people who were safe as they remained faithful to God.

Like the apostle Paul, Ellen White experienced a violent storm while on a boat voyage. During the storm, many people were fearful that the boat would be broken apart or sink. But she remained calm and fearless in her knowledge that she was doing God's will. Read her personal account of the situation in the following paragraph.

"A few weeks after this, on our way to Boston we took the steamer at Portland. A violent storm came up, and we were in great peril. The boat rolled fearfully, and the waves dashed into the cabin windows. There was great fear in the ladies' cabin. Many were confessing their sins, and crying to God for mercy. Some were calling upon the Virgin Mary to keep them, while others were making solemn vows to God that if they reached land they would devote their lives to His service. It was a scene of terror and confusion. As the boat rocked, a lady turned to me and said: 'Are you not terrified? I suppose it is a fact that we may never reach land.' I told her that I had made Christ my refuge, and if my work was done, I might as well lie in the bottom of the ocean as in any other place; but if my work was not done, all the waters of the ocean could not drown me. My trust was in God; He would bring us safe to land if it was for His glory." *Testimonies for the Church Volume 1* p. 80–81

Here is another boat and storm story.

"John and Charles Wesley, after being ordained to the ministry, were sent on a mission to America. On board the ship was a company of Moravians. Violent storms were encountered on the passage, and John Wesley, brought face to face with death, felt that he had not the assurance of peace with God. The Germans, on the contrary, manifested a calmness and trust to which he was a stranger.

'I had long before,' he says, 'observed the great seriousness of their behavior. Of their humility they had given a continual proof, by performing those servile offices for the other passengers which none of the English would undertake; for which they desired and would receive no pay, saying it was good for their proud hearts, and their loving Saviour had done more for them. And every day had given them occasion of showing a meekness which no injury could move. If they were pushed, struck, or thrown about, they rose again and went away; but no complaint was found in their mouth. There was now an opportunity of trying whether they were delivered from the spirit of fear, as well as from that of pride, anger, and revenge. In the midst of the psalm wherewith their service began, the sea broke over, split the mainsail in pieces, covered the ship, and poured in between the decks as if the great deep had already swallowed us up. A terrible screaming began among the English. The Germans calmly sang on. I asked one of them afterwards, "Were you not afraid?" He answered, "I thank God, no." I asked, "But were not your women and children afraid?" He replied mildly, "No; our women and children are not afraid to die." '—Whitehead, *Life of the Rev. John Wesley*, page 10." *The Great Controversy* p. 254–255

Many of the martyrs faced a horrible death fearlessly. They remained committed to God and faithful to Him even as they were burned or drowned or beheaded because they knew that the only safe path is the path of loyalty and obedience to God. They might save themselves from a comparatively brief trial, an unsafe and life-threatening situation here on earth, only to lose out on eternal life. But no, they chose to endure danger and death, believing that they were safe—that they were in God's hand and that He would bring them safely to heaven and eternal life.

Look at this account of the death of Mr. Tilleman who lived in the Netherlands. Notice how he remained faithful and fearless to the end, secure in the safety of eternal life. Notice also that God seemed to give him extra strength and peace to endure his last trial on earth.

"Giles Tilleman, a cutler of Brussels, was a man of great humanity and piety. Among others he was apprehended as a Protestant, and many endeavors were made by the monks to persuade him to recant. He had once, by accident, a fair opportunity of escaping from prison and being asked why he did not avail himself of it, he replied, 'I would not do the keepers so much injury, as they must have answered for my absence, had I gone away.' When he was sentenced to be burnt, he fervently thanked God for granting him an opportunity, by martyrdom, to glorify His name. Perceiving, at the place of execution, a great quantity of fagots, he desired the principal part of them might be given to the poor, saying, 'A small quantity will suffice to consume me.' The executioner offered to strangle him before the fire was lighted, but he would not consent, telling him that he defied the flames; and, indeed, he gave up the ghost with such composure amidst them, that he hardly seemed sensible of their effects."
Fox's Book of Martyrs p. 113

Here is another account from the Netherlands.
"A.D. 1568, three persons were apprehended in Antwerp, named Scoblant, Hues, and Coomans. During their confinement they behaved with great fortitude and

cheerfulness, confessing that the hand of God appeared in what had befallen them, and bowing down before the throne of his providence. In an epistle to some worthy Protestants, they expressed themselves in the following words: 'Since it is the will of the Almighty that we should suffer for His name, and be persecuted for the sake of His Gospel, we patiently submit, and are joyful upon the occasion; though the flesh may rebel against the spirit, and hearken to the council of the old serpent, yet the truths of the Gospel shall prevent such advice from being taken, and Christ shall bruise the serpent's head. We are not comfortless in confinement, for we have faith; we fear not affliction, for we have hope; and we forgive our enemies, for we have charity. Be not under apprehensions for us, we are happy in confinement through the promises of God, glory in our bonds, and exult in being thought worthy to suffer for the sake of Christ. We desire not to be released, but to be blessed with fortitude; we ask not liberty, but the power of perseverance; and wish for no change in our condition, but that which places a crown of martyrdom upon our heads.' " *Fox's Book of Martyrs* p. 113

"We do not know what great interests may be at stake in the proving of God. There is no safety except in strict obedience to the word of God. All His promises are made upon condition of faith and obedience, and a failure to comply with His commands cuts off the fulfillment to us of the rich provisions of the Scriptures. We should not follow impulse, nor rely on the judgment of men; we should look to the revealed will of God and walk according to His definite commandment, no matter what circumstances may surround us. God will take care of the results; by faithfulness to His word we may in time of trial prove before men and angels that the Lord can trust us in difficult places to carry out His will, honor His name, and bless His people." *Patriarchs and Prophets* p. 621

My Experience

My wife and I face multiple situations in Chad that are not considered to be safe by many. For example, I am a pilot. Some people say that aviation is not safe, that too many people die in airplane crashes. In Chad, there are not numerous airports to divert to in an emergency or in bad weather. Also, we come across many poisonous snakes and scorpions. We live in a place where there is a high risk of malaria. Traveling by overloaded and crowded bus is dangerous, as is driving a motorcycle every day.

So why are we here in this unsafe place? My wife and I have chosen not to make physical circumstances and physical safety our sole guide in making decisions. Jesus did not ask, "Where is the safest place to work?" He asked, "What is God's work for me and where does He want me to labor next?"

We recognize that no matter where we live, we face unsafe circumstances. But God knows how to deal with these and protect us. Yes, God expects us to be wise and not foolish, but we can never find a place that is perfectly safe by human standards. In the States, it is not safe to drive on the Interstate at seventy-five miles per hour, and many people die on the road every year. Even though driving on the road is not as safe as walking, most people choose to take the risk and drive because driving is far more efficient than walking.

Similarly, we choose to use the airplane as a tool to accomplish God's work more quickly. A motorcycle or car is not equipped to serve in a capacity as an airplane. In many circumstances the airplane is a far more efficient means of transportation. We choose to do thorough maintenance on the plane and take whatever safety precautions we can to remain accident-free.

God gave us intelligence to use, and we believe that we should do what we reasonably can to be safe. At night we use flashlights to avoid scorpions and snakes. We use a mosquito net at night. We minimize travel by bus and are careful on the motorcycle. We filter our drinking water.

When God called us to Chad, how could we respond, "No God, we cannot work there; it is dangerous; let those people die without knowing You"? We can be in no safer place than in obedience to God.

WHAT IS YOUR RESPONSE?

I choose to constantly look to Jesus and be safe. I choose to safely trust Him and not my own feelings. I choose to cultivate a habit of continual conversation with my Father, realizing that without this I am living in danger and am not safe. Father, give me courage to accept Your will for my life and help me to understand that in so doing I am safe.

FURTHER READING FOR YOU

"Our only safe course is to render obedience to all His requirements, at whatever cost. All are founded in infinite love and wisdom." *Messages to Young People* p. 442

"You are safe only as you trust in God. We have a vigilant foe to contend against." *Our High Calling* p. 25

"Amidst all life's perplexities and dangers and conflicting claims the one safe and sure rule is to do what God says." *Education* p. 229

"The only safety for any of us is to plant our feet upon the Word of God and study the Scriptures, making God's Word our constant meditation." *This Day with God* p. 292

"When men separate from God, they place themselves under the control of Satan. Talents have been given to men that they may be used in God's service.... There is only one safe way for any man, and that is the way of obedience to a 'Thus saith the Lord.' " *Conflict and Courage* p. 34

"Holy angels often visited the garden, and gave instruction to Adam and Eve concerning their employment and also taught them concerning the rebellion and fall of Satan. The angels warned them of Satan and cautioned them not to separate from each other in their employment, for they might be brought in contact with this fallen foe. The angels also enjoined upon them to follow closely the directions God had given them, for in perfect obedience only were they safe. Then this fallen foe could have no power over them." *Early Writings* p. 147

"If we are to learn of Christ, we must pray as the apostles prayed when the Holy Spirit was poured upon them. We need a baptism of the Spirit of God. We are not safe for one hour while we are failing to render obedience to the word of God." *Fundamentals of Christian Education* p. 537

"Satan is well aware that the weakest soul who abides in Christ is more than a match for the hosts of darkness, and that, should he reveal himself openly, he would be met and resisted. Therefore he seeks to draw away the soldiers of the cross from their strong fortification, while he lies in ambush with his forces, ready to destroy all who venture upon his ground. Only in humble reliance upon God, and obedience to all his commandments, can we be secure. "No man is safe for a day or an hour without prayer. Especially should we entreat the Lord for wisdom to understand his Word. Here are revealed the wiles of the tempter, and the means by which he may be successfully resisted. Satan is an expert in quoting Scripture, placing his own interpretation upon passages by which he hopes to cause us to stumble. We should study the Bible with humility of heart, never losing sight of our dependence upon God. While we must constantly guard against the devices of Satan, we should pray in faith continually, 'Lead us not into temptation.' " *The Great Controversy* p. 530

"The things of this world would be enjoyable, were it not for the curse of sin; but crime, sorrow, suffering, and death meet us everywhere. Property, and even life itself, is not safe.... It is only in obedience to God's law that true happiness can be found. We must submit our will to God if we would have his divine and eternal harmony in our souls." *Historical Sketches of the Foreign Missions of the Seventh-day Adventists* p. 187

"I implore you to trust wholly in God. 'Resist the devil, and he will flee from you. Draw nigh to God, and he will draw nigh to you.' James 4:7–8 The Christian life is a life of conflict, or self-denial and conquest. It is a continual battle and a march. Every act of obedience to Christ, every victory obtained over self, is a step in the march to glory and final victory. Take Christ for your Guide and He will lead you safely along. The pathway may be rough and thorny and the ascents steep, requiring toil. You may have to press on when weary, when you long for rest. You may have to fight on when faint and hope on when discouraged, but, with Christ as your Guide, you cannot lose the path of immortal life. You cannot fail to reach the exalted seat by the side of your Guide, whose own feet trod the rough path before you, evening the way for your feet. If you follow pride and selfish ambition you will find it pleasant at first, but the end is pain and sorrow. You may follow selfishness, which will promise you much but will poison and embitter your life. To follow Christ is safe. He will not suffer the powers of darkness to hurt one hair of your head. Trust in your Redeemer and you are safe." *Our High Calling* p. 25

"It is as true now as when the words were spoken to Israel of obedience to His commandments: 'This is your wisdom and your understanding in the sight of the nations.' Deuteronomy 4:6. Here is the only safeguard for individual integrity, for the purity of the home, the well-being of society, or the stability of the nation. Amidst all life's perplexities and dangers and conflicting claims, the one safe and sure rule is to do what God says. 'The statutes of the Lord are right,' and 'he that doeth these things shall never be moved.' Psalm 19:8; 15:5." *Prophets and Kings* p. 83

"Students, you are safe only as, in perfect submission and obedience, you connect yourselves with Christ." *Selected Messages Book 1* p. 242

"We must not allow our minds to drift and come to no point. We know that the Lord is soon to come, and we must serve God from principle and be firm as a rock to follow in the path of obedience, because it is the only safe path." *That I May Know Him* p. 203

"Some have so long sacrificed principle that they cannot see the difference between the sacred and the common. Those who refuse to give heed to the Lord's instruction will go steadily downward in the path of ruin. The day of test and trial is just before us. Let every man put on his true colors. Do you choose loyalty or rebellion? Show your colors to men and to angels. We are safe only when we are committed to the right. Then the world knows where we shall be found in the day of trial and trouble." *Testimonies for the Church Volume 8* p. 96

"Our only safety is to follow where the steps of the Master lead the way, to trust for protection implicitly to Him who says, 'Follow me.' Our constant prayer should be, 'Hold up my goings in thy path, O Lord, that my footsteps slip not.' " *Sons and Daughters of God* p. 154

FURTHER READING FOR YOU

Conflict and Courage p. 92 "A Safe Path"
That I May Know Him p. 223 "A Safe Place for Our Treasures"
The Great Controversy chapter 37 "The Scriptures a Safeguard"
SDA Bible Commentary Volume 4, Isaiah 58

"My brethren, you need to study more carefully the fifty-eighth chapter of Isaiah. This chapter marks out the only course that we can follow with safety." *S.D.A. Bible Commentary Volume 4* p. 1149

Suffer.
Are You Willing?

*"Yes, and all who desire to live godly in Christ Jesus
will suffer persecution."*
2 Timothy 3:12

I am a missionary because...

- I am not afraid of suffering. I have committed my soul to God's keeping.
- Jesus knows what it is to suffer; He will give me strength.
- To suffer for God's sake is an honor.
- I cannot in any other way be joyful in suffering.

...What about you?

*"If ten men are carrying a log — nine of them on the little end and
one at the heavy end — and you want to help,
which end will you lift on?"*
William Borden

Jesus did not enjoy suffering. But He lived to relieve others' suffering of all kinds—physical, mental, and spiritual. He did not come for people to serve Him, but to serve others.

Jesus was more interested in relieving other peoples' suffering than in avoiding His own suffering. He would suffer so that others would not suffer.

God did not intend for humans to suffer. But since Adam and Eve sinned, humanity has suffered. Our hearts also suffer sympathetically when we see other people suffering.

What are you doing about other people's suffering? How does your attitude toward the suffering compare to Jesus' attitude?

■ Wherever there is suffering, there is a need for missionary work. Will you fill that need somewhere? Ask yourself, "Where are the suffering people near me?" or "Where are people suffering the greatest in the world?" God is calling us to minister to the suffering.

While we could study Bible the teaching regarding our duty to relieve the suffering, we will leave that to another study. Here, we will look primarily at personal suffering that is a result of loyalty to God. We do not like to suffer. We try to avoid suffering at all cost. It is not fun to be uncomfortable or hungry or in pain or in mental anguish.

■ In our attempts to avoid suffering, are we compromising God's plan for our lives and our mission work?

Jesus' Attitude Toward Suffering

Jesus knew in advance that coming to earth on His mission trip would cause Him suffering. His suffering was clearly described in the prophecies. But He did not shrink back.

> *"Those things which God foretold by the mouth of all His prophets, that the Christ would suffer, He has thus fulfilled."*
> Acts 3:18

To Jesus, the thought of His sons and daughters being safe for eternity was a joy much greater in magnitude than that of His sufferings. He loves us that much! He was willing to suffer greatly because of His love for us.

> *"...looking unto Jesus, the author and finisher of our faith, who for the joy that was set before Him endured the cross, despising the shame, and has sat down at the right hand of the throne of God. For consider Him who endured such hostility from sinners against Himself, lest you become weary and discouraged in your souls." Hebrews 11:2-3*

Jesus is our example, even in His sufferings. But our sufferings will never come close to the magnitude of Jesus' sufferings.

> " 'The world cannot hate you,' He said, 'but Me it hateth, because I testify of it, that the works thereof are evil.' The world does not hate those who are like it in spirit; it loves them as its own. The world for Christ was not a place of ease and self-aggrandizement." *The Desire of Ages* p. 451

Study Jesus' attitude toward suffering. He did not fear discomfort or persecution. When people mocked Him He did not respond in like manner. He did not threaten to "get even" with those who were causing Him to suffer. When He spoke, He remained peaceful.

> *"He was oppressed and He was afflicted, yet He opened not His mouth; He was led as a lamb to the slaughter, and as a sheep before its shearers is silent, so He opened not His mouth." Isaiah 53:7*

> *"His visage was marred more than any man, and His form more than the sons of men." Isaiah 52:14*

> *"I gave My back to those who struck Me, and My cheeks to those who plucked out the beard; I did not hide My face from shame and spitting." Isaiah 50:6*

"Christ also suffered for us, leaving us an example, that you should follow His steps: 'who committed no sin, nor was deceit found in His mouth'; who, when He was reviled, did not revile in return; when He suffered, He did not threaten, but <u>committed Himself to Him</u> who judges righteously." 1 Peter 2:21–23

According to the verse you just read in 1 Peter, what was the secret of how Jesus endured suffering without fear? Jesus committed Himself to God the righteous Judge. Jesus knew that God sees and records everything and will give to everybody their reward in the final judgment. God will preserve truth and will deal with individually everybody who does wrong. As Jesus remained 100% committed to God, He did not have any reason to fear or to become agitated under suffering.

Jesus' commitment was so solid and genuine that at the peak of His suffering, while nailed to the cross and experiencing punishment of the sins of you and me and everyone, while evil men tortured Him, He prayed,

"Father, forgive them, for they do not know what they do."
Luke 23:34

It was not the physical suffering that affected Jesus the most but the mental suffering of bearing the sins of all the world and feeling the separation from God that those sins brought. Yet through all this, He did not show fear or react with anger, for He had committed His life to God.

BIBLE ATTITUDE TOWARD SUFFERING

We all face suffering of various types, though none of the suffering is on the level that Jesus suffered. And unlike Jesus' example, sometimes we suffer from our own mistakes. But there is genuine suffering that comes as a result of being missionaries—because of being Christlike. The fervent Christian missionary is going to get more than his fair share of trials and suffering.

"Yes, and all who desire to live godly in Christ Jesus will suffer persecution." 2 Timothy 3:12

"For to you it has been granted on behalf of Christ, not only to believe in Him, but also to suffer for His sake." Philippians 1:29

As Jesus committed His life to God, so we should follow His example. We will likely fear suffering when our lives are not 100% committed to Him. But if our lives are committed fully to God, we can be like Daniel before he was thrown into the lions' den and like his three friends before they were thrown into the fiery furnace, who, in the face of suffering and death, were not scared or timid but bold and strong remaining faithful to God even to death.

The key to a Christ-like attitude in suffering is to follow His example of 100% commitment. When we do this, we do not need to fear suffering. In fact, we can be joyful and content in suffering. We have no need to be ashamed.

"So [Peter and the other apostles] departed from the presence of the council, rejoicing that they were counted worthy to suffer shame for His name." Acts 5:41

"I now rejoice in my sufferings for you, and fill up in my flesh what is lacking in the afflictions of Christ, for the sake of His body, which is the church." Colossians 1:24

"Beloved, do not think it strange concerning the fiery trial which is to try you, as though some strange thing happened to you; but rejoice to the extent that you partake of Christ's sufferings, that when His glory is revealed, you may also be glad with exceeding joy. If you are reproached for the name of Christ, blessed are you, for the Spirit of glory and of God rests upon you. On their part He is blasphemed, but on your part He is glorified. But let none of you suffer as a murderer, a thief, an evildoer, or as a busybody in other people's matters. Yet if anyone suffers as a Christian, let him not be ashamed, but let him glorify God in this matter.... Therefore let those who suffer according to the will of God

commit their souls to Him in doing good, as to a faithful Creator."
1 Peter 4:12–16, 19

"Therefore do not be ashamed of the testimony of our Lord, nor of me His prisoner, but share with me in the sufferings for the gospel according to the power of God.... For this reason [preaching and teaching the Gospel] I also suffer these things; nevertheless I am not ashamed, for I know whom I have believed and am persuaded that He is able to keep what I have committed to Him until that Day." 2 Timothy 1:8, 12

Notice how commitment to God is the key to experiencing joy in suffering.

Suffering also helps us to hate sin. The more we endure suffering, the more we experience the results of sin. God allowed the Israelites to endure slavery for a long time until they were finally ready to leave. Even then, they were wanting to return to slavery only a few short days after liberation. We do not hate sin or Satan enough. Suffering can lead us to hate sin and Satan.

Unfortunately, we sometimes suffer as a result of our own selfish actions, not as a result of our commitment to God. This type of suffering is not desirable.

"For this is commendable, if because of conscience toward God one endures grief, suffering wrongfully. For what credit is it if, when you are beaten for your faults, you take it patiently? But when you do good and suffer, if you take it patiently, this is commendable before God. For to this you were called, because Christ also suffered for us, leaving us an example, that you should follow His steps." 1 Peter 2:19–21

"But even if you should suffer for righteousness' sake, you are blessed. 'And do not be afraid of their threats, nor be troubled.' But sanctify the Lord God in your hearts, and always be ready to give a defense to everyone who asks you a reason for the hope that is in you, with meekness and fear; having a good conscience,

that when they defame you as evildoers, those who revile your good conduct in Christ may be ashamed. For it is better, if it is the will of God, to suffer for doing good than for doing evil."
1 Peter 3:14-17

When we face suffering for God, we would do well to keep our eyes focused on Jesus and the prize before us, not on our sufferings or difficulties.

"But what things were gain to me, these I have counted loss for Christ. Yet indeed I also count all things loss for the excellence of the knowledge of Christ Jesus my Lord, for whom I have suffered the loss of all things, and count them as rubbish, that I may gain Christ." Philippians 3:7-8

"But recall the former days in which, after you were illuminated, you endured a great struggle with sufferings: partly while you were made a spectacle both by reproaches and tribulations, and partly while you became companions of those who were so treated; for you had compassion on me in my chains, and joyfully accepted the plundering of your goods, knowing that you have a better and an enduring possession for yourselves in heaven. Therefore do not cast away your confidence, which has great reward." Hebrews 10:32-35

You might be thinking, "How could I joyfully accept the plundering of my possessions?" To lose your possessions would seem to be something terrible, like a calamity or a large trial. How were they joyful?

- o   They recognized the principle of God's ownership.

- o   Their goals and attention were fixed on an enduring place in heaven, not on their temporary things here. Because their focus was on heaven, losing things on earth was not such a trial.

- o   More importantly, they relied on God and His grace for strength.

> *"But may the God of all grace, who called us to His eternal glory by Christ Jesus, after you have suffered a while, perfect, establish, strengthen, and settle you."* 1 Peter 5:10

The more we contemplate eternal things, the less we value temporary things. The more we study Jesus' sufferings, the more we realize how little we suffer. Paul was a man who suffered much during his life including lashings, imprisonment, and shipwreck. Yet, he did not consider his great sufferings to be worth comparing to the future reward. They were insignificant.

> *"[We are] joint heirs with Christ, if indeed we suffer with Him, that we may also be glorified together. For I consider that the sufferings of this present time are not worthy to be compared with the glory which shall be revealed in us."* Romans 8:17-18

> *"But even after we had suffered before and were spitefully treated at Philippi, as you know, we were bold in our God to speak to you the gospel of God in much conflict."* 1 Thessalonians 2:2

In the context of Paul's sufferings, we read this following paragraph.

> "Reformatory action is always attended with loss, sacrifice, and peril. It always rebukes love of ease, selfish interests, and lustful ambition. Hence, whoever initiates or prosecutes such action must encounter opposition, calumny, and hatred from those who are unwilling to submit to the conditions of reform. It is no easy matter to overcome sinful habits and practices. The work can be accomplished only with the help of divine grace; but many neglect to seek such help, and endeavor to bring down the standard to meet their deficiencies, instead of bringing themselves up to meet the standard of God." *Sketches from the Life of Paul* p. 305–306

Some people are called to suffer a little and others are called to suffer greatly, perhaps even in death at the stake. But God knows how to give us the comfort and help that we need. The more suffering we endure for Christ's sake, the more comfort He supplies. With this knowledge, we can choose to be steadfast in our decision to follow Christ.

"For as the suffering_s of Christ abound in us, so our consolation also abounds through Christ. Now if we are afflicted, it is for your consolation and salvation, which is effective for enduring the same sufferings which we also suffer. Or if we are comforted, it is for your consolation and salvation. And our hope for you is steadfast, because we know that as you are partakers of the sufferings, so also you will partake of the consolation."
2 Corinthians 1:5–7

If you would like to study the topic of suffering more, try following the advice of James and study the lives of the prophets.

"My brethren, take the prophets, who spoke in the name of the Lord, as an example of suffering and patience." James 5:10

It can also be helpful to learn about some of the martyrs who were faithful to death.

MARTYRS' ATTITUDE TOWARD SUFFERING

"Do not fear any of those things which you are about to suffer. Indeed, the devil is about to throw some of you into prison, that you may be tested, and you will have tribulation ten days. Be faithful until death, and I will give you the crown of life." Revelation 2:10

"O Lord, You know; Remember me and visit me, And take vengeance for me on my persecutors. In Your enduring patience, do not take me away. Know that for Your sake I have suffered rebuke. Your words were found, and I ate them, And Your word was to me the joy and rejoicing of my heart; For I am called by Your name, O Lord God of hosts." Jeremiah 15:15–16

Below are a few short accounts of various martyrs who chose to suffer a relatively short time in comparison to the eternal reward. They were not fearful of suffering and were faithful to death.

"The year following the martyrdoms of the before-mentioned persons, viz. 1539, two others were apprehended on a suspicion of heresy; namely, Jerome Russell and Alexander Kennedy, a youth about eighteen years of age.

"These two persons, after being some time confined in prison, were brought before the archbishop for examination. In the course of which Russell, being a very sensible man, reasoned learnedly against his accusers; while they in return made use of very opprobrious language.

"The examination being over, and both of them deemed heretics, the archbishop pronounced the dreadful sentence of death, and they were immediately delivered over to the secular power in order for execution.

"The next day they were led to the place appointed for them to suffer; in their way to which, Russell, seeing his fellow-sufferer have the appearance of timidity in his countenance, thus addressed him: 'Brother, fear not; greater is He that is in us, than He that is in the world. The pain that we are to <u>suffer</u> is short, and shall be light; but our joy and <u>consolation</u> shall never have an end. Let us, therefore, strive to enter into our Master and Savior's joy, by the same straight way which He hath taken before us. Death cannot hurt us, for it is already destroyed by Him, for whose sake we are now going to suffer.'

"When they arrived at the fatal spot, they both kneeled down and prayed for some time; after which being fastened to the stake, and the fagots lighted, they cheerfully resigned their souls into the hands of Him who gave them, in full hopes of an everlasting reward in the heavenly mansions." *Fox's Book of Martyrs* p. 129

The story of Faninus gives us another illustration of an inspirational attitude toward suffering.

"Faninus, a learned layman, by reading controversial books, became of the reformed religion. An information being exhibited against him to the pope, he was apprehended, and cast into prison. His wife, children, relations, and friends visited him in his confinement, and so far wrought upon his mind, that he renounced his faith, and obtained his release. But he was no sooner free from confinement than his mind felt the heaviest of chains; the weight of a guilty conscience. His horrors were so great that he found them insupportable, until he had returned from his apostasy, and declared himself fully convinced of the errors of the Church of Rome. To make amends for his falling off, he now openly and strenuously did all he could to make converts to Protestantism, and was pretty successful in his endeavors. These proceedings occasioned his second imprisonment, but he had his life offered him if he would recant again. This proposal he rejected with disdain, saying that he scorned life upon such terms. Being asked why he would obstinately persist in his opinions, and leave his wife and children in distress, he replied, 'I shall not leave them in distress; I have recommended them to the care of an excellent trustee.' 'What trustee?' said the person who had asked the question, with some surprise: to which Faninus answered, 'Jesus Christ is the trustee I mean, and I think I could not commit them to the care of a better.' On the day of execution he appeared remarkably cheerful, which one observing, said, 'It is strange you should appear so merry upon such an occasion, when Jesus Christ himself, just before his death, was in such agonies, that he sweated blood and water.' To which Faninus replied: 'Christ sustained all manner of pangs and conflicts, with hell and death, on our accounts; and thus, by his sufferings, freed those who really believe in him from the fear of them.' He was then strangled, his body was burnt to ashes, and then scattered about by the wind." *Fox's Book of Martyrs* p. 58

MY EXPERIENCE

Honestly, it is hard for me to find something to write about for this section. When I view the sufferings of Christ and what He went through, I feel as though I have not really suffered.

In the chapter on sacrifice, I mentioned a few things we have left behind or sacrificed. Some would say that these sacrifices caused us to suffer. But suffering to what magnitude?

Cold-water bucket baths each evening are not always pleasant. During the cooler part of the year, cold baths are somewhat shocking. Yes, I grew up taking hot showers, and that is what I prefer. But is it really suffering to bathe in cold water? I don't think so.

I suffer when I see other people suffering. I see much more suffering here in Chad than I do back in the States. But how much does God suffer? He sees all the suffering all over the world. How can my suffering compare with that?

People say, "How can you survive in such intense heat? It must be awful." Well, it is true that I have spent many days welding in the full sun in temperatures around 105–110 degrees F with welding gear (long pants, long sleeves, thick gloves, helmet, shoes). Undoubtedly, that is a hot job. But I do not consider that suffering. I just drink lots of water and try to keep my mind on pleasant things like the breeze or the goal of completing the job.

Some say we suffer because of the limited options for food. But how can we say we suffer when God always provides for our needs? Who are we to complain about what God has given us to eat? Surely, some of the food we eat is not our favorite food. But we are not starving, and we get to eat many things that are very good.

All of these things are just trivial, temporary inconveniences. My lifetime is short compared to eternity. To suffer a little bit now on the road to heaven is insignificant, for my sights are on greater goals than this life. My greatest sufferings are far less in magnitude than those of Jesus. His physical sufferings were greater than anything I have ever experienced. But my mental suffering is even less comparable to His. How can I complain?

WHAT IS YOUR RESPONSE?

With God's strength, I will not shrink back from suffering in my life. I choose to keep my goals on heavenly things. I will not let suffering interfere with God's plan for me. Even if called to suffer to death, I want to remain faithful to God and depend on Him for courage to remain joyful always.

FURTHER READING FOR YOU

"God looked upon His faithful martyrs with great approbation. The Christians who lived in that fearful time were greatly beloved of Him, because they were willing to suffer for His sake. Every suffering endured by them increased their reward in heaven....The sufferings that they endured only drove them closer to the Lord, leading them to love one another, and causing them to fear more than ever to offend Him." *Early Writings* p. 210

"It was through <u>suffering</u> that Jesus obtained the ministry of <u>consolation</u>. In all the affliction of humanity He is afflicted; and 'in that He Himself hath suffered being tempted, He is able to succor them that are tempted.' Isaiah 63:9; Hebrews 2:18. In this ministry every soul that has entered into the fellowship of His sufferings is privileged to share. 'As the sufferings of Christ abound in us, so our consolation also aboundeth by Christ.' 2 Corinthians 1:5." *Thoughts from the Mount of Blessing* p. 13

"Heaven will be cheap enough, if we obtain it through suffering. We must deny self all along the way, die to self daily, let Jesus alone appear, and keep His glory continually in view. I saw that those who of late have embraced the truth would have to know what it is to suffer for Christ's sake, that they would have trials to pass through that would be keen and cutting, in order that they may be purified and fitted through suffering to receive the seal of the living God, pass through the time of trouble, see the King in His beauty, and dwell in the presence of God and of pure, holy angels.

"As I saw what we must be in order to inherit glory, and then saw how much Jesus had suffered to obtain for us so rich an inheritance, I prayed that we might be baptized into Christ's sufferings, that we might not shrink at trials, but bear them with patience and joy, knowing what Jesus had suffered that we through His poverty and sufferings might be made rich." *Early Writings* p. 67

"A man whose heart is stayed upon God will be the same in the hour of his greatest trial as he is in prosperity, when the light and favor of God and of man beam upon him. Faith reaches to the unseen, and grasps eternal realities.

"Heaven is very near those who suffer for righteousness' sake. Christ identifies His interests with the interests of His faithful people; He suffers in the person of His saints, and whoever touches His chosen ones touches Him. The power that is near to deliver from physical harm or distress is also near to save from the greater evil, making it possible for the servant of God to maintain his integrity under all circumstances, and to triumph through divine grace." *Prophets and Kings* p. 545

"Christ's earthly life, so full of toil and sacrifice, was cheered by the thought that He would not have all His travail for nought. By giving His life for the life of men, He would win the world back to its loyalty. Although the baptism of blood must first be received, although the sins of the world were to weigh upon His innocent soul, yet, for the joy that was set before Him, He chose to endure the cross and despised the shame.

"Study Christ's definition of a true missionary: 'Whosoever will come after Me, let him deny himself, and take up his cross, and follow Me.' Mark 8:34 Following Christ, as spoken of in these words, is not a pretense, a farce. Jesus expects His disciples to follow closely in His footsteps, enduring what He endured, suffering what He suffered, overcoming as He overcame. He is anxiously waiting to see His professed followers revealing the spirit of self-sacrifice.

"Those who receive Christ as a personal saviour, choosing to be partakers of His suffering, to live His life of self-denial, to endure shame for His sake, will understand what it means to be a genuine medical missionary." *Testimonies for the Church Volume 8* p. 209

"Stand on the threshold of eternity and hear the gracious welcome given to those who in this life have co-operated with Christ, regarding it as a privilege and an honor to suffer for His sake. With the angels, they cast their crowns at the feet of the Redeemer, exclaiming, 'Worthy is the Lamb that was slain to receive power, and riches, and wisdom, and strength, and honor, and glory, and blessing.... Honor, and glory, and power, be unto Him that sitteth upon the throne, and unto the Lamb for ever and ever.' Revelation 5:12–13" *The Ministry of Healing* p. 506

FURTHER READING FOR YOU

God's Amazing Grace p. 90 "Sharing Christ's Suffering"
God's Amazing Grace p. 165 "Infinite Suffering"
Testimonies for the Church Volume 2 p. 200-215 "The Sufferings of Christ"

Christi-like Examples

"Brethren, join in following my example,
and note those who so walk
as you have us for a pattern."
Philippians 3:17

I am a missionary because...

O I am inspired by the lives of other missionaries.
O Stories of Bible characters give me courage to be
obedient to God no matter what.

...What about you?

"The spirit of Christ is the spirit of missions.
The nearer we get to Him,
the more intensely missionary we become."
Henry Martyn, missionary to India and Persia

Christ is the best Example of a missionary. His example is a perfect example, and that is why we have studied His example as first priority in this book.

"Therefore be imitators of God as dear children." Ephesians 5:1

But we can also find inspiration by studying people who were Christ-like. In the Bible, we find many other examples of Christ-like people who, though not perfect, left behind examples that are worthy of study and thought. In areas of their lives where they are Christ-like, they are worthy of imitation.

Paul said,

"Imitate me, just as I also imitate Christ." 1 Corinthians 11:1

"And we desire that each one of you show the same diligence to the full assurance of hope until the end, that you do not become sluggish, but imitate those who through faith and patience inherit the promises." Hebrews 6:11–12

Below you will find a few introductory comments for a few Bible characters. You will benefit from a deeper study of these and other examples in the Bible.

Noah, the Persevering Missionary

For a hundred and twenty years Noah faithfully delivered the warnings that God had given him. He lived a godly life. People mocked him. They said he was preaching things that were scientifically impossible. Even though Noah had never seen rain before, he acted on God's word and persevered.

God's work was not popular in Noah's day. Only a few (eight total) people believed the message and were saved.

Our message may not be popular. People may mock us and say that their science is more authoritative than the Bible. Our work may be discouraging and unsuccessful. It may be that nobody but our family accepts the message. But we can

choose to remain faithful to God's call and persevere like
Noah.

Abram, the Faithful Missionary

One of the earlier missionaries sent was Abram. Look at
Abram's "great commission" found in Genesis 12:1–3. Abram
was to get out of his country and move away from his family
to some unknown land out near "somewhere." With the
command to move, the Lord included some promises in verse
2 that his descendants would become a great nation. The Lord
would bless Abram and make his name great. Then at the end
of verse 2 we see some results of Abram's missionary move.
Abram would be a blessing. Those who blessed Abram would
be blessed as well. We can observe God's cycle of blessings in
these verses as we see how being a blessing to someone is a
two-way street. The one who blesses is blessed as well as the
one who is blessed. Those who blessed Abram were blessed,
Abram was blessed, and Abram was to bless others in his life.
This cascade of blessings was to continue until all the families
of the earth would be blessed. Ultimately, one of Abram's
descendants was Jesus. What a wide influence Abram had
when he was committed to obeying God! Moving away from
his home was unsettling and a move of faith, but his
obedience to God led to much blessing.

Could one man really have that much influence for good, so
much that all the families of the earth would be blessed? No,
not alone; humans are not naturally good. Notice who was
enabling all this good. Abram traveled to the land God showed
him. God would make him a great nation and bless him. God
would bless those who blessed Abram. So all this blessing was
only possible because God was enabling it to happen.

Abram was seventy-five years old when this happened. Age
does not hinder the Lord from using us to bless others.
Families and circumstances under which we grew up do not
prevent the Lord from using us to bless others. God is on the

lookout for anybody who will believe His promises and who will follow His bidding.

Immediately after this message from the Lord, Abram left as the Lord had commanded him to. He did not delay once he knew what the Lord wanted him to do. A clear Divine command was enough to rouse him to immediate action. Hebrews 11:8

JOSEPH, THE FOCUSED MISSIONARY

When Joseph faced the trial of being sold as a slave early in his life, he did not turn away from God. He chose to understand that even though the future was not clear to him, it was clear to God and God had a plan for his life. He chose to focus on God's work for him rather than all the trials that came his way.

No matter where Joseph was, he was a missionary. His missionary work in Egypt first included being a servant and doing things like washing the dishes and sweeping the floor and doing house chores for Potiphar. Later, he was promoted to more responsibility. After being tempted and resisting the temptation, then being falsely accused, he was thrown in jail, but chose to be a missionary even in the dungeon. Eventually he was promoted to a top government position, and continued to serve God and be a witness there. God used his life to witness to many thousands of people in a heathen land.

ELISHA, THE SACRIFICING MISSIONARY

Elisha was out plowing his field when Elijah came and put his mantle on him. Elisha had a choice. He knew that this was a sign that God was calling him to ministry, but there was no force involved. Elisha was free to make his decision either way.

Elisha could have decided to stay with his family and enjoy an easier life. He loved his family, and his family loved him.

Staying at home had a lot of advantages. But he chose to leave behind people he loved and easy circumstances to work with Elijah and obey God's call to service.

Joshua and Caleb, the Courageous Missionaries

Joshua and Caleb were among the group of twelve spies who were sent to spy out the land. God had clearly promised victory ahead of time, but ten of the spies rejected God's promises. They said that the territory was too difficult, that there were challenges bigger than they, that the people were scary, that they were afraid.

Had God promised ease? No. Were the challenges bigger than God? No. Was there need to fear when God had promised protection and success? No.

When everybody else was giving advice to not risk their safety and lives, these two men were strong and faithful to God. It is good to accept advice when advice is in accordance with God's will. But this advice was directly contrary to God's command. God's command did not appear easy, but that didn't matter. "God commanded, we must do it," was the attitude of Joshua and Caleb. The challenges were large and the danger was great, but that didn't matter. "God is bigger than any challenge we face," was the attitude of Joshua and Caleb. The likelihood of defeat and harm seemed high, but that didn't matter. "God has promised protection and success," was the attitude of Joshua and Caleb.

Timothy, the Student Missionary

Timothy was:
- appreciative of the sacredness of the work of a minister.
- willing to be taught.
- knowledgeable in Scriptures from his youth.

- O pure in speech and unsullied by the evil influences with which he was surrounded.
- O faithful, steadfast, and true.
- O young, but responsible.
- O constantly seeking Paul's advice and instruction.
- O constantly asking, "Is this the way of the Lord?"
- O learning and applying lessons from Scripture.

Timothy was not:
- O appalled at the prospect of suffering and persecution.
- O impulsive or self-reliant.
- O gifted with specially brilliant talents.

(Excerpted from *The Acts of the Apostles* 203–205.)

HEALED DEMONIACS, THE "IGNORANT" MISSIONARIES

The two demon-possessed men were healed by Jesus and were completely changed. That morning they had been under the control of and in the service of Satan. Soon after their healing, Jesus sent them as Christian missionaries to Decapolis. They had not spent much time with Him. They had only heard a little bit of Jesus' teaching.

Yet, Jesus sent them as missionaries. They had a personal experience with Jesus. Personal experience and evidence of God's work in your life is more important than a lot of knowledge or information. These two men could tell about their personal experience, what they had seen, and what they had heard.

We do not have to know a lot or have a long training experience to be effective missionaries for God. Start now. Learn to have an experience with God, and then share it with others. Test His promises, and share with others how the promises are true.

PETER, THE BOLD MISSIONARY

Although Peter thought he was a brave man, and that he would even follow Jesus to death if necessary, he was really a coward. When an opportunity for bravery and courage came, he failed and denied that he even knew Jesus. He may have been willing to do great things for Jesus, but when others scorned and ridiculed him, he gave in.

Shortly after Peter denied Jesus, their eyes met and Jesus communicated immense love and forgiveness to Peter. Peter's heart was melted, and he became a changed man. He no longer trusted in himself, but from then on he trusted in God. He repented of his sin and humbled himself before God.

Peter became a strong, courageous, brave man. When he was later brought before the judges and accused of preaching Jesus, he was not cowardly but brave, bold, and fearless. He was a converted man.

> *"Now when they saw the boldness of Peter and John, and perceived that they were uneducated and untrained men, they marveled. And they realized that they had been with Jesus."*
> Acts 4:13

This was the same Peter. Many of his habits were the same. He still knew how to fish. His accent didn't change. He was still Peter, with the same personality traits. But he had spent time with Jesus and was now changed.

We, too, need to spend time with Jesus. God can change our unholy character traits and convert our hearts. We can be fearless, bold workers for Him.

JOHN THE BAPTIST, THE LONELY MISSIONARY

John was not accustomed to much social life. He grew up in the wilderness and spent much of his time, even during his ministry days, in isolation from society. His parents had been instructed to give him a careful and strict upbringing, not allowing him to even have grape juice. When he became of age, he chose to continue a strict and simple life. His food was simple. He had been dedicated to God from his birth.

Living in the lonely wilderness had many advantages for John. He was not influenced by friends and church people. He wanted to be separated from the influence of pride and envy and so many other common evil character traits. A simple life did not lead to boredom, but to a happy state of communion with God. While not busy with the average activities of the population, he had extra time to develop his relationship with God and to prepare himself for the work that God had for him to do. When he did mingle with people, his message was clear, plain, and uncompromising.

God does not call everybody to live in the wilderness. But if He calls you to a lonely place, do not be afraid of loneliness. Jesus will be your constant companion as He prepares you for a special work.

Paul, the Selfless Missionary

Paul knew a life of self-denial. His life was full of hardship and inconvenience. He naturally preferred an easier life, but knew that he must persevere in God's work no matter how difficult it seemed.

Why did Paul endure so much in his life? Multiple times he was attacked by a mob or beaten or put in prison. He endured a life of constant travel. He didn't settle in one place and enjoy a comfortable life of ease. Sometimes he endured cold. Sometimes he was hungry. Sometimes he faced life-threatening situations on the sea. What pushed him to endure all those trials?

Paul was not self-focused. His one goal was to preach Jesus to those who did not know or understand Him. He had learned lessons of self-denial. Because he was intensely focused on the salvation of others and not on his own trials, it pained him to see people backslide or reject truth. He wrote many letters of instruction and encouragement to struggling Christians.

"Paul was not alone in the trials which he endured from the love of ease and desire for worldly gain in his professed brethren. His experience is still shared by the faithful servants of Christ. Many, even of those who profess to believe the solemn truths for this time, feel but little moral responsibility. When they see that the path of duty is beset with perplexities and trials, they choose a way for themselves, where there is less effort needed; where there are fewer risks to run, fewer dangers to meet. By selfishly shunning responsibilities, they increase the burdens of the faithful workers, and at the same time separate themselves from God, and forfeit the reward they might have won. All who will work earnestly and disinterestedly, in his love and fear, God will make co-laborers with himself. Christ has hired them at the price of his own blood, the pledge of an eternal weight of glory. Of every one of his followers he requires efforts that shall in some degree correspond with the price paid and the infinite reward offered." *Sketches from the Life of Paul* p. 284

See also *Sketches from the Life of Paul* p. 147–149.

OTHERS

Study other Bible characters. There are plenty more not covered here. Where they are Christlike, be encouraged by their examples and imitate them.

Questions and Answers

Chapter Contents

WHAT IS A MISSIONARY?

The term "missionary" can refer to anyone who attempts to convert others to a certain doctrine or program. Everyone is a missionary. Some missionaries represent Satan's character and lead others to Satan. Other missionaries represent God's character and lead others to God. In this book, I use the term "missionary" in its commonly understood meaning of Christian missionary.

WHAT IS A CHRISTIAN MISSIONARY?

A Christian missionary is anyone who follows the mission given to him by God: to live a Christ-like life that leads people to Jesus and eternal life. Wherever you work, however you work, whatever your work, whether you are a child or an old person, you are a missionary as you lead people to Jesus. This work extends from your own house to the ends of the world: from siblings, parents, children, relatives, neighbors, fellow countrymen, to foreigners on a different continent.

A missionary is not necessarily just someone who goes somewhere else or tells people about Jesus, but is someone who lives the truth. He verifies the truth of his words by his life.

WHAT DOES IT MEAN TO BE A MISSIONARY?

Being a missionary means living a Christ-like life, following His example for us. Are you a missionary?

HOW CAN I BECOME A MISSIONARY?

A young person may feel inspired to ask this question after hearing a miraculous mission story, but this question is not just for him or her. Church members planning a mission trip to build a school in a foreign country may ask this question, but they are not the only ones who should ask it, either. Literature evangelists may ask the question, but they are not the only group of people God wants as His missionaries.

In some churches, if missionaries are ever mentioned, the idea is indirectly conveyed that being a missionary is reserved for a select few qualified individuals specially called by God to do a special work. This question of how to become a missionary, however, applies to a much larger group of people. If you are a Christian, you are included in this group. Becoming a missionary is simply the same as becoming Christ-like. If you are a true Christian, than you are a missionary for God! You can become a missionary by becoming Christ-like.

How do I become Christ-like? Here are a few examples.

O By studying His example, in His life and His character.

O By praying for strength to imitate His example.

O By studying nature.

O By acting on truth that I know.

O By praying for others.

How can I get training to be a missionary?

In an article in *The Signs of the Times,* July 19, 1905 entitled "Fishers of Men," we find some answers that apply to the old and young alike.

O By following Jesus' example.

O By practicing Jesus' virtues.

O By studying Jesus' teachings.

O By studying Jesus' works of healing.

O By applying the simplicity of faith in pure, humble service.

O By learning daily from Christ the mystery of saving and serving souls.

O By practicing how to show Christ's love and compassion in our lives.

O By practicing sternness against all evil doing.

- ○ By separating from business entanglements that hinder us spiritually.
- ○ By recognizing that it is Christ who sees in us the qualifications for His purpose and by putting our hearts into the work as continual learners.

WHO IS CALLED TO BE A MISSIONARY?

If you are a believer on Christ's name, you are called to be a missionary. See *Christian Service* p. 9.

If you are a child, you are called to be a missionary. See *Prophets and Kings* p. 245.

If you are a youth, God has a work for you to do "for the honor of God and the uplifting of humanity." *The Adventist Home* p 280

All of God's people alike are called to missionary work. See *The Ministry of Healing* p. 395.
"Let every soul copy the Pattern, and become missionaries in the highest sense, winning souls to Jesus." *Sons and Daughters of God* p. 150

WHEN IS THE BEST TIME TO BECOME A MISSIONARY?

Whether you are old or young, weak or strong, now is the time to respond to God's call.

"And do this, knowing the time, that now it is high time to awake out of sleep; for now our salvation is nearer than when we first believed." *Romans 13:11*

"As the Holy Spirit says: 'Today, if you will hear His voice, do not harden your hearts.' " *Hebrews 3:7-8*

WHERE DO I START?

When we recognize that God has given us a mission, we usually want to know the details right away. It is as if we owe a debt and must unload this debt by spreading the gospel to others. Often, however, our calling is without immediate details (like Abraham's call to a place called "I-will-show-you-later").

- O Start by studying Jesus' life and character, and ask Him to make you like Him now, where you are, and in what you think and say and do.
- O Pray that God will lead and guide you in your search for direction. Follow His leading, even if the steps feel small or laboriously slow.
- O Be faithful even in the little things that seem insignificant.

JONATHAN, HOW DID YOU DECIDE TO BECOME A MISSIONARY?

Being a missionary is not something I can do on my own. Everything from the reason for being a missionary to the results of being a missionary come from God's power. For me, being a missionary is a result of a miracle of character transformation. It is not something that I directly chose to do, but rather the natural result of another choice.

> *"If anyone is in Christ, he is a new creation; old things have passed away; behold, all things have become new.... Now then, we are ambassadors for Christ, as though God were pleading through us." 2 Corinthians 5:17, 20*

> *"A city that is set on a hill cannot be hidden." Matthew 5:14*

First, I began to appreciate the value of a relationship with God. I tend to share with others things that I value. It is only through a relationship with Him that He can help me with my will. As God continues to work miracles of character transformation in my life, I want to share with others how they can have a similar experience.

I learn to value my relationship with God the same way I learn to value relationships with my friends—by spending time talking with them and getting to know who they are and what they are like. The primary method for growing my relationship with God is spending time in Scripture and prayer. By doing this, I learn more about God and become more like Him. I read what He has communicated, and I talk to Him about what I just read. He replies either through thoughts inspired by the Holy Spirit or by guiding my attention to other passages from Scripture. He also can reply through counsel or circumstances or through "open" and "closed" doors.

Once I value my relationship with God, I naturally want to share with others how they, too, can experience the same. A light on a hill cannot be hidden.

WHAT IS THE TRUE MISSIONARY SPIRIT?

"The true missionary spirit is the spirit of Christ. The world's Redeemer was the great model missionary. Many of His followers have labored earnestly and unselfishly in the cause of human salvation; but no man's labor can bear comparison with the self-denial, the sacrifice, the benevolence, of our Exemplar." *Testimonies for the Church Volume 5* p. 385

"Many suppose that the missionary spirit, the qualification for missionary work, is a special gift or endowment bestowed upon the ministers and a few members of the church and that all others are to be mere spectators. Never was there a greater mistake. Every true Christian will possess a missionary spirit, for to be a Christian is to be Christlike." *Testimonies for the Church Volume 5* p. 385–386

"You can prove by faithful performance of the little things that seem to you unimportant that you have a true missionary spirit." *The Adventist Home* p. 300

"If we would have the true missionary spirit we must be imbued with the love of Christ; we must look to the Author and Finisher of our faith, study His character, cultivate His spit of meekness and humility, and walk in His footsteps." *Testimonies for the Church Volume 5* p. 385

WHAT HINDERS THE MISSIONARY SPIRIT?

"It is Satan's work to excite envy and jealousy, to alienate affection, weaken confidence, and engender distrust and suspicion. All this hinders unity of faith in intercession with God for the weak and the desponding, for the grace of Christ, for the conversion of sinners, and thus shuts away the blessing which might be ours." *The Review and Herald*, July 10, 1883

"The work of whole-souled soldiers of Christ is as far-reaching as eternity. Then why is it that there is such a lack of the missionary spirit in our churches? It is because there is a neglect of home piety." *The Adventist Home* p. 33

"Many of the professed followers of Christ feel no more burden for souls than do the world. The lusts of the eye, and the pride of life, the love of display, the love of ease, separate the professed Christians from God, and the missionary spirit in reality exists in but few. What can be done to open the eyes of these sinners in Zion, and make hypocrites tremble?" *Christian Service* p. 35–36

HOW IMPORTANT IS THE MISSIONARY SPIRIT?

"The world needs missionaries, consecrated home missionaries, and no one will be registered in the books of heaven as a Christian who has not a missionary spirit." *Christian Service* p. 86

(Continue to next question.)

WHAT IS THE RELATIONSHIP BETWEEN SALVATION AND MISSIONARY WORK?

Scripture is clear: we are not saved by works, but by grace. We are saved by what Jesus has done for us, not by what we do for Him. How then do we understand the quote in the last question that says there will be nobody in heaven who did not have a missionary spirit?

Study faith and works. A really good place to start is James 2. Basically, faith and works are inseparable. But works is the evidence of faith. That means that although we are not saved by missionary work, when we are saved, we will do missionary work. Doing missionary work is a natural result of being a Christian.

> "All who are on the Lord's side are to confess Christ. 'Ye are My witnesses, saith the Lord.' The faith of the genuine believer will be made manifest in purity and holiness of character. Faith works by love and purifies the soul, and with faith there will be corresponding obedience, a faithful doing of the words of Christ. Christianity is always intensely practical, adapting itself to all the circumstances of actual life. 'Ye are My witnesses.' To whom?—To the world; for you are to bear about with you a holy influence. Christ is to abide in your soul, and you are to talk of Him and make manifest the charms of His character…. If Christ is abiding in the heart by faith, you cannot keep silent. If you have found Jesus, you will be a true missionary."
> *Messages to Young People* p. 200

WHAT IS OUR MISSION?

> "Our mission in this world is to live for the good of others. And it is little things which test the character. It is the unpretending acts of daily self-denial, performed heartily and cheerfully, that God smiles upon. We should cherish love and forbearance, and should be a blessing to others by our forgetfulness of self and our care for their welfare."
> *The Signs of the Times*, September 2, 1886

> "We are to labor both for the health of the body and for the saving of the soul. Our mission is the same as that of our Master, of whom it is written that He went about doing good and healing all who were oppressed by Satan. Acts

10:38. ... As we follow Christ's example of labor for the good of others we shall awaken their interest in the God whom we love and serve." *Testimonies for the Church Volume 6* p. 225

"There is a great work to be done, and the nearer we live to Jesus, the better fitted we shall be for fulfilling our mission in the world. We are to gather sheaves for the Master. We cannot afford to live simply to please ourselves, and to seek our own will. 'Even Christ pleased not himself.' He lived a life of self-denial and sacrifice.... It is only in proportion to the devotion and consecration to Christ, that the Christian exerts an influence for the blessing and uplifting of mankind." *The Review and Herald*, June 12, 1888

"We are Christ's representatives upon the earth. How do we fulfill our mission? Christ's representatives will be in daily communion with Him. Their words will be select, their speech seasoned with grace, their hearts filled with love, their efforts sincere, earnest, persevering, to save souls for whom Christ has died." *Testimonies on Sabbath School Work* p. 14

"The object of our mission is the same as the object of Christ's mission. Why did God send His Son to the fallen world? To make known and to demonstrate to mankind His love for them. Christ came as a Redeemer. Throughout His ministry He was to keep prominent His mission to save sinners....

"God's purpose in committing to men and women the mission that He committed to Christ is to disentangle His followers from all worldly policy and to give them a work identical with the work that Christ did." *Medical Ministry* p. 24–25

WHAT DOES A MISSIONARY DO ALL DAY?

Missionaries are usually busy people, often doing much the same work as others, but with a different focus. A missionary may sew tents like Paul or fish like Peter or sell clothing dye like Lydia. He may settle in one place like Noah or he may travel around like Abraham. But no matter what he does to earn a living or to fill his time, his focus is helping people get ready for Jesus to come.

The life and work of the missionary who lives in a third-world country is often more busy with routine duties than those who live in a first-world country. In the States, people are accustomed to many time-saving things. They cook minute rice out of a bag, use a microwave to heat up food, push a button on the machine to wash clothes, and turn the faucet handle to get water. In a third-world country, you might sort the beetles and rocks and sand out of the rice, wash it, start the charcoal fire, cook the rice for twenty minutes, and then eat it. Without electricity to run a microwave, you might go out into the bush with your ax, chop some wood, carry it home, dry it in the sun, go to the neighbors to borrow a hot coal, start the fire, then cook your food over the fire. Washing clothes is hard work: pulling water out of the well in a bucket, scrubbing all the stains by hand, washing and rinsing all the dirt out in a bucket, then hanging them up to dry. When you are thirsty you don't just get water from a faucet: you haul it up from the well, filter or boil it, then drink it. (Here in Chad, we can usually get propane bottles for cooking from one of the bigger towns. The locals help us wash our laundry and pump water from the well.)

No matter where a missionary lives, he must spend time arranging for certain basic needs. He needs to sleep, eat food, drink water, bathe, communicate, go places, etc. He also needs to spend time alone with God reading Scripture and praying.

Other than those things, some of the most common activities that take the missionary's time include:

- Helping people with their medical problems.
- Building or fixing things.
- Making or building friendships with people.
- Teaching reading, writing, or Bible classes.
- Working as a pastor or Bible worker.
- Translating material into the local language.
- Digging wells for cleaner water.

Whatever your work is, use it as a tool to help others and lead them to Jesus.

WHAT ARE SOME TYPES OF MISSIONARY WORK?

- Sabbath School. (*Counsels on Sabbath School Work* p. 10)
- Missionary correspondence. (*Christian Service* p. 131)
- Pen and voice. (*Christian Service* p. 130)
- Bible readings in homes. (*Gospel Workers* p. 192)
- Go where you can help in a weak church. (*The Review and Herald*, December 18, 1888)
- Cooking school and health training. (*Counsels on Diet and Foods* p. 476)
- Minister of the Word. (*Christian Service* p. 13)
- Nurse. (*Christian Service* p. 13)
- Christian physician. (*Christian Service* p. 13)
- Medical missionary. (*Healthful Living* p. 252)
- Merchant. (*Christian Service* p. 13)
- Farmer. (*Christian Service* p. 13)
- Professional work. (*Christian Service* p. 13)
- Mechanic. (*Christian Service* p. 13)

- Caring for needy fathers, widows, old people, etc. (*Counsels on Stewardship* p. 46)
- Parents maintaining peaceful countenances. (*Peter's Counsel to Parents* p. 28)
- Child education and training at home. (*Peter's Counsel to Parents* p. 28)

WHAT KIND OF PEOPLE MAKE GOOD MISSIONARIES?

"Those who enter the missionary field should be <u>men and women who walk and talk with God</u>." *The Review and Herald*, November 10, 1885

"The work of the Lord is a great work, and <u>wise men</u> are needed to engage in it. God calls for <u>earnest</u>, <u>unselfish</u>, <u>disinterested</u> laborers, who will keep up the various branches of the work. <u>Sacrifice</u>, <u>self-denial</u>, <u>toil</u>, and <u>disinterested benevolence</u> characterized the life of Christ, who is our example in all things. He laid aside his glory, his high command, his honor, and his riches, and <u>humbled</u> himself to our necessities. The work and character of a true laborer will be in accordance with the life of Christ. We cannot equal the example, but we should copy it." *The Signs of the Times*, September 2, 1886

"The laborer for souls needs <u>consecration</u>, <u>integrity</u>, <u>intelligence</u>, <u>industry</u>, <u>energy</u>, and <u>tact</u>. Possessing these qualifications, no man can be inferior; instead, he will have a commanding influence for good." *Gospel Workers* p. 111

"God does not bid the youth to be less aspiring. The elements of character that make a man successful and honored among men—the <u>irrepressible desire for some greater good</u>, the <u>indomitable will</u>, the <u>strenuous exertion</u>, the <u>untiring perseverance</u>—are not to be crushed out. By the grace of God they are to be directed to objects as much higher than mere selfish and temporal interests as the heavens are higher than the earth. And the education

begun in this life will be continued in the life to come."
Patriarchs and Prophets p. 602

"He who <u>faithfully performs small duties</u> will be prepared to answer the demands of larger responsibilities. The man who is <u>kind</u> and <u>courteous</u> in the daily life, who is <u>generous</u> and <u>forbearing</u> in his family, whose <u>constant aim it is to make home happy</u>, will be the first to deny self and make sacrifices when the Master calls." *Messages to Young People* p. 143

"In the work of soul-winning, <u>great tact and wisdom</u> are needed. The Saviour never suppressed the truth, but He uttered it always in love. In His intercourse with others, He exercised the greatest tact, and He was always kind and thoughtful. He was never rude, never needlessly spoke a severe word, never gave unnecessary pain to a sensitive soul. He did not censure human weakness. He fearlessly denounced hypocrisy, unbelief, and iniquity, but tears were in His voice as He uttered His scathing rebukes. He never made truth cruel, but ever manifested a deep tenderness for humanity. Every soul was precious in His sight. He bore Himself with divine dignity; yet He bowed with the tenderest compassion and regard to every member of the family of God. <u>He saw in all, souls whom it was His mission to save.</u>" *Gospel Workers* p. 117

"<u>Courtesy</u> is one of the graces of the Spirit. To deal with human minds is the greatest work ever given to man; and he who would find access to hearts must heed the injunction, 'Be <u>pitiful</u>, be <u>courteous</u>.' [1 Peter 3:8.] Love will do that which argument will fail to accomplish. But a moment's petulance, a single gruff answer, a lack of Christian <u>politeness</u> and <u>courtesy</u> in some small matter, may result in the loss of both friends and influence." *Gospel Workers* p. 121

"Independent men of earnest endeavor are needed, not men as impressible as putty. Those who want their work made ready to their hand, who desire a fixed amount to do and a fixed salary, and who wish to prove an exact fit without the trouble of adaptation or training, are not the men whom God calls to work in His cause. A man who cannot adapt his abilities to almost any place, if necessity requires, is not the man for this time. Men whom God will connect with His work are not limp and fiberless, without muscle or moral force of character." *Gospel Workers* p. 133

WHAT IS THE DAILY CYCLE OF MISSIONARY LIFE?

We gain strength from Jesus, the Water of Life. Then we share Jesus with others. Then we again replenish our strength from Him again.

Here's another way to put it. We are converted every day. Then we lead others to Jesus and they are converted. Then we are re-converted as we reconsecrate our lives to His service.

"I die daily." 1 Corinthians 15:31

"We want a new conversion daily. We want the love of Jesus throbbing in our hearts, that we may be instrumental in saving many souls." *Christian Service* p. 91

Daily, we need the attitude of Jesus, who lived by this motto:

"Not My will, but Yours be done." Luke 22:42

We should make this our daily motto. God, today show me how to do not what I want to do but what You want me to do. Teach me to say "No" to what I want to do and say "Yes" to what You want me to do.

WHAT IS ONE WAY I CAN REMEMBER TO REMAIN COMMITTED TO GOD THROUGHOUT THE DAY?

It is easy to say, "I gave my heart to God." That is good theory, but how do we do that practically? We can only become Christ-like as He gives us the power. When we ask for help, He will give us help. But our part requires effort.

We could answer this question from many angles, but for now, we will use our bodies to help us remember to give ourselves completely to God during the day. For example, when you comb your hair on your head, meditate on how God wants you to think. Remember that He cares for you and that He knows how many hairs you have. When you put on your glasses or contact lenses, think about how God wants to use your eyes that day. When you scratch an itch on your foot, think about where God wants you to go today.

"Or do you not know that your body is the temple of the Holy Spirit who is in you, whom you have from God, and you are not your own? For you were bought at a price; therefore glorify God in your body and in your spirit, which are God's."
1 Corinthians 6:19-20

○ Head/Thoughts. Choose to recognize Christ as your Head. He is over you and will direct you.
(Ephesians 4:15; 1 Corinthians 11:3; Philippians 4:8)

○ Ears. Listen to God. Pay attention to Him. Learn to recognize His voice. (John 10:27; James 1:22; Isaiah 50:4-5)

○ Eyes. Keep focused on Jesus. Do not get distracted. Continue on the straight and narrow way.
(Proverbs 4:25; Psalm 119:37; 101:3)

○ Mouth/Tongue/Lips. Determine to use your mouth to bring blessing and good news to others. Please God with the words you speak. (James 3:10; Joshua 1:8; Isaiah 50:4; Psalm 19:4)

○ Neck. Do not be stiff-necked and rebellious, but be willing to hear God's voice and be obedient.
(Jeremiah 17:23; 2 Chronicles 30:8)

○ Heart. Ask God to direct your heart and give you a love for souls. (Deuteronomy 5:29; Psalm 19:14; 51:10; Proverbs 3:5-6; Proverbs 4:4; also, study the prayers of

Moses and Daniel, in Exodus 32 and Daniel 9 respectively)

o   Arms/Hands. Commit to do whatever God asks you to do with your whole heart, not partially.
(Ecclesiastes 9:10; Luke 9:62; James 2:17; James 4:17)

o   Legs/Feet. Jesus has given us an example to follow. Commit to go wherever God asks you to go.
(1 Peter 2:21; Isaiah 52:7; Isaiah 6:8; Proverbs 4:18–19, 26–27)

o   Food. Regularly take in the highest quality spiritual nourishment from the Word of God. (Matthew 4:4; John 6:51; Psalm 19:10)

o   Water. Regularly drink from the Water of Life.
(John 4:10; Revelation 22:17)

o   Clothing. Wear the armor of God. Accept His robe of righteousness. (Ephesians 6; Matthew 22:11–14)

How can I lead and not push somebody to Jesus?

By allowing Jesus to help you be patient, kind, unselfish, cheerful, trusting, you will make Christianity so attractive as people see the "power of godliness." If we say we are Christians, but do not let God help us overcome sin, we are what Paul called, "having a form of godliness but denying the power."

God has given us instructions and laws to follow, but these are not heavy and burdensome requirements. They are not intended to make us feel restricted or to make us feel gloomy. The source of these laws is God's strong love for us. He wants us to be happy. He wants us to be free from sin.

> "For this is the love of God, that we keep His commandments. And His commandments are not burdensome." 1 John 5:3

Too often we misrepresent God's law to others because we misunderstand the purpose of God's law. We use the law more like a whip and tell them they must do this and do that and do the other. But God never uses force. He leads people and allows them to choose. His laws are designed to help bring us closer to Him. They point us to Jesus where we find help. If we are willing to be led to Jesus, it is there that we will be changed.

So what is the difference between pushing and leading?

Presenting the truth with the attitude of "do this" is like pushing. One may agree with the texts and believe that something is true, but unless He knows Jesus personally, his mental knowledge is ultimately not valuable. His brain accepts the information, but his heart is not ready to accept it.

"Even the demons believe—and tremble!" James 2:19

Presenting the truth in the context of God's love and Jesus' sacrifice for us is like leading. Simple truth is powerful and attractive; it is truth and the Holy Spirit that work together to convert and change people. We do not convert.

If you want to lead people to Jesus and not push them, here are some helpful concepts:

- Be Christlike. Choose to be converted in your own heart every day. We do not want people to be attracted to this or that method, or to us, except as they see Jesus there. By being Christlike, you make Christianity attractive.

- When you make an appeal, remember that angels and the Holy Spirit come with power to convince and convert. Our job is to present truth; the Holy Spirit's job is to convert the heart. (See *Evangelism* p. 38.)

- Learn to guide conversations by asking questions. Rather than tell them what they should believe, lead them to come to the conclusion in their own minds. Patiently allow the Holy Spirit time to work on their hearts.

○ Teach them first how to yield to the Holy Spirit's power. Knowing facts does not convert a person. But the Holy Spirit can make their decision for truth deep and solid if they accept His work in their hearts.

○ Watch for the best timing to present truth. If they are not ready, they might feel like we are pushing or forcing them along. Learn to read facial expressions, body language, tone of voice, etc. Listen to their questions to judge their interest and level of understanding. Be alert to the Holy Spirit's promptings in your own heart for when to make an appeal and when to leave a subject for later discussion.

WHAT IF THEY ASK A HARD QUESTION?

Do not be afraid of hard questions. Sometimes people ask me a question that I have not heard before or ask me to explain something that I have not studied or do not know well. I simply respond: "That is a good question. I could tell you what I think, but what really matters is what the Bible says. I'll study my Bible and bring you an answer the next time we meet." Or if there is enough time, I say: "I don't know, but let's study that together right now."

Learn to welcome hard questions because they:

○ ...encourage you to grow spiritually.

○ ...encourage you to study your Bible more deeply.

○ ...increase your reliance on the Holy Spirit.

○ ...remind you of how little you really know.

○ ...keep you humble.

○ ...indicate that your Bible study is causing them to think.

"Now when they bring you to the synagogues and magistrates and authorities, do not worry about how or what you should

answer, or what you should say. For the Holy Spirit will teach you in that very hour what you ought to say." Luke 12:11-12

"But sanctify the Lord God in your hearts, and always be ready to give a defense to everyone who asks you a reason for the hope that is in you, with meekness and fear." 1 Peter 3:15

Do not be afraid to explain simply, but tactfully why you believe the way you do. (If you can't explain why you believe the way you do, you need to study more.) Giving a Biblical reason why you are different is not an embarrassment, but an opportunity to share truth.

For example, sometimes as I eat a meal with others, they notice that I do not eat certain things they eat—things they view as part of a normal diet. "What DO you eat, anyway?" they sometimes ask. Rather than be embarrassed, I view this as an opportunity to explain to them why I choose to eat the way I do. I might say something like, "I am a vegetarian because I believe that is the best way to keep my mind and body strong. God gave this diet as His first choice, and for over two thousand years, people before the flood lived long and healthy lives on this diet."

IF I AM NOT WELL EDUCATED, IS THERE STILL WORK FOR ME?

"In this closing work of the gospel there is a vast field to be occupied; and more than ever before, the work is to enlist helpers from the common people. Both the youth and those older in years will be called from the plow, from the vineyard, and from various other branches of labor, and sent forth by the Master to give His message. Many of these have had little opportunity for education. To human wisdom the outlook for them would seem discouraging. But Christ sees in them qualifications that will enable them to take their place in His vineyard. If they put their hearts into the work, and continue to be learners, He will fit them to labor for Him...

"There is no line of work in which it is possible for the youth to receive greater benefit. All who engage in ministry are God's helping-hand. They are <u>co-workers with the angels</u>; rather, they are the human agencies through whom the angels accomplish their mission. Angels speak through their voices, and work by their hands. And the human workers, co-operating with heavenly agencies, have the benefit of their education and experience. <u>As a means of education, what 'university course' can equal this?</u>" *General Conference Bulletin*, July 1, 1902

WHAT IF *I* DO NOT KNOW ENOUGH?

When God called Jeremiah, he felt inadequate for the work God had asked him to do. He felt as if he did not know enough. Here's the conversation between Jeremiah and God:

" '*Ah, Lord God! Behold, I cannot speak, for I am a youth.'*
But the Lord said to me:
'*Do not say, "I am a youth," For you shall go to all to whom I send you, And whatever I command you, you shall speak. Do not be afraid of their faces, For I am with you to deliver you,' says the Lord.*
Then the Lord put forth His hand and touched my mouth, and the Lord said to me:
'*Behold, I have put My words in your mouth. See, I have this day set you over the nations and over the kingdoms, To root out and to pull down, To destroy and to throw down, To build and to plant.'* " *Jeremiah 1:6–10*

PRACTICALLY, HOW CAN *I* BE A MISSIONARY EVERY DAY?

Being a good missionary is being Christlike. Simply ask yourself, "What would Jesus do? How would He act?" If you do not know the answers to these questions, ask Him to help you and spend more time studying His life and character.

With every event in life ask, "How will this shape my character?" and "Why did God bring me in contact with this person?"

"Jesus says, 'If any man thirst, let him come unto me, and drink.' 'The water that I shall give him, shall be in him a well of water springing up unto everlasting life.' Never let amusements, or the companionship of others, come between you and Jesus, your best Friend. Set the Lord always before you. When natural inclination draws you in the direction of fulfilling some selfish desire, set the Lord before you as your counselor, and ask,

Will this please Jesus?

Will this increase my love for my best Friend?

Will this course grieve my dear Saviour?

Will it separate me from his company?

Will Jesus accompany me to the pleasure party, where all will be lightness and gaiety, where there will be nothing of a religious nature, nothing serious, no thought of the things of God?

If Jesus sends me there as a missionary to warn some soul of his danger, then I am sure Jesus will not separate from me; but if I go simply to please myself, I cannot be sure of my Saviour's presence. If I choose to go where Jesus cannot enter, where he cannot make his abode, where the hearts of those present are saying, 'Cause the Holy One of Israel to cease from before us,' I choose another counselor than Jesus." *The Youth's Instructor*, July 19, 1894

WHAT WORK WILL BRING THE GREATEST SATISFACTION AND JOY TO GOD?

"When men and women have formed characters which God can endorse, when their self-denial and self-sacrifice have been fully made, when they are ready for the final test, ready to be introduced into God's family, what service will stand highest in the estimation of Him who gave Himself a willing offering to save a guilty race? What enterprise will be most dear to the heart of infinite love? What work will bring the greatest satisfaction and joy to

the Father and the Son? The salvation of perishing souls."
A Call to Medical Evangelism and Health Education p. 47

WHAT IS THE MOST IMPORTANT KIND OF MISSIONARY WORK?

"If you are truly converted, if you are children of Jesus, you
will honor your parents; you will not only do what they tell
you but will watch for opportunities to help them. In doing
this you are working for Jesus. He considers all these
care-taking, thoughtful deeds as done to Himself. This is
the most important kind of missionary work; and those
who are faithful in these little everyday duties are gaining
a valuable experience." *The Adventist Home* p. 295

"The mother who has children to train and prepare for the
heavenly mansions should not place her responsibilities
upon some one else in order that she may be a missionary.
In her own home she can do the very highest kind of
missionary work." *The Review and Herald*, December 18,
1900

"If the Word of God is obeyed, the home will be the center
of the highest kind of missionary work, but those who are
at a disagreement in the home life, do not practice the
words of the Lord, and will never be fit to enter the
heavenly mansions, unless they are transformed by the
grace of Christ." *Manuscript Releases Volume 13* p. 78

WHAT ARE SOME CHALLENGES THAT THE MISSIONARY WILL FACE?

- O   Discouragement. Often the work does not go as we
    think it should or people do not accept truth
    according to our plan. We must remember that God
    is in control.

- O   Sickness. Missionaries minister to all people. Being
    with people increases the chance of getting a
    disease. Also, some countries have diseases that our
    country of origin does not have. We must be wise

and do what we can to prevent disease, and we must also trust in God's protection.

○ Overwork. The work is great and the laborers are few, but God still expects us to take care of our bodies and live a balanced lifestyle. Intemperate living causing an early death does not please God.

○ Social stresses. Working closely with other believers can be a great help, blessing, and encouragement. But not everyone believes the same way, and this can lead to unkind thoughts and feelings toward each other. Satan would love to disturb the unity and decrease the efficiency of a group. Our goal should be to live in unity by focusing on Jesus, and not on each other's problems.

○ Language and culture. When we step outside the comfort zone of our friends and family who are like us, we are challenged. A poor person visiting someone who lives in a mansion feels uncomfortable. Some people have different customs, eat different food, and speak a different language. God will give us the ability to learn what we need to know and go where He sends us, whether it is to our neighbor's house or across the world to another continent.

○ Distractions. Life is full of fascinating activities. The missionary will prioritize these activities and tasks based on how they fit the Gospel Commission and God's specific call for them. An activity may be good and profitable, but may have to be neglected for one of greater priority.

○ Pride. When we see the work progressing well and we see success, it is easy to begin thinking of ourselves and how we have things figured out. We must always remember that we depend on God for success. We continue praying. We continue our faith in God.

○ Loneliness. When moving to a new place where there are few or no other believers, it is easy to feel alone. Living in a strange place away from friends and family, and without a local church for support, a missionary could easily feel lonely. He needs to remember that God is ever present and will supply his every need.

○ Indifference of other Christians. The missionary often labors intensely and longs for encouragement and help from other Christians and fellow church members. Yet often he meets with a spirit of criticism, indifference, or even active opposition of the work.

○ Opposition of the wicked. Wicked people sometimes feel conviction when they see the contrast of their own life with a Christlike life. The more Christlike a person is, the more Satan and wicked men oppose his work and his life.

WHAT ARE SOME GOOD ACTIVITIES TO PREPARE FOR OVERSEAS MISSION WORK?

○ Practice being Christlike to your family. It is often easier to be nicer to strangers than to our own families. Family members are often the most difficult people to get along with because we are so familiar with their good qualities and their faults.

○ Develop a strong and stable habit of spending time with God. Study your Bible. Pray to God. Exercise faith even in the little things in life.

○ Team up with your local church to give Bible studies to someone in the community. Often, you will encounter questions and you might not know the answers. This gives you the incentive to study more for yourself and perhaps ask help from your pastor or other church members.

o   Literature Evangelism is another excellent preparation for overseas mission work. In this occupation, you will often encounter rejection, such as Jesus did during His ministry, and learn how to deal with it.

SHORT-TERM OR LONG-TERM SERVICE?

God calls many people to work in their own country without traveling much. Noah preached in one place for one hundred and twenty years. We need missionaries in our homes and schools and churches.

But God also calls us to go into all the world. When God calls you to travel, one decision you need to make is the duration of your trip. There are definite advantages and disadvantages to short-term and long-term trips, and we will highlight a few here.

God calls each of us to long-term service, life-long service. As long as we have life, God has a work for us to do. But practically speaking, sometimes we have an opportunity to make a special trip focused especially on missionary work, and that is what we will look at here.

Long-term trip (more than 1 year)

o   Pros

   o   You can become closer friends and build trust with the people and thus address their true spiritual needs better.

   o   You will better understand the culture and the way the people think.

   o   Travel expense per day of service is minimized. (Example: Round-trip ticket from USA to Chad is

$2300. Ticket cost for a two-year stay based on this ticket price is $3.15 per day.)

- Cons
  - Many people are not willing to make a long-term commitment.
  - You are more isolated from family and friends.
  - You can get discouraged more easily.

Short-term trip (less than 1 year)

- Pros
  - More convenient. Fits into school and work schedules and vacation time. Does not require much of a time commitment.
  - Much can be accomplished in an intensive, well-organized effort.
  - Helps a person decide if he is called to long-term service in that place.
  - Can change the long-term outlook on life and adjust priorities when back at home.
- Cons
  - Travel expense per day of service is relatively high. (Example: Round-trip ticket from USA to Chad is $2300. Ticket cost for a two-week stay based on this ticket price is $164.29 per day.)
  - Often there is not time to address the true spiritual needs of the people.
  - It is easy to think, "I've been a missionary now..." and slip back into the previous lifestyle at home.

IS SOMETHING WRONG WITH ME IF I DON'T ENJOY SELF-DENIAL, SACRIFICE, AND SUFFERING?

"The one absorbing aim of the life of Christ was to do the will of his heavenly Father. He did not become offended with God; for he lived not to please himself. The human will of Christ would not have led him to the wilderness of temptation, to fast, and to be tempted of the devil. It would not have led him to endure humiliation, scorn, reproach, suffering, and death. His human nature shrank from all these things as decidedly as ours shrinks from them. He endured the contradiction of sinners against himself. The contrast between the life and character of Christ and our life and character is painful to contemplate. What did Christ live to do? It was the will of his heavenly Father. Christ left us an example, that we should follow in his steps. Are we doing it?" *The Signs of the Times*, October 29, 1894

"[Paul's] experience had been one of poverty, self-denial, and suffering. With a sensitive nature, that thirsted for love and sympathy, he had braved misrepresentation, reproach, and abuse. Shrinking with nervous dread from pain and peril, he had fearlessly endured both. Like his Master, he had been a homeless wanderer; he had lived and suffered for the truth's sake, seeking to bless humanity and to live the Christ-life." *The Youth's Instructor*, July 3, 1902

WHAT HAPPENS IF I REJECT MY CALL TO MISSIONS?

God has called each of us to missionary life. He has called us to be like a fruitful tree. When we claim to be Christians, yet are not active in missions, we are like the fig tree which had many leaves but no fruit. (Matthew 21:19) It looked like a good tree, but it had no fruit.

To ignore or reject God's call is to disobey God. It is insulting to God when we effectively say, "No God, I can't be a missionary. My priorities and goals are more important than Yours." On the topic of how God views our neglect of missions we read:

"Oh, I felt so sorry for my Saviour! His searching for fruit amid the leaf-covered branches of the fig tree and His disappointment in finding nothing but leaves seemed so vivid before my eyes. I felt that I could not have it so. I could in no way be reconciled to the past years of neglect of duty on the part of ministers and people. I feared that the withering curse passed upon the fig tree might be the fate of these careless ones. The terrible neglect of doing the work and fulfilling the mission which God has entrusted to them incurs a loss which none of us can afford to sustain. It is running a risk too fearful to contemplate and too terrible to be ventured at any time in our religious history, but especially now, when time is so short and so much is to be done in this day of God's preparation. All heaven is earnestly engaged for the salvation of men; light is coming from God to His people, defining their duty, so that none need err from the right path. But God does not send His light and truth to be lightly esteemed and trifled with. If the people are inattentive, they are doubly guilty before Him." *Testimonies for the Church Volume 5* p. 257–258

WHAT IS THE MEANING OF THE CURSE OF MEROZ?

" 'Curse Meroz,' said the angel of the Lord, 'Curse its inhabitants bitterly, Because they did not come to the help of the Lord, To the help of the Lord against the mighty.' " *Judges 5:23*

"There is a class that are represented by Meroz. The missionary spirit has never taken hold of their souls. The calls of foreign missions have not stirred them to action. What account will those render to God, who are doing nothing in His cause,—nothing to win souls to Christ? Such will receive the denunciation, 'Thou wicked and slothful servant.' " *Christian Service* p. 36

"The curse of God rested upon them for what they had not done. They had loved that work which would bring the greatest profit in this life; and opposite their names in the ledger devoted to good works there was a mournful blank." *Christian Service* p. 88

Should missionaries go only to people who are likely to listen?

No. Missionaries should go wherever God sends them.

"Then He said to me: 'Son of man, go to the house of Israel and speak with My words to them.... Surely, had I sent you to them, they would have listened to you. But the house of Israel will not listen to you, because they will not listen to Me; for all the house of Israel are impudent and hard-hearted.... Speak to them and tell them, "Thus says the Lord God," whether they hear, or whether they refuse.'" Ezekiel 3:4-11

What if the people do not accept me or try to kill me?

Read Luke 4:29. Why was the reaction of the people to kill Jesus? (See *The Desire of Ages* p. 237–239) At first, the people were happy to see Someone who was the fulfillment of prophecy. But almost immediately they returned to thinking selfish thoughts. They liked to think of themselves as more important than the surrounding nations. But Jesus described them as being captive and blind and bruised. Although they knew that this description was true, their pride was hurt. They did not want people looking closely at their actions for fear their hypocrisy would be uncovered.

"Truth was unpopular in Christ's day. It is unpopular in our day." *The Desire of Ages* p. 242

As missionaries we need to first ask ourselves how we respond to truth. How do I respond when Christ tries to help me learn a lesson by showing me a deficiency in my character? Am I willing to change my habits and practices? Am I willing to sacrifice personal goals and plans and even the respect of my friends in order to honor God? Am I so narrow-minded in my goals that I am unable to expand to share Christ's goals? Human nature tends to selfishly shy away from the light of truth which illuminates deficiencies of character.

Recognizing this tendency to shy away from the light of truth can help us have more patience with those to whom we present light. We can expect that their pride will be hurt and that they will have some natural resistance to light. Many will resist accepting the light. We can pray that God will give us wisdom to know how to be an example and how to teach in a way that will make service to God appear worthwhile.

An interesting article on missions

The Signs of the Times, August 21, 1901

Calls to Service

"The harvest truly is great,
but the laborers are few;
therefore pray the Lord of the harvest
to send out laborers into His harvest."
Luke 10:2

I am a missionary because...

○ God's call is clear and I cannot ignore it.

○ No other call is more authoritative than the call of God.

○ Being a Christian and being a missionary are inseparable. Every Christian is given a mission.

...What about you?

"If Jesus Christ be God and died for me,
then no sacrifice can be too great for me to make for Him."
C.T. Studd

This chapter is a small compilation of calls to service found in the Scriptures and Ellen G. White's writings.

"Peace to you! As the Father has sent Me, I also send you."
John 20:21

"Many of the professed followers of Christ feel no more burden for souls than do the world. The lusts of the eye, and the pride of life, the love of display, the love of ease, separate the professed Christians from God, and the missionary spirit in reality exists in but few. What can be done to open the eyes of these sinners in Zion, and make hypocrites tremble?" *Christian Service* p. 35–36

"God's people must take warning and discern the signs of the times. The signs of Christ's coming are too plain to be doubted; and in view of these things every one who professes the truth should be a living preacher. God calls upon all, both preachers and people, to awake. All heaven is astir. The scenes of earth's history are fast closing. We are amid the perils of the last days. Greater perils are before us, and yet we are not awake. This lack of activity and earnestness in the cause of God is dreadful. This death stupor is from Satan." *Christian Service* p. 37

"The harvest truly is great, but the laborers are few; therefore pray the Lord of the harvest to send out laborers into His harvest." Luke 10:2

"Men are in peril. Multitudes are perishing. But how few of the professed followers of Christ are burdened for these souls. The destiny of a world hangs in the balance; but this hardly moves even those who claim to believe the most far-reaching truth ever given to mortals. <u>There is a lack of that love which led Christ to leave His heavenly home</u> and take man's nature, that humanity might touch humanity, and draw humanity to divinity. There is a stupor, a paralysis, upon the people of God, which prevents them

from understanding the duty of the hour."
Christian Service p. 37–38

"Christians should be preparing for what is soon to break upon the world as an overwhelming surprise, and this preparation they should make by diligently studying the word of God, and striving to conform their lives to its precepts.... God calls for a revival and a reformation. "A revival of true godliness among us is the greatest and most urgent of all our needs. To seek this should be our first work." *Christian Service* p. 41

"A distinct work is assigned to every Christian....
"Were every one of you a living missionary, the message for this time would speedily be proclaimed in all countries, to every people and nation and tongue....
"God expects personal service from every one to whom He has intrusted a knowledge of the truth for this time. Not all can go as missionaries to foreign lands, but all can be home missionaries in their families and neighborhoods."
Christian Service p. 9

"Long has God waited for the spirit of service to take possession of the whole church, so that every one shall be working for Him according to his ability....
"Wherever a church is established, all the members should engage actively in missionary work. They should visit every family in the neighborhood, and know their spiritual condition....
"We are not, as Christians, doing one-twentieth part that we might do in winning souls to Christ. There is a world to be warned, and every sincere Christian will be a guide and an example to others in faithfulness, in cross-bearing, in prompt and vigorous action, in unswerving fidelity to the cause of truth, and sacrifices and labors to promote the cause of God." *Christian Service* p. 11–12

"Do not hesitate to work for the Lord because you think you can do but little. Do your little with fidelity; for God will work with your efforts. He will write your name in the book of life as one worthy to enter into the joy of the Lord. Let us earnestly entreat the Lord that laborers may be raised up, for the fields are white to the harvest; the harvest is great, and the laborers are few." *Messages to Young People* p. 23

"We are Christ's witnesses, and we are not to allow worldly interests and plans to absorb our time and attention." *Christian Service* p. 15

"Every one who is connected with God will impart light to others. If there are any who have no light to give, it is because they have no connection with the Source of light." *Christian Service* p. 21

"And Jesus came and spoke to them, saying, 'All authority has been given to Me in heaven and on earth. Go therefore and make disciples of all the nations, baptizing them in the name of the Father and of the Son and of the Holy Spirit, teaching them to observe all things that I have commanded you; and lo, I am with you always, even to the end of the age.' Amen." Matthew 28:18-20

"The gospel commission is the great missionary charter of Christ's kingdom. The disciples were to work earnestly for souls, giving to all the invitation of mercy. They were not to wait for the people to come to them; they were to go to the people with their message....

"The commission given to the disciples is given also to us. Today, as then, a crucified and risen Saviour is to be uplifted before those who are without God and without hope in the world. The Lord calls for pastors, teachers, and evangelists. From door to door His servants are to proclaim the message of salvation. To every nation, kindred, tongue, and people the tidings of pardon through Christ are to be carried. Not with tame, lifeless utterances is the message to be given, but with clear, decided, stirring utterances. Hundreds are waiting for the warning to escape for their lives. The world needs to see in Christians an evidence of the power of Christianity. Not merely in a few places, but throughout the world, messages of mercy are needed." *Christian Service* p. 23

"Then the master said to the servant, 'Go out into the highways and hedges, and compel them to come in, that my house may be filled.' " Luke 14:23

"Those in the highways are not to be neglected; neither are those in the hedges; and as we journey about from place to place and pass by house after house, we should often inquire, 'Have the people who are living in these places heard the message? Has the truth of God's Word been brought to their ears? Do they understand that the end of all things is at hand, and that the judgments of God are impending? Do they realize that every soul has been bought with an infinite price?' As I meditate upon these things, my heart goes out in deep longing to see the truth carried in its simplicity to the homes of these people along the highways and places far removed from the crowded centers of population.... It is our privilege to visit them and acquaint them with God's love for them and with His wonderful provision for the salvation of their souls." *Evangelism* p. 45

"Repeatedly God has called upon His people to go out into the highways and hedges, and compel men to come in, that His house may be full, yet even within the shadow of our own doors are families in which we have not shown sufficient interest to lead them to think that we cared for their souls. It is this work lying nearest us that the Lord now calls upon the church to undertake." *Christian Service* p. 39

"For your soul's sake, for Christ's sake, who gave Himself to save you from ruin, pause on the threshold of your life, and weigh well your responsibilities, your opportunities, your possibilities. God has given you an opportunity to fill a high destiny. Your influence may tell for the truth of God; you may be a co-laborer with God in the great work of human redemption." *Messages to Young People* p. 21

"Also I heard the voice of the Lord, saying: 'Whom shall I send, And who will go for Us?' Then I said, 'Here am I! Send me.' "
Isaiah 6:8

"Christ's work is to be done. Let those who believe the truth consecrate themselves to God. Where there are now a few who are engaged in missionary work, there should be hundreds. Who will feel the importance, the divine greatness, of the call? Who will deny self? When the Saviour calls for workers, who will answer, 'Here am I, send me'?" ...

"There is need of both home and foreign missionaries. There is work right at hand that is strangely neglected by many. All who have tasted 'the good word of God, and the powers of the world to come' (Hebrews 6:5), have a work to do for those in their homes and among their neighbors. The gospel of salvation must be proclaimed to others. Every man who has felt the converting power of God becomes in a sense a missionary. There are friends to whom he can speak of the love of God. He can tell in the church what the Lord is to him, even a personal Saviour; and the testimony given in simplicity may do more good than the most eloquent discourse. There is a great work to be done, too, in dealing justly with all and walking humbly with God. Those who are doing the work nearest them are gaining an experience that will fit them for a wider sphere of usefulness. There must be an experience in home missionary work as a preparation for foreign work."
Counsels on Health p. 32–33

"Wherever we may be, there the lost piece of silver awaits our search. Are we seeking for it? Day by day we meet with those who take no interest in religious things; we talk with them, we visit among them; do we show an interest in their spiritual welfare? Do we present Christ to them as the sin-pardoning Saviour? With our own hearts warm with the love of Christ, do we tell them about that love? If we do not, how shall we meet these souls—lost, eternally lost— when with them we stand before the throne of God? "The value of a soul, who can estimate? Would you know its worth, go to Gethsemane, and there watch with Christ through those hours of anguish, when He sweat as it were great drops of blood. Look upon the Saviour uplifted on the cross. Hear that despairing cry, 'My God, My God, why hast Thou forsaken Me?' Mark 15:34. Look upon the wounded head, the pierced side, the marred feet. Remember that Christ risked all. For our redemption, heaven itself was imperiled. At the foot of the cross, remembering that for one sinner Christ would have laid down His life, you may estimate the value of a soul." *Christ's Object Lessons* p. 196

"When the appeals of the Holy Spirit come to the heart, our only safety lies in responding to them without delay. When the call comes, 'Go work today in My vineyard,' do not refuse the invitation. 'Today if ye will hear His voice, harden not your hearts.' Hebrews 4:7. It is unsafe to delay obedience. You may never hear the invitation again." *Christ's Object Lessons* p. 280

"While there is an awakening among our people in regard to foreign missions, there should also be much more interest than is now shown in home missions. This zeal for foreign work should kindle zeal for home work also. Some who have long professed to be Christians, and yet have felt no responsibility for the souls of those who are perishing right around them, within the shadow of their own homes, may feel a burden to go to foreign lands, to take hold of a work far off; but where is the evidence of their fitness for such a work? Wherein have they manifested a burden for souls? Let such begin the work at home, in their own household, in their own neighborhood, among their own friends. Here they will find a favorable missionary field. This home missionary work is a test, revealing their ability or inability for service in a wider field.

"This is the work that the Lord is constantly keeping before me. Who is carrying this burden? Who is doing this kind of missionary work? It is left undone. Children of Sabbath-keepers are not brought up in the nurture and admonition of the Lord. Those who feel no real burden for the souls in their own houses, who cannot educate and discipline their children, in the kindness, patience, and forbearance of Christ, have no work to do in larger missions. Let them do their home-work in the fear and love of God, showing their tact and wisdom by presenting to the church and the world a well-ordered, well-disciplined family. Such a family will indeed be a power for good; its influence will be far-reaching." *The Review and Herald*, January 6, 1891

"The burden of labor for these needy ones in the rough places of the earth, Christ lays upon those who can feel for the ignorant and for such as are out of the way. He will be present to help those whose hearts are susceptible to pity, tho their hands may be rough and unskilled. He will work through those who can see mercy in misery, and gain in loss. When the Light of the world passes by, privilege will be discerned in hardship, order in confusion, success in apparent failure. Calamities will be seen as disguised blessings; woes, as mercies. Laborers from the common people, sharing the sorrows of the whole human race, will by faith see Him working with them." *The Signs of the Times*, July 19, 1905

FURTHER READING FOR YOU

Christian Service chapter 1 "God's Call to Service"
Messages to Young People chapter 2 "A Call to the Youth"
The Youth's Instructor, January 23, 1902 "The Fair Flowers of Promise"
The Signs of the Times, July 19, 1905 "Fishers of Men"
Genesis 12:1–5 Abraham's call
1 Kings 19:19–21 Elisha's call

Promises of Success

"[Abraham] did not waver at the promise of God through unbelief,
but was strengthened in faith, giving glory to God,
and being fully convinced
that what He had promised He was also able to perform.
And therefore 'it was accounted to him for righteousness.'"
Romans 4:20–22

I am a missionary because...

○ God's promises are reliable; they do not fail.
○ To not claim God's promises is to disbelieve His word.

...What about you?

"The prospects are as bright as the promises of God."
Adoniram Judson

We are given many promises of success. Promises come with conditions. If you want to be successful, comply with the conditions and the promise will come true. As you read through these promises and as you find others, look for the conditions. Then practice applying those promises to your life. Here are a few examples.

> *"Delight yourself also in the Lord, and He shall give you the desires of your heart. Commit your way to the Lord, trust also in Him, and He shall bring it to pass." Psalm 37:4–5*

- O Condition: Commitment to God.
- O Promise: Fulfillment of our desires.
  <u>As I commit myself to God, He will fulfill my desires.</u>

> "Missionary success will be proportionate to wholehearted, thoroughly consecrated effort." *Testimonies to Ministers and Gospel Workers* p. 205

- O Condition: Consecrated effort.
- O Promise: Missionary success.
  <u>The more I consecrate my efforts and put my heart into the work, the more successful I will be in missionary work.</u>

> "Love for souls for whom our Lord made this great sacrifice should stimulate his people to self-denying effort for their salvation. When this spirit actuates ministers and people, their labors will be fruitful; for the power of God will be seen upon them in the gracious influences of his Holy Spirit." *The Signs of the Times*, September 2, 1886

- O Condition: Love for souls, self-denying effort.
- O Promise: Fruitful labors; power of God seen.
  <u>When I love souls and am willing to deny self, my work will be successful through God's power.</u>

"Those who consecrate body, soul, and spirit to God, will constantly receive a new endowment of physical, mental, and spiritual power. The inexhaustible supplies of heaven are at their command. Christ gives them the breath of His own Spirit, the life of His own life. The Holy Spirit puts forth His highest energies to work in heart and mind. The grace of God enlarges and multiplies their faculties, and every perfection of the divine nature comes to their assistance in the work of saving souls. Through co-operation with Christ, they are made complete in Him, and in their human weakness they are enabled to do the deeds of Omnipotence." *Gospel Workers* p. 112–113

- Condition: Consecrate body, soul, spirit to God.
- Promise: Receive new physical, mental, spiritual power.
  I choose to consecrate myself completely to God. He will give me power in my body, mind, and spiritual life.

"Perfect oneness—a union as close as the union existing between the Father and the Son—this is what will give success to the efforts of God's workers." *Reflecting Christ* p. 200

- Condition: Unity.
- Promise: Success to God's workers.
  As I work, I will continue learning how to work undividedly with others recognizing that disunity hinders success.

"The worker for God should put forth the highest mental and moral energies with which nature, cultivation, and the grace of God have endowed him; but his success will be proportionate to the degree of consecration and self-sacrifice in which his work is done, rather than to either natural or acquired endowments. Earnest, continuous endeavor to acquire qualifications for usefulness is necessary; but unless God works with humanity, nothing good can be accomplished." *Counsels to Parents, Teachers, and Students* p. 537–538

- ○ Condition: Consecration and self-sacrifice.
- ○ Promise: Success proportionate to the degree of the condition.
  I choose to be willing to sacrifice anything God asks for and give myself 100% to His work so that He can use me more successfully.

"Individual, constant, united efforts will be rewarded by success." *Messages to Young People* p. 369

- ○ Condition: Individual, constant, united efforts.
- ○ Promise: Success.
  I will personally do my part, not sporadically, but faithfully. God will give success.

"Success in any line demands a definite aim. He who would achieve true success in life must keep steadily in view the aim worthy of his endeavor. Such an aim is set before the youth of today. The heaven-appointed purpose of giving the gospel to the world in this generation is the noblest that can appeal to any human being. It opens a field of effort to everyone whose heart Christ has touched." *Education* p. 262

- ○ Condition: Maintain a definite and steady goal of giving the gospel to the world.
- ○ Promise: True success in life.
  From now on I will stay focused on telling others about Jesus and not get distracted with my own desires. Then I will feel fulfilled in life because Jesus will give me true success.

"As we seek to win others to Christ, bearing the burden of souls in our prayers, our own hearts will throb with the quickening influence of God's grace; our own affections will glow with more divine fervor; our whole Christian life will be more of a reality, more earnest, more prayerful." *Christ's Object Lessons* p. 354

   o   Condition: Search for souls to win for Christ.

   o   Promise: Our Christian life will grow stronger.

In my prayers I choose to take more time to pray for others. In my daily tasks I choose to take more time in seeking to win others to Christ. Then my whole personal Christian experience will blossom and grow in fervor.

"It is conscientious attention to what the world terms 'little things' that makes life a success. Little deeds of charity, little acts of self-denial, speaking simple words of helpfulness, watching against little sins,—this is Christianity." *Messages to Young People* p. 143

   o   Condition: Conscientious attention to little things.

   o   Promise: Life will be successful.

During my day, I choose to make a conscientious effort to look for ways in which I can put aside my plans and help others, making them feel more cared for and loved. I will be very careful not to even do "little" things that are wrong because this hurts others and myself. I will ask God for help and He will prosper my life.

"True success in any line of work is not the result of chance or accident or destiny. It is the outworking of God's providences, the reward of faith and discretion, of virtue and perseverance. Fine mental qualities and a high moral tone are not the result of accident. God gives opportunities; success depends upon the use made of them." *Conflict and Courage* p. 247

- Condition: Make good use of God-given opportunities.
- Promise: You will be successful.
  If I choose to use and not ignore the opportunities God gives me, I will be successful.

Now What?

"Therefore,
to him who knows to do good
and does not do it,
to him it is sin."
James 4:17

I am a missionary because...

- O I can do nothing else with a clear conscience.
- O I know about the Great Commission.

...What about you?

"I have but one candle of life to burn,
and I would rather burn it out in a land filled with darkness
than in a land flooded with light."
John Keith Falconer

We have come to the close of this study on why I am a missionary. But this is only the beginning of our missionary activity. I hope you will join me in continuing to study and read and grow and learn about what it means to be a missionary. I hope you are inspired to be a missionary for God. I hope you will commit your life to God here, now, completely.

If you recognize God calling you to make some changes in your life, and if you see that your life is not as Christ-like as it should be, do not hesitate to take action. Do not be like Felix who said,

> *"Go away for now; when I have a convenient time I will call for you."* Acts 24:25

Now is the most convenient time. A more convenient time will not come. Be like the people in Berea who

> *"received the word with all readiness, and searched the Scriptures daily to find out whether these things were so."* Acts 17:11

It is not me who is calling you to be a missionary. It is Jesus, and He has given us His own wonderful example to follow.

Look up some Bible promises on guidance and pray that God will guide and direct you. Take time to listen for His voice as you open your Bible in prayer. Hear His voice guiding and directing you during the day.

Learn the lesson of self-distrust from the story of Peter. After studying Jesus' example, you know there is such a difference between your life and the life of Jesus. You yield to the conviction of the Holy Spirit and, like Peter, promise to follow Jesus wherever He leads you. You decide right now that you will remain faithful even to death. But if you are self-confident, if you think you can do this on your own, you are only tempting Satan to tempt you. Then you face a crisis. When it is important to remain faithful, you may fall under temptation, as Peter did when he denied Jesus.

When we are self-sufficient and depend on our own ideas of what we think a faithful missionary should be, we will fail just as Peter did. But when we realize our insufficiency and weakness, we will not depend on self. We will look to God. And as we depend on God instead of self, we are safe from Satan's temptations.

❚❚ Will you deny Jesus or will you deny self? These are the only two options. If we deny self, we are confessing Jesus. If we do not deny self, we are denying Jesus.

Keep your eyes fixed on Jesus and not on your own capabilities or supposed greatness. Depend on Him continually to remain faithful to your commission.

Pray for a willingness to do anything God wants you to do. Pray for the willingness of Esther who risked her life in order to save her people. Pray for the courage of Daniel who was not ashamed of his calling and was willing to be eaten by lions rather than deny his God. Pray for the resolve of Daniel's three friends who were thrown into the furnace. Pray that you will be like Joseph who chose to see God's working in all situations.

And don't just pray—get to work! Don't wait for God to give you some big, fancy job to do for Him, or you might wait until you die. Start with what He gives you now, wherever you are. He will give you little tests and little jobs to see if you are really committed to Him. He sees your missionary activity in your home and at work. He sees how you treat your spouse or your siblings. He observes your interaction with your neighbors. He notes your attention to details. As you are faithful doing small things, God can trust you with bigger responsibilities.

The Bible teaches us that Jesus is coming back soon. How thoroughly do you believe this? How will He find you? Will He find you busily caring for self and improving your temporal life and possessions? Or will He find you watching and waiting for His return, preparing yourself and others to live with Him eternally? As you work and do other activities during the day, ask yourself if this is what you would like Jesus to find you doing when He returns.

Have you ever wished to choose what is right but felt compelled to make the wrong choice? When you are tempted, do you always choose wisely, or do you sometimes make wrong choices leading to guilt and the consequences of sin? Do you ever feel powerless to do what you know is right? Jesus lived as a human; how did He make His choices? How did He overcome every temptation without sin? If we are to become effective missionaries, we need to know the answers to these questions. If we are to teach others to become like Christ, we need to become more like Him. By studying His character, we will become more like the greatest Missionary who ever lived—from deciding to be a missionary, to benefiting from mission training, to being sent to work in the mission field. "But we all, with unveiled face, beholding as in a mirror the glory of the Lord, are being transformed into the same image from glory to glory, just as by the Spirit of the Lord." 2 Corinthians 3:18

Looking Back

"Well done, good and faithful servant;
you have been faithful over a few things,
I will make you ruler over many things.
Enter into the joy of your lord."
Matthew 25:23

I am a missionary because...

○ I want to add to Jesus' eternal glory.
○ I do not want to regret time wasted in other occupations.
○ I want to enlarge the family of heaven and increase eternal happiness.

...What about you?

"Only one life, 'twill soon be past,
only what's done for Christ will last."
Anonymous

Missionaries do not live for the here and now. We work toward an eternal and everlasting reward. It is easy to become focused on our work, our trials, our troubles, and lose sight of our goal of heaven.

Just for a few minutes, pretend with me that Jesus has already come and we are already home—home in heaven, our final home.

As we relax, enjoying some luscious fruit under a tree by a clear stream, we try to think back to our life on earth. What a contrast between our earthly life and our new life in heaven! The melody of the birds is so much sweeter here than on earth. The climate is comfortable and the air pure. It is far more peaceful here than on earth.

We try to think back on our hard life on earth. We thought that we really suffered and sacrificed a lot. But now we struggle to even remember our deepest disappointment, our deepest pain, our deepest sorrow. "Is that all?" we think to ourselves, "Was that all we had to endure? Oh why did we come so close to giving up the fight to surrender self? Why did we love our own ways and think our own thoughts so many times?" Now, everything appears in proper perspective. We are overwhelmed with thankfulness for God's grace that we chose to accept.

We notice something interesting about the crowns that Jesus has given each of us. Each person's crown is decorated perfectly with at least one star. Some crowns are full of stars. Every star represents another soul that has been led to accept eternal life through our influence. (See *Christian Experience and Teachings of Ellen G. White p. 59.*) No matter how many stars each person has, everyone is content, knowing that he has been influential in bringing others to heaven with him. We recognize that nobody's crown is without stars. Solemnly, we realize that if we had not led people to Jesus, we would not be here in heaven.

Jesus' crown is especially heavy with stars. (See *Testimonies for the Church Volume 6* p. 296.) Then we recognize that for every star on one of our crowns, a star is on Jesus' crown as a memorial for the work we had done for Him. What a privilege and honor we had to add stars to Jesus' crown!

Our thoughts about stars are interrupted as we see a familiar African boy running up to us. How many times did he grab our motorcycle and nearly tip us over, and how many times did he disrupt Sabbath School? He recognizes us, too, and says,

"Lapia, lapia (local greeting in our region of Chad), Jonathan and Melody. How are you?"

"Well, lapia to you, too! It is a happy sight to see you here," we reply.

Then he tells us a bit of his story. "I was a big troublemaker in your Sabbath School. My parents did not train me. But I learned many lessons from the Bible and from nature. I saw how you treated me, and how you lived your life, and I decided to give my life to God. He helped me to change my ways, and because of you, I am here today. Thank you!"

Then we see a middle-aged lady. She has been looking for me and now that our eyes meet, she starts running towards me with excitement.

"Do you remember me? We couldn't talk much because I didn't know French," she says. "But my foot was badly infected. My husband was always drunk and didn't care about me. But you washed and changed the bandage almost every day for about six weeks. During that time my baby fell ill. You sent him to the hospital, but he died on the way. But I could see that you really cared for me. When my foot healed, I thanked you. But you said, 'Thank God. It is God, not me, who healed you.' "

Our eyes well up with tears of joy. How could we have known the lasting results of caring for this lady?

We see another man over there, waiting to speak with us. We remember how he had tried to pass his exams ten times, each time failing. He had been very discouraged, and ready to give up on God. He stopped coming to church. But we let him know that we would not stop praying for him and that we wanted to be neighbors in heaven someday. We walk over to him. "Well, here I am," he says. "Thank you for your persevering prayers." Our joy could not be more full. "Where is your new house?" we ask. "I live just across the golden street from you. We're neighbors!"

It is a grand reunion. People come to visit and say, "Thank you." Some we had known from the market. Some we had met in a distant village. Some we had never known, but they had heard the good news of salvation through one of the Bible students we trained.

We meet others who had prayed perseveringly for us. Our parents, our brothers, our sisters, and friends. We now realize more fully the effect of their prayers in our lives as we recognize times when we were encouraged or protected.

Now, a strangely familiar being approaches. We think we recognize him, but how could we recognize him? He is a shining angel with a beaming smile. He is closely followed by another angel. "We are your guardian angels," they say to us. We seem to recognize the face of one of them; he gave us a ride to help us escape from a dangerous situation on the street in Kinshasa. At the time we had wondered if he was an angel. He was dressed like a man, but he was especially kind and warm. Now we speak with our angels face to face! They say, "You were in danger so many times. You didn't know it, but we jammed the guns of bandits, held your vehicle together, guided the plane, blinded the thief, canceled curses and witchcraft, and stayed with you as your personal body guards wherever you went."

The other angel added, "We worked together in the Bible studies you gave. We put words in your mouths and helped

you lead others to know Jesus. Thank you for being
co-workers with us on Earth!"

The first angel continued, "We encouraged you to make good
decisions and to choose the right and shun the wrong. You
struggled many times, but through Jesus' power were
triumphant. Welcome to heaven! We will have to talk and
share more stories later."

As we socialize with the angels, we begin to understand so
much more. We have been working with them as a team in
our work on earth, but did not knowingly see them. But now,
we see them and realize what a privilege we had to work with
them. We thought we were challenged to work with some
people, but what a challenge they had working with us!
Angels have been patiently and interestedly working with
wretched and ungrateful humans for thousands of years.
They practiced self-denial more than any of us. Now all
creatures are freed from dealing with the problem of sin.

No other work would have brought such a reward as this. But
why had we wasted so much time? Why did we spend so
much time in search of temporal advantages and possessions?
Why were we interested in entertainment rather than
soul-saving? Why were we so busy with things?—unimportant
things when compared to eternity. We thought we were
making a sacrifice to spend a little time reaching souls. But
now we regret so much time not spent winning souls to Jesus.

Above all, we value the privilege of walking and talking
directly with Jesus. We have talked with Him so often
throughout our labors and have longed to be with Him face to
face. All of our trials fade into nothingness when we begin to
understand more about Jesus and His love for us. To finally
meet Him for whom we have labored and suffered is a reward
valued far above anything else.

Jesus picks a fruit, and as we eat together, He says to us again
with eyes so full of love,

"Well done, good and faithful servant; you have been faithful over a few things, I will make you ruler over many things. Enter into the joy of your lord." Matthew 25:23

And so, in my imagination, begins some of our first few hours in heaven. We look back and are thrilled to have been workers together with God and with angels. We also sadly note the absence of some people who rejected their call and selfishly pursued their careers or hobbies. We are filled with gratitude for making the decision to sacrifice for God. The reward is much sweeter since we have sacrificed for it.

FURTHER READING FOR YOU

"Stand on the threshold of eternity, and hear the gracious welcome given to those who in this life have co-operated with Christ, regarding it as a privilege and an honor to suffer for His sake.... There the redeemed ones greet those who directed them to the uplifted Saviour. They unite in praising Him who died that human beings might have the life that measures with the life of God. The conflict is over. All tribulation and strife are at an end. Songs of victory fill all heaven, as the redeemed stand around the throne of God. All take up the joyful strain, 'Worthy, worthy is the Lamb that was slain,' and hath redeemed us to God.

"If the record shows that this has been their life, that their characters have been marked with tenderness, self-denial, and benevolence, they will receive the blessed assurance and benediction from Christ, 'Well done.' 'Come, ye blessed of My Father, inherit the kingdom prepared for you from the foundation of the world.' ...

"In our life here, earthly, sin-restricted, though it is, the greatest joy and the highest education are in service. And in the future state, untrammeled by the limitations of sinful humanity, it is in service that our greatest joy and our highest education will be found,—witnessing, and ever as we witness learning anew 'the riches of the glory of this mystery,' 'which is Christ in you, the hope of glory.'

"They share in the sufferings of Christ, and they will share also in the glory that shall be revealed. One with Him in His work, drinking with Him the cup of sorrow, they are partakers also of His joy.

"Every impulse of the Holy Spirit leading men to goodness and to God, is noted in the books of heaven, and in the day of God every one who has given himself as an instrument for the Holy Spirit's working will be permitted to behold what his life has wrought.

"When the redeemed stand before God, precious souls will respond to their names who are there because of the faithful, patient efforts put forth in their behalf, the entreaties and earnest persuasions to flee to the Stronghold. Thus those who in this world have been laborers together with God will receive their reward.

"What rejoicing there will be as these redeemed ones meet and greet those who have had a burden in their behalf! And those who have lived, not to please themselves, but to be a blessing to the unfortunate who have so few blessings —how their hearts will thrill with satisfaction! They will realize the promise, 'Thou shalt be blessed; for they cannot recompense thee: for thou shalt be recompensed at the resurrection of the just.'

"In heaven we shall see the youth whom we helped, those whom we invited to our homes, whom we led from temptation. We shall see their faces reflecting the radiance of the glory of God.

"To be a coworker with Christ and the heavenly angels in the great plan of salvation! What work can bear any comparison with this! From every soul saved, there comes to God a revenue of glory, to be reflected upon the one saved, and also upon the one instrumental in his salvation....

"If the time seems long to wait for our Deliverer to come; if, bowed by affliction and worn with toil, we feel impatient for our commission to close, and to receive an honorable release from the warfare, let us remember—and let the remembrance check every murmur—that God leaves us on earth to encounter storms and conflicts, to perfect Christian character, to become better acquainted with God our Father and Christ our Elder Brother, and to do work for the Master in winning many souls to Christ, that with glad heart we may hear the words, 'Well done, good and faithful servant; enter thou into the joy of thy Lord.'

"Be patient, Christian soldier. Yet a little while, and He that shall come, will come. The night of weary waiting, and watching, and mourning is nearly over. The reward will soon be given; the eternal day will dawn. There is no time to sleep now—no time to indulge in useless regrets. He who ventures to slumber now will miss precious opportunities of doing good. We are granted the blessed privilege of gathering sheaves in the great harvest; and every soul saved will be an additional star in the crown of Jesus, our adorable Redeemer. Who is eager to lay off the armor, when by pushing the battle a little longer, he will achieve new victories and gather new trophies for eternity?" *Christian Service* p. 271–275

The Missionary

by Jennifer Dietrich

He was rich. He had lots of servants.
Everybody knew him.
He had everything going for him.
A good job. A comfortable home. Great friends.

His announcement was a shock.
"I'm leaving here and going there."

They said,
"Why would you leave your nice home
and go to that miserable place?"
"Those people don't love God,
and they aren't even interested in Him."
"Why would you waste your time?"
"Shouldn't someone else go?"
"They're happy with their religion."
"Why not help those who already love God?"
"They're too degraded. Not worth your time."
"You'll come right back."

He decided to go anyway.

When he talked to his dad about it, his dad said, "Son, how
can I let you go there? Think of what might happen to you.
It's a terrible place to live. You could be a failure, too. Are you
sure you don't want to stay here and do some missionary
work at home? I can't bear to think of losing you."

But he had made up his mind. He thought,
"I can't enjoy anything anymore, knowing they are so
miserable."
"How can I keep all my things when they have nothing?"
"I love God. I want them to have a chance to love Him, too."

He quit his good job.
He left all his servants.
He left all his money.
He left his church and his friends who loved God.

Yes, he left. Alone.

Saying good-by was hard. Would he ever come back?

He finally arrived. A stranger.
No one knew who he was.
No one cared.
No one helped him.
No one even gave him a place to stay.
Everything was so different.
The rampant degradation was repulsive to him.

Soon after he arrived, political problems forced him to flee to
another country for a while.
As soon as it was safe, he went back again.

Then there were the religious leaders.
They felt threatened by the new teacher.
"We're not having any new religion around here," they said.
While he was in the capital city,
they made plans to assassinate him.
He went to work in another city not far away.

The poor people became interested.
"Who is this new teacher?"
"Is he telling the truth?"
"Where did he come from?"
"What can he do for us?"

"Rice Christians," they are called.
Soon they came in droves.
For money. For food. For clothes.
For help when they were sick.
They would listen if they thought they would get something.

Then they figured out that he hadn't come to give handouts.
So they quit coming, since that's all they wanted.
They quit listening to what he had to say.

True, a few were really interested in learning about God.
But their culture held them in an iron grip.
"What will you give us?" even they asked.

They couldn't ever seem to "get it."

Sometimes he was tempted to think,
"I should go back home."
"Everyone here hates me."
"It's hard to be so poor."
"At home I could have everything I want."
"My friends would be nice to me."
"No one wants my help."
"They're happy the way they are."
"Give it up. It's hopeless."

But he didn't go back home.
Even though almost everyone hated him.
He didn't go back home.
Even though he didn't have a decent place to live.
He didn't go back home.
Even though he was dreadfully lonely.
He didn't go back home.
Because he knew they weren't really happy.
He didn't give up.
Because he knew it wasn't hopeless, even though it seemed
so.

He learned important lessons.
Depend on God continually.
Always obey the promptings of the Holy Spirit.
Know your Bible.
Pray.
Work hard.
Teach by example.

His work provoked endless disputes and contentions.
Political and religious tension increased.
Anyone in that country who was identified with him could be
accused of treason or excommunicated.
They turned the rabble against him.
He was murdered.
Only a few were brave enough to bury his body.

Was he a success or a failure?